SHAKESPEARE'S TRAGEDY

OF

ROMEO AND JULIET

SHAKESPEARE'S

TRAGEDY OF

ROMEO AND JULIET.

115057

Edited, with Notes,

by

WILLIAM J. ROLFE, Litt. D.,

FORMERLY HEAD MASTER OF THE HIGH SCHOOL, CAMBRIDGE, MASS.

WITH ENGRAVINGS.

NEW YORK ·:· CINCINNATI ·:· CHICAGO

AMERICAN BOOK COMPANY

PR 2754
S52N

ENGLISH CLASSICS.

EDITED BY WM. J. ROLFE, LITT. D.

Illustrated. 12mo, Cloth, 56 cents per volume.

SHAKESPEARE'S WORKS.

The Merchant of Venice.	Richard III.
Othello.	Henry VIII.
Julius Cæsar.	King Lear.
A Midsummer-Night's Dream.	The Taming of the Shrew.
Macbeth.	All 's Well that Ends Well.
Hamlet.	Coriolanus.
Much Ado about Nothing.	The Comedy of Errors.
Romeo and Juliet.	Cymbeline.
As You Like It.	Antony and Cleopatra.
The Tempest.	Measure for Measure.
Twelfth Night.	Merry Wives of Windsor.
The Winter's Tale.	Love's Labour 's Lost.
King John.	Two Gentlemen of Verona.
Richard II.	Timon of Athens.
Henry IV. Part I.	Troilus and Cressida.
Henry IV. Part II.	Pericles, Prince of Tyre.
Henry V.	The Two Noble Kinsmen.
Henry VI. Part I.	Venus and Adonis, Lucrece, etc.
Henry VI. Part II.	Sonnets.
Henry VI. Part III.	Titus Andronicus.

GOLDSMITH'S SELECT POEMS.   BROWNING'S SELECT POEMS.
GRAY'S SELECT POEMS.   BROWNING'S SELECT DRAMAS.
MINOR POEMS OF JOHN MILTON.   MACAULAY'S LAYS OF ANCIENT ROME.
WORDSWORTH'S SELECT POEMS.

LAMBS' TALES FROM SHAKESPEARE'S COMEDIES.
LAMBS' TALES FROM SHAKESPEARE'S TRAGEDIES.

EDITED BY WM. J. ROLFE, LITT. D.

Illustrated. Cloth, 12mo, 50 cents per volume

Romeo and Juliet.
W. P. 2

CONTENTS.

his Seruants.* | LONDON, | Printed by Iohn Danter. 1597.

This was followed in 1599 by a second quarto edition, the title-page of which is as follows:

THE | MOST EX- | cellent and lamentable | Tragedie, of Romeo | and *Iuliet.* | *Newly corrected, augmented, and* | *amended:* | As it hath bene sundry times publiquely acted, by the | right Honourable the Lord Chamberlaine | his Seruants | LONDON | Printed by Thomas Creede, for Cuthbert Burby, and are to | be sold at his shop neare the Exchange. | 1599.

A third quarto appeared in 1609 with the following title-page:

THE | MOST EX- | CELLENT AND | Lamentable Tragedie, of | *Romeo and Juliet.* | As it hath beene sundrie times publiquely Acted, | by the KINGS Maiesties Seruants | at the Globe. | Newly corrected, augmented, and amended: | LONDON | Printed for IOHN SMETHVVICK, and are to be sold | at his Shop in Saint *Dunstanes* Church-yard, | in Fleetestreete vnder the Dyall | 1609.

A fourth quarto has no date, and there is some doubt whether it was a reprint of the one of 1609, or that a reprint of this. The Camb. editors consider that "internal evidence conclusively proves" the former; Halliwell thinks "it is very difficult to say which is the earlier," but inclines to the opinion that the undated copy was published in 1608. The text is more correct than that of the quarto of 1609. The earlier of the two, whichever it may have been, was undoubtedly a reprint of the second quarto with some corrections, and the later was a reprint of the earlier.

The undated quarto is the first that bears the name of the author. On the title-page, which in other respects is

* Here follows a vignette, with the motto *AVT NVNC AVT NVN-QVAM.*

This quarto is reprinted in full in Furness's "New Variorum" ed. of the play, and also in the Camb. ed.

substantially identical with that of the third quarto, "Written by W. *Shake-speare*" is inserted as a separate line after the word "Globe." According to Halliwell, this line is found only in early copies of the edition, having been suppressed before the rest were printed.*

The above are the only editions known to have been issued before the folio of 1623, in which the play occupies pages 53–79 in the division of "Tragedies." The text of the folio seems to have been taken from the third quarto.

A fifth quarto, evidently reprinted from the fourth, and with substantially the same title-page, except that it is said to be printed "by *R. Young* for *John Smethwicke*," was published in 1637.

The first quarto is much shorter than the second, the former having only 2232 lines, including the prologue, while the latter has 3007 lines (Daniel). Some editors (among whom are Knight and Verplanck) believe that the first quarto gives the author's first draught of the play, and the second the form it assumed after he had revised and enlarged it ; but the majority of the best critics (including Collier, White, the Cambridge editors, Mommsen, Furness, Daniel, Dowden, and Stokes) agree substantially in the opinion that the first quarto was a pirated edition, and represents in an abbreviated and imperfect form the play subsequently printed in full in the second. The former was "made up partly from copies of portions of the original play, partly from recollection and from notes taken during the performance ;" the latter was from an authentic copy, and a careful comparison of the text with the earlier one shows that in the meantime the play "underwent revision, received some slight augmentation, and in some few places must have been entirely rewritten."†

* The copy in the British Museum is without the author's name (Daniel).

¹ See the introduction to Mr. P. A. Daniel's *Romeo and Juliet: Par-*

The date of the play is placed by all the critics some years earlier than the publication of the first quarto. They generally agree that it was probably begun as early as 1591, though it may not have assumed its final form until 1596 or 1597. Romeo is alluded to as a popular character of Shakespeare's by Weever in an epigram, written probably before 1595. The title-page of the first quarto tells us in 1597 that the play had been "often plaid publiquely;" and from the additional statement that "Lord Hunsdon's servants" were the performers, Malone shows that it must have been acted between July, 1596, and April, 1597. The Lord Chamberlain, Henry Lord Hunsdon, died July 22, 1596; his son, George Lord Hunsdon, was appointed Chamberlain in April, 1597. It was only in the interval between these dates that the company would have been called "Lord Hunsdon's servants" instead of the more honourable designation of "the Lord Chamberlain's servants." This, however, does not prove that the play was then *first* brought out; and Weever's epigram proves that it had been put on the stage at least a year earlier.

The Nurse's allusion in i. 3. 23 ("'T is since the earthquake now eleven years") has been quoted in support of the assumed date of 1591, a memorable earthquake having been felt in London in 1580; and the repetition of the "eleven years" (in i. 3. 35), as Stokes remarks, favours this view, in spite of the fact that the Nurse is somewhat confused in her reckoning as to Juliet's age.*

---

allel Texts of the First Two Quartos, published for the New Shakspere Society in 1874; also White's introduction to the play in his ed. of Shakespeare, vol. x. p. 10 fol. On this subject and on the question of the date of the play, cf. the summary of the views of the leading editors in F. p. 408 fol.

* Other historical allusions have been suspected to exist. For instance, the reference in v. 2. 8 fol. to the sealing-up of plague-stricken houses has been thought to be connected with the pestilence of 1593;

The internal evidence confirms this opinion that the tragedy was an early work of the poet, and that it was subsequently "corrected, augmented, and amended." There is a
good deal of rhyme, and much of it in the form of alternate
rhyme. The alliteration, the frequent playing upon words,
and the lyrical character of many passages also lead to the
same conclusion.*

II. THE SOURCES OF THE PLOT.

Girolamo della Corte, in his *Storia di Verona,* 1594, relates the story of the play as a true event occurring in 1303;
but he is very untrustworthy as a historian, and the earlier
annalists of the city are silent on the subject. A tale in

and ii. 2. 82 fol. may have been suggested by the voyages of Drake and
Hawkins in 1594-5 or of Raleigh in 1595, etc.

* White sees traces of another hand than Shakespeare's in the earlier
version of the play—"not many," but "quite unmistakable;" and he believes that the difference between the two versions "is owing partly to
the rejection by him of the work of a colaborer, partly to the surrepti-
tious and inadequate means by which the copy for the earlier edition
was obtained, and partly, perhaps, but in a much less degree, to Shakespeare's elaboration of what he himself had written." The date of the
first form of the play W. is inclined to put as early as 1591. He says:
"that in 1591 Shakespeare and one or more other 'practitioners for the
stage' composed a *Romeo and Juliet* in partnership, and that in 1596
Shakespeare 'corrected, augmented, and amended' it, making it to all
intents and purposes entirely his own, and that it then met with such
great success that an unscrupulous publisher obtained as much as he
could of it, by hook or by crook, and had the deficiencies supplied, as
well as could be, by bits from the play of 1591, and, when that failed, by
poets as unscrupulous as himself, is entirely accordant with the practices
of that day, and reconciles all the facts in this particular case; even the
two that the play contains a reference which indicates 1591 as the year
when it was written, and that in 1596 it was published in haste to take
advantage of a great and sudden popularity." Fleay (*Shakespeare Man-
ual,* p. 32) expresses the opinion "that G. Peele wrote the early play
about 1593; that Shakespeare in 1596 corrected this up to the point
where there is a change of type in the 1st quarto (end of ii. 3), and in
1597 completed his corrections as in the 2d quarto."

some respects similar is found in the *Ephesiaca* of Xeno-phon of Ephesus, a Greek romance - writer of the Middle Ages; and one essentially the same, the scene of which is laid in Siena, appears in a collection of novels by Masuccio di Salerno, printed at Naples in 1476. Luigi da Porto, in his *La Giulietta*, published about 1530, is, however, the first to call the lovers Romeo and Juliet, and to make them children of the rival Veronese houses. The story was retold in French by Adrian Sevin, about 1542; and a poetical version of it was published at Venice in 1553. It is also found in Bandello's *Novelle*, 1554; and five years later Pierre Bois-teau translated it, with some variations, into French in his *Histoire de Deux Amans*. The earliest English version of the romance appeared in 1562 in a poem by Arthur Brooke founded upon Boisteau's novel, and entitled *Romeus and Juliet.* A prose translation of Boisteau's novel was given in Paynter's *Palace of Pleasure,* in 1567. It was undoubtedly from these English sources, and chiefly from the poem by Brooke, that Shakespeare drew his material. It is to be noted, however, that Brooke speaks of having seen "the same argument lately set forth on stage;" and it is possible that this lost play* may also have been known to Shake-speare, though we have no reason to suppose that he made any use of it. That he followed Brooke's poem rather than Paynter's prose version is evident from a careful compari-son of the two with the play. Malone sums up the results of such a comparison as follows :

* It is not unlikely that there was more than one English play on the subject before Shakespeare's. Coll. says : "We can scarcely suppose that no other drama would be founded upon the same interesting inci-dents between 1562 and the date when Shakespeare wrote his tragedy, a period of probably more than thirty years ; but no hint of the kind is given in any record, and certainly no such work, either manuscript or printed, has come down to us."

Some critics believe that the "stage" to which Brooke refers was a foreign one, but this is improbable.

Romeo and Juliet owes to Shakespeare only its dramatic form and its poetic decoration. But what an exception is the latter! It is to say that the earth owes to the sun only its verdure and its flowers, the air only its perfume and its balm, the heavens only their azure and their glow. Yet this must not lead us to forget that the original tale is one of the most truthful and touching among the few that have entranced the ear and stirred the heart of the world for ages, or that in Shakespeare's transfiguration of it his fancy and his youthful fire had a much larger share than his philosophy or his imagination.

"The only variations from the story in the play are the three which have just been alluded to : the compression of the action, which in the story occupies four or five months, to within as many days, thus adding impetuosity to a passion which had only depth, and enhancing dramatic effect by quickening truth to vividness; the conversion of Mercutio from a mere courtier, 'bolde emong the bashfull maydes,' 'courteous of his speech and pleasant of devise,' into that splendid union of the knight and the fine gentleman, in portraying which Shakespeare, with prophetic eye piercing a century, shows us the fire of faded chivalry expiring in a flash of wit; and the bringing-in of Paris (forgotten in the story after his bridal disappointment) to die at Juliet's bier by the hand of Romeo, thus gathering together all the threads of this love entanglement to be cut at once by Fate."

III. CRITICAL COMMENTS ON THE PLAY.

[*From Schlegel's " Dramatic Literature."**]

Romeo and Juliet is a picture of love and its pitiable fate, in a world whose atmosphere is too rough for this tenderest blossom of human life. Two beings created for each other feel mutual love at first glance; every consideration dis-

* *Lectures on Dramatic Art and Literature,* by A. W. Schlegel ; as quoted by Verplanck, p. 63.

"1. In the poem the prince of Verona is called *Escalus;* so also in the play. In Painter's translation from Boisteau he is named *Signor Escala,* and sometimes *Lord Bartholomew of Escala.* 2. In Painter's novel the family of Romeo are called the *Montesches;* in the poem and in the play, the *Montagues.* 3. The messenger employed by friar Lawrence to carry a letter to Romeo is in Painter's translation called *Anselme;* in the poem and in the play, friar *John* is employed in this business. 4. The circumstance of Capulet's writing down the names of the guests whom he invites to supper is found in the poem and in the play, but is not mentioned by Painter, nor is it found in the original Italian novel. 5. The residence of the Capulets, in the original and in Painter, is called *Villa Franca;* in the poem and in the play, *Freetown.* 6. Several passages of *Romeo and Juliet* appear to have been formed on hints furnished by the poem, of which no traces are found either in Painter's novel, or in Boisteau, or the original; and several expressions are borrowed from thence."*

White remarks on the same subject: "The tragedy follows the poem with a faithfulness which might be called slavish, were it not that any variation from the course of the old story was entirely unnecessary for the sake of dramatic interest, and were there not shown in the progress of the action, in the modification of one character, and in the disposal of another, all peculiar to the play, self-reliant dramatic intuition of the highest order. For the rest, there is not a personage or a situation, hardly a speech, essential to Brooke's poem, which has not its counterpart—its exalted and glorified counterpart—in the tragedy. . . . In brief,

---

* On the other hand, as Fleay notes, the statement of the exact duration of Juliet's sleep (iv. 1. 105 : " two and forty hours ") is given in the novel ("forty houres at the least "), but not in the poem ; which shows that Shakespeare, while generally following the latter, occasionally made use of the former.

of prelude, shown the laughable absurdity of the evil by the contagion of it reaching the servants, who have so little to do with it, but who are under the necessity of letting the superfluity of sensorial power fly off through the escape-valve of wit-combats, and of quarrelling with weapons of sharper edge, all in humble imitation of their masters. Yet there is a sort of unhired fidelity, an *ourishness* about all this that makes it rest pleasant on one's feelings. All the first scene, down to the conclusion of the Prince's speech, is a motley dance of all ranks and ages to one tune, as if the horn of Huon had been playing behind the scenes.

Benvolio's speech—

> "Madam, an hour before the worshipp'd sun
> Peer'd forth the golden window of the east"—

and, far more strikingly, the following speech of old Montague—

> "Many a morning hath he there been seen
> With tears augmenting the fresh morning dew"—

prove that Shakspeare meant the Romeo and Juliet to approach to a poem, which, and indeed its early date, may be also inferred from the multitude of rhyming couplets throughout. And if we are right, from the internal evidence, in pronouncing this one of Shakspeare's early dramas, it affords a strong instance of the fineness of his insight into the nature of the passions, that Romeo is introduced already love-bewildered. The necessity of loving creates an object for itself in man and woman; and yet there is a difference in this respect between the sexes, though only to be known by a perception of it. It would have displeased us if Juliet had been represented as already in love, or as fancying herself so; but no one, I believe, ever experiences any shock at Romeo's forgetting his Rosaline, who had been a mere name for the yearning of his youthful imagination, and rushing into his passion for Juliet. Rosaline was a mere creation of his fancy; and we should remark the boastful positiveness of Romeo in a love of his own making, which is never shown where love is really near the heart.

> "When the devout religion of mine eye
>   Maintains such falsehood, then turn tears to fires;
> And these, who often drown'd could never die,
>   Transparent heretics, be burnt for liars!
> One fairer than my love! the all-seeing sun
> Ne'er saw her match since first the world begun."

The character of the Nurse is the nearest of anything in Shakspeare to a direct borrowing from mere observation; and the reason is, that as in infancy and childhood the individual in nature is a representative of a class—just as in describing one larch-tree, you generalize a grove of them— so it is nearly as much so in old age. The generalization is done to the poet's hand. Here you have the garrulity of age strengthened by the feelings of a long-trusted servant, whose sympathy with the mother's affections gives her privileges and rank in the household; and observe the mode of connection by accidents of time and place, and the child-like fondness of repetition in a second childhood, and also that happy, humble, ducking under, yet constant resurgence against, the check of her superiors!

In the fourth scene we have Mercutio introduced to us. O! how shall I describe that exquisite ebullience and overflow of youthful life, wafted on over the laughing waves of pleasure and prosperity, as a wanton beauty that distorts the face on which she knows her lover is gazing enraptured, and wrinkles her forehead in the triumph of its smoothness! Wit ever wakeful, fancy busy and procreative as an insect, courage, an easy mind that, without cares of its own, is at once disposed to laugh away those of others, and yet to be interested in them—these and all congenial qualities, melting into the common *copula* of them all, the man of rank and the gentleman, with all its excellences and all its weaknesses, constitute the character of Mercutio!

[From Mrs. Jameson's " Characteristics of Women."*]

Romeo and Juliet are not poetical beings placed on a prosaic background ; . . . but every circumstance, and every personage, and every shade of character in each tends to the development of the sentiment which is the subject of the drama.   The poetry, too, the richest that can possibly be conceived, is interfused through all the characters ; the splendid imagery lavished upon all with the careless prodigality of genius ; and the whole is lighted up into such a sunny brilliance of effect as though Shakspeare had really transported himself into Italy, and had drunk to intoxication of her genial atmosphere.   How truly it has been said that "although Romeo and Juliet are in love, they are not love-sick !"   What a false idea would anything of the mere whining amoroso give us of Romeo, such as he really is in Shakspeare—the noble, gallant, ardent, brave, and witty !   And Juliet—with even less truth could the phrase or idea apply to her !   The picture in *Twelfth Night* of the wan girl dying of love, "who pined in thought, and with a green and yellow melancholy," would never surely occur to us when thinking on the enamoured and impassioned Juliet, in whose bosom love keeps a fiery vigil, kindling tenderness into enthusiasm, enthusiasm into passion, passion into heroism !   No, the whole sentiment of the play is of a far different cast.   It is flushed with the genial spirit of the South : it tastes of youth, and of the essence of youth ; of life, and of the very sap of life.   We have indeed the struggle of love against evil destinies and a thorny world ; the pain, the grief, the anguish, the terror, the despair ; the aching adieu ; the pang unutterable of parted affection ; and rapture, truth, and tenderness trampled into an early grave : but still an Elysian grace lingers round the whole, and the blue sky of Italy bends over all.

* American ed. (Boston, 1857), p. 123 fol.

In the delineation of that sentiment which forms the groundwork of the drama, nothing in fact can equal the power of the picture but its inexpressible sweetness and its perfect grace: the passion which has taken possession of Juliet's whole soul has the force, the rapidity, the resistless violence of the torrent; but she is herself as "moving delicate," as fair, as soft, as flexible as the willow that bends over it, whose light leaves tremble even with the motion of the current which hurries beneath them. But at the same time that the pervading sentiment is never lost sight of, and is one and the same throughout, the individual part of the character in all its variety is developed, and marked with the nicest discrimination. For instance, the simplicity of Juliet is very different from the simplicity of Miranda; her innocence is not the innocence of a desert island. The energy she displays does not once remind us of the moral grandeur of Isabel, or the intellectual power of Portia: it is founded in the strength of passion, not in the strength of character; it is accidental rather than inherent, rising with the tide of feeling or temper, and with it subsiding. Her romance is not the pastoral romance of Perdita, nor the fanciful romance of Viola; it is the romance of a tender heart and a poetical imagination. Her inexperience is not ignorance; she has heard that there is such a thing as falsehood, though she can scarcely conceive it. . . .

Our impression of Juliet's loveliness and sensibility is enhanced when we find it overcoming in the bosom of Romeo a previous love for another. His visionary passion for the cold, inaccessible Rosaline forms but the prologue, the threshold, to the true, the real sentiment which succeeds to it. This incident, which is found in the original story, has been retained by Shakspeare with equal feeling and judgment; and, far from being a fault in taste and sentiment, far from prejudicing us against Romeo by casting on him, at the outset of the piece, the stigma of inconstancy, it becomes, if properly considered, a beauty in the drama, and adds a fresh stroke of truth to the portrait of the lover. Why, after all, should we be offended at what does not offend Juliet herself? for in the original story we find that her attention is first attracted towards Romeo by seeing him "fancy-sick and pale of cheer," for love of a cold beauty. We must remember that in those times every young cavalier of any distinction devoted himself, at his first entrance into the world, to the service of some fair lady, who was selected to be his fancy's queen ; and the more rigorous the beauty and the more hopeless the love, the more honourable the slavery. To go about "metamorphosed with a mistress," as Speed humorously expresses it [*T. G. of V.* ii. 1. 32]—to maintain her supremacy in charms at the sword's point, to sigh, to walk with folded arms, to be negligent and melancholy, and to show a careless desolation—was the fashion of the day. The Surreys, the Sidneys, the Bayards, the Herberts of the time—all those who were the mirrors "in which the noble youth did dress themselves," were of this fantastic school of gallantry—the last remains of the age of chivalry ; and it was especially prevalent in Italy. Shakspeare has ridiculed it in many places with exquisite humour ; but he wished to show us that it has its serious as well as its comic aspect. Romeo, then, is introduced to us with perfect truth of costume, as the thrall of a dreaming, fanciful passion for the scornful Rosaline, who had forsworn to love ; and on her charms and coldness, and on the power of love generally, he descants to his companions in pretty phrases, quite in the style and taste of the day.*

---

* There is an allusion to this court language of love in *A. W.* i. 1. 181, where Helena says,—

> "There shall your master have a thousand loves—
> A guide, a goddess, and a sovereign ;
> A counsellor, a traitress, and a dear,
> His humble ambition, proud humility,
> His jarring concord, and his discord dulcet,
> His faith, his sweet disaster, with a world

But when once he has beheld Juliet, and quaffed intoxicating draughts of hope and love from her soft glance, how
all these airy fancies fade before the soul-absorbing reality.
The lambent fire that played round his heart burns to that
heart's very core. We no longer find him adorning his lamentations in picked phrases, or making a confidant of his
gay companions : he is no longer "for the numbers that Petrarch flowed in ;" but all is consecrated, earnest, rapturous,
in the feeling and the expression. . . .

His first passion is indulged as a waking dream, a reverie
of the fancy ; it is depressing, indolent, fantastic ; his second
elevates him to the third heaven, or hurries him to despair.
It rushes to its object through all impediments, defies all
dangers, and seeks at last a triumphant grave, in the arms
of her he so loved. Thus Romeo's previous attachment to
Rosaline is so contrived as to exhibit to us another variety
in that passion which is the subject of the poem, by showing us the distinction between the fancied and the real sentiment. It adds a deeper effect to the beauty of Juliet ; it
interests us in the commencement for the tender and ro-
mantic Romeo ; and gives an individual reality to his character by stamping him, like an historical as well as a dramatic portrait, with the very spirit of the age in which he
lived. . . .

In the extreme vivacity of her imagination, and its influence upon the action, the language, the sentiments of the
drama, Juliet resembles Portia ; but with this striking difference. In Portia, the imaginative power, though developed
in a high degree, is so equally blended with the other intellectual and moral faculties, that it does not give us the idea
of excess. It is subject to her nobler reason ; it adorns

> Of pretty fond adoptious Christendoms
> That blinking Cupid gossips."

The courtly poets of Elizabeth's time, who copied the Italian sonnet-
teers of the sixteenth century, are full of these quaint conceits.

and heightens all her feelings ; it does not overwhelm or mislead them. In Juliet, it is rather a part of her Southern temperament, controlling and modifying the rest of her character ; springing from her sensibility, hurried along by her passions, animating her joys, darkening her sorrows, exaggerating her terrors, and, in the end, overpowering her reason. With Juliet, imagination is, in the first instance, if not the source, the medium of passion ; and passion again kindles her imagination. It is through the power of imagination that the eloquence of Juliet is so vividly poetical ; that every feeling, every sentiment, comes to her clothed in the richest imagery, and is thus reflected from her mind to ours. The poetry is not here the mere adornment, the outward garnishing of the character ; but its result, or rather blended with its essence. It is indivisible from it, and interfused through it like moonlight through the summer air. . . .

With regard to the termination of the play, which has been a subject of much critical argument, it is well known that Shakspeare, following the old English versions, has departed from the original story of Da Porta ;* and I am inclined to believe that Da Porta, in making Juliet waken from her trance while Romeo yet lives, and in his terrible final scene between the lovers, has himself departed from the old tradition, and, as a romance, has certainly improved it ; but that which is effective in a narrative is not always calculated for the drama ; and I cannot but agree with Schlegel, that Shakspeare has done well and wisely in adhering to the old story. . . .

It is in truth a tale of love and sorrow, not of anguish and terror. We behold the catastrophe afar off with scarcely a

---

* In the novel of Da Porta the catastrophe is altogether different. After the death of Romeo, the Friar Lorenzo endeavors to persuade Juliet to leave the fatal monument. She refuses ; and throwing herself back on the dead body of her husband, she resolutely holds her breath and dies.

wish to avert it. Romeo and Juliet *must* die ; their destiny is fulfilled ; they have quaffed off the cup of life, with all
its infinite of joys and agonies, in one intoxicating draught.
What have they to do more upon this earth ? Young, inno-
cent, loving and beloved, they descend together into the
tomb ; but Shakspeare has made that tomb a shrine of
martyred and sainted affection consecrated for the worship
of all hearts, not a dark charnel vault haunted by spec-
tres of pain, rage, and desperation. Romeo and Juliet are
pictured lovely in death as in life ; the sympathy they inspire does not oppress us with that suffocating sense of hor-
ror which in the altered tragedy makes the fall of the curtain a relief, but all pain is lost in the tenderness and poetic beauty of the picture.

[*From Philarète Chasles's "Études sur Shakespeare."**]

Who cannot recall lovely summer nights when the forces
of nature seem ripe for development and yet sunk in drowsy
languor—intense heat mingled with exuberant vigour, fer-
vid force, and silent freshness ?

The nightingale's song comes from the depths of the
grove. The flower-cups are half closed. A pale lustre il-
lumines the foliage of the forest and the outline of the hills.
This profound repose conceals, we feel, a fertile force ; beneath the retiring melancholy of nature lies hidden burning
emotion. Beneath the pallor and coolness of night we divine restrained ardours ; each flower brooding in silence is
longing to bloom forth.

Such is the peculiar atmosphere with which Shakespeare

* As quoted by F., p. 141, with a few verbal changes. For another
translation of a part of the same passage, see Dowden's *Shakspere*, p. 101.
Dowden remarks : " The external atmosphere of the tragedy of *Romeo
and Juliet*, its Italian colour and warmth, have been so finely felt by M.
Philarète Chasles that his words deserve to be a portion of every criticism of that play."

has enveloped one of his most wonderful creations, *Romeo and Juliet.*

Not only the story upon which the drama is founded, but the very form of the language comes from the South. Italy was the inventor of the tale; it breathes the very spirit of her national records, her old family feuds, the amorous and bloody intrigues which fill her annals. No one can fail to recognize Italy in its lyric rhythm, its blindness of passion, its blossoming and abundant vitality, in its brilliant imagery, its bold composition. Romeo's words flow like one of Petrarch's sonnets, with a like delicate choice, a like antithesis, a like grace, and a like delight in clothing his passion in tender allegory. Juliet, too, is wholly Italian ; with small gift of forethought, and absolutely ingenuous in her *abandon*, she is at once passionate and pure. . . .

With Friar Laurence, we foresee that the lovers will be conquered by fate ; Shakespeare does not close the tomb upon them until he has intoxicated them with all the happiness that can be crowded into human existence. The balcony scene is the last gleam of this fleeting bliss. Heavenly accents float upon the air, the fragrance of the pomegranate blossoms is wafted aloft to Juliet's chamber, the sighing plaint of the nightingale pierces the leafy shadows of the grove ; nature, dumb and impassioned, can only in rustling and fragrance add her assent to that sublime, sad hymn upon the frailty of human happiness. . . .

In a deserted street of deserted Verona stands, half hidden, an old smoke-stained hostelry, where there is shouting, and swearing, and smoking, where macaroni and sour wine are dealt out to labourers. It was once the palace of the Capulets. The little hat sculptured above the door-way is the escutcheon of the Capulets, the *cappelletto.* Here Juliet lived. At the end of a court-yard there is an ancient tomb, the burial-place, they tell you, of Romeo and Juliet. It looks now like an empty horse-trough. Every year thousands of

curious people come on a pilgrimage hither to see this fragment of stone.

It is due to Shakespeare that the traveller now visits Verona solely to look for traces of Romeo and Juliet.*

[*From Maginn's "Shakespeare Papers."†*]

I consider Romeo designed to represent the character of
an *unlucky* man—a man, who, with the best views and fairest intentions, is perpetually so unfortunate as to fail in every aspiration, and, while exerting himself to the utmost in
their behalf, to involve all whom he holds dearest in misery
and ruin. Had any other passion or pursuit occupied Romeo, he would have been equally unlucky as in his love. Ill-
fortune has marked him for her own. From beginning to

* "The Veronese," says Lord Byron, in one of his letters from Verona,
"are tenacious to a degree of the truth of Juliet's story, insisting on the
fact, giving the date 1303, and showing a tomb. It is a plain, open, and
partly decayed sarcophagus, with withered leaves in it, in a wild and des-
olate conventual garden—once a cemetery, now ruined, to the very graves!
The situation struck me as very appropriate to the legend, being blighted
as their love."

Since Byron's day the tomb has remained in the garden of the Or-
fanotrofio delle Franceschine, where it is still shown to tourists for a
fee of 25 centesimi (5 cents in our money). Howells (*Italian Journeys*,
p. 307) asks : "Does not the fact that this relic has to be protected from
the depredations of travellers, who could otherwise carry it away piece-
meal, speak eloquently of a large amount of vulgar and rapacious innocence drifting about the world?"

The same writer thus refers to the House of the Capulets : "We found
it a very old and time-worn edifice, built round an ample court, and we
knew it, as we had been told we should, by the cap carven in stone above
the interior of the grand portal. The family, anciently one of the principal in Verona, has fallen from much of its former greatness. . . . There
was a great deal of stable litter, and many empty carts standing about in
the court ; and if I might hazard the opinion formed upon these and
other appearances, I should say that old Capulet has now gone to keeping a hotel, united with the retail liquor business, both in a small way."

† *Shakespeare Papers*, by **William Maginn** (London, 1860), quoted by
F. p. 427.

end he intends the best; but his interfering is ever for the worst. Everything glides on in smooth current at Capulet's feast till the appearance of him whose presence is deadly. Romeo himself is a most reluctant visitor. He apprehends that the consequences of the night's revels will be the vile forfeit of a despised life by an untimely death, but submits to his destiny. He foresees that it is no wit to go, but consoles himself with the reflection that he " means well in going to this masque." His intentions, as usual, are good; and, as usual, their consequences are ruinous. Vainly does Romeo endeavour to pacify the bullying swordsman, Tybalt; vainly does he decline the ~~proffered~~ duel. His good intentions are again doomed to be frustrated. There stands by his side as mad-blooded a spirit as Tybalt himself, and Mercutio takes up the abandoned quarrel. The star of the unlucky man is ever in the ascendant. His ill-omened interference slays his friend. Had he kept quiet the issue might have been different; but the power that had the steerage of his course had destined that the uplifting of his sword was to be the signal of death to his very friend. And when the dying Mercutio says, "Why the devil came you between us? I was hurt under your arm," he can only offer the excuse, which is always true and always unavailing, " I thought all for the best." . .

The mode of his death is chosen by himself, and in that he is unlucky as in everything else. Utterly loathing life, the manner of his leaving it must be instantaneous. He stipulates that the poison by which he shall die shall not be slow of effect. He leaves himself no chance of escape. Instant death is in his hand; and thanking the true apothecary for the quickness of his drugs, he scarcely leaves himself a moment with a kiss to die. If he had been less in a hurry—if he had not felt it impossible to delay posting off to Verona for a single night—if his riding had been less rapid, or his medicine less sudden in its effect, he might

have lived. The Friar was at hand to release Juliet from
her tomb the very instant after the fatal vial had been emp-
tied. That instant was enough; the unlucky man had effected his purpose just when there was still a chance that
things might be amended. Haste is made a remarkable
characteristic of Romeo—because it is at once the parent
and the child of uniform misfortune. As from the acorn
springs the oak, and from the oak the acorn, so does the
temperament that inclines to haste predispose to misadventure, and a continuance of misadventure confirms the habit
of haste. A man whom his rashness has made continually
unlucky is strengthened in the determination to persevere
in his rapid movements by the very feeling that the "run"
is against him, and that it is of no use to think. In the
case of Romeo, he leaves it all to the steerage of Heaven—
that is, to the heady current of his own passions; and he
succeeds accordingly. . . . With all the qualities and emotions which can inspire affection and esteem,—with the
most honourable feelings and the kindliest intentions,—he
is eminently an unlucky man. . . . If we desired to moralize
with the harsh-minded satirist, who never can be suspected
of romance, we should join with him in extracting as a moral from the play—

> "Nullum numen habes, si sit prudentia; nos te
>   Nos facimus, Fortuna, deam, caeloque locamus;"

and attribute the mishaps of Romeo, not to want of fortune,
but of prudence. Philosophy and poetry differ not in es-
sentials, and the stern censure of Juvenal is just. But still,
when looking on the timeless tomb of Romeo, and contem-
plating the short and sad career through which he ran, we
cannot help recollecting his mourning words over his dying
friend, and suggest as an inscription over the monument of
the luckless gentleman,

"I THOUGHT ALL FOR THE BEST."

[*From Dowden's "Shakspere."**]

Few critics of the play have omitted to call attention to
the fact that Shakspere represents Romeo as already in
love before he gives his heart to Juliet—in love with the
pale-cheeked, dark-eyed, disdainful Rosaline. . . . The circumstance is not of Shakspere's invention. He has retained it from Brooke's poem ; but that he thought fit to
retain the circumstance, fearlessly declaring that Romeo's
supreme love is not his first love, is noteworthy. . . . Of
what character is the love of Romeo for Rosaline? Romeo's is not an active practical nature like Henry V. ; neither is he great by intellect, a thinker in any high sense of
the word. But if he lives and moves and has his being
neither heroically in the outward world, like Henry V., nor
in the world of the mind like Hamlet, all the more he lives,
moves, and has his being in the world of mere emotion. To
him emotion which enriches and exalts itself with the imagination, emotion apart from thought and apart from action,
is an end in itself. Therefore it delights him to hover over
his own sentiment, to brood upon it, to feed upon it richly.
Romeo must needs steep his whole nature in feeling, and if
Juliet does not appear, he must love Rosaline.

Nevertheless the love of Rosaline cannot be to Romeo
as the love of Juliet. It is a law in moral dynamics, too
little recognized, that the breadth and height and perma-
nence of a feeling depend in a certain degree at least upon
the actual force of its external cause. . . . Shakspere's cap-
ital discovery was this — that the facts of the world are
worthy to command our highest ardour, our most resolute
action, our most solemn awe ; and that the more we pene-
trate into fact the more will our nature be quickened, en-
riched, and exalted. The moral theme of the play is the

* *Shakspere: a Critical Study of his Mind and Art,* by Edward Dowden (2d ed. London, 1876), p. 106 fol. (by permission).

deliverance of a man from dream into reality. In Romeo's love of Rosaline we find represented the dream-life as yet undisturbed, the abandonment to emotion for emotion's sake. Romeo nurses his love ; he sheds tears ; he cultivates solitude ; he utters his groans in the hearing of the comfortable friar ; he stimulates his fancy with the sought-out phrases, the curious antitheses of the amorous dialect of the period :*

> " Why, then, O brawling love ! O loving hate!
>   O any thing, of nothing first create !
>   O heavy lightness ! serious vanity !
>   Misshapen chaos of well-seeming forms !
>   Feather of lead, bright smoke, cold fire, sick health !"

And then Romeo meets Juliet. Juliet is an actual force beyond and above himself, a veritable fact of the world. Nevertheless there remains a certain clinging self-consciousness, an absence of perfect simplicity and directness even in Romeo's very real love of Juliet. This is placed by Shakspere in designed contrast with the singleness of Juliet's nature, her direct unerroneous passion which goes straight to its object, and never broods upon itself. It is Romeo who says in the garden scene,

> " How silver-sweet sound lovers' tongues by night,
>   Like softest music to attending ears."

He has overheard the voice of Juliet, and he cannot answer her call until he has drained the sweetness of the sound. He is one of those men to whom the emotional atmosphere which is given out by the real object, and which surrounds it like a luminous mist, is more important than the reality itself . . . It is Juliet who will not allow the utterance of any oath because the whole reality of that night's

---

* Mrs. Jameson has noticed that in *A. W.* i. 1. 180–189, Helena mockingly reproduces this style of amorous antitheses. Helena, who lives so effectively in the world of fact, is contemptuous towards all unreality and affectation.

event, terrible in its joy, has flashed upon her, and she, who lives in no golden haze of luxurious feeling, is aroused and alarmed by the sudden shock of too much happiness.   It is Juliet who uses direct and simple words—

> " Farewell compliment !
> Dost thou love me? I know thou wilt say ay,
> And I will take thy word."

She has declared that her bounty is measureless, that her love is infinite, when a sudden prosaic interruption occurs ; the nurse calls within, Juliet leaves the window, and Romeo is left alone.   Is this new joy a dream?

> "O blessed, blessed night ! I am afeard,
> Being in night, all this is but a dream,
> Too flattering-sweet to be substantial."

But Juliet hastily reappears with words upon her lips which make it evident that it is no dream of joy in which she lives:

> "Three words, dear Romeo, and good night indeed.
> If that thy bent of love be honourable,
> Thy purpose marriage, send me word to-morrow,
> By one that I 'll procure to come to thee,
> Where and what time thou wilt perform the rite,
> And all my fortunes at thy foot I 'll lay,
> And follow thee, my lord, throughout the world."

The wholeness and crystalline purity of Juliet's passion is flawed by no double self.   She is all and entire in each act of her soul ; while Romeo, on the contrary, is as yet but half delivered from self-consciousness. . . .

The moment that Romeo receives the false tidings of Juliet's death is the moment of his assuming full manhood. Now, for the first time, he is completely delivered from the life of dream, completely adult, and able to act with an initiative in his own will, and with manly determination.   Accordingly, he now speaks with masculine directness and energy :

> "Is it even so? Then I defy you, stars !"

Yes; he is now master of events; the stars cannot alter his course :

> "Thou know'st my lodgings : get me ink and paper,
> And hire post-horses; I will hence to-night.
>   *Balthasar.* I do beseech you, sir, have patience;
> Your looks are pale and wild, and do import
> Some misadventure.
>   *Romeo.*   Tush! thou art deceiv'd.
> Leave me, and do the thing I bid thee do.
> Hast thou no letters for me from the Friar?
>   *Balthasar.* No, my good lord.
>   *Romeo.*   No matter: get thee gone,
> And hire those horses; I 'll be with thee straight."

"Nothing," as Maginn has observed, "can be more quiet than his final determination, 'Well, Juliet, I will lie with thee to night.' . . . It is plain Juliet. There is nothing about 'Cupid's arrow' or 'Dian's wit;' no honeyed word escapes his lips, nor again does any accent of despair. His mind is made up; the whole course of the short remainder of his life so unalterably fixed that it is perfectly useless to think more about it." These words because they are the simplest are amongst the most memorable that Romeo utters. Is this indeed the same Romeo who sighed, and wept, and spoke sonnet-wise, and penned himself in his chamber, shutting the daylight out for love of Rosaline? Now passion, imagination, and will are fused together, and Romeo who was weak has at length become strong.

ROMEO AND JULIET.

DRAMATIS PERSONÆ.

ESCALUS, prince of Verona.

PARIS, a young nobleman, kinsman to the prince.

MONTAGUE, } heads of two houses at va-
CAPULET, } riance with each other.

An old man of the Capulet family.

ROMEO, son to Montague.

MERCUTIO, kinsman to the prince, and friend to Romeo

BENVOLIO, nephew to Montague, and friend to Romeo.

TYBALT, nephew to Lady Capulet.

FRIAR LAURENCE, } Franciscans.
FRIAR JOHN, }

BALTHASAR, servant to Romeo.

SAMPSON, } servants to Capulet.
GREGORY, }

PETER, servant to Juliet's nurse.

ABRAM, servant to Montague.

An Apothecary

Three Musicians.

Page to Paris; another Page; an Officer.

LADY MONTAGUE, wife to Montague.

LADY CAPULET, wife to Capulet.

JULIET, daughter to Capulet.

Nurse to Juliet.

Citizens of Verona; Kinsfolk of both houses; Maskers, Guards, Watchmen, and Attendants.

Chorus.

SCENE: *Verona; Mantua.*

VERONA.

PROLOGUE.

Two households, both alike in dignity,
   In fair Verona, where we lay our scene,
From ancient grudge break to new mutiny,
   Where civil blood makes civil hands unclean.
From forth the fatal loins of these two foes
   A pair of star-cross'd lovers take their life,
Whose misadventur'd piteous overthrows
   Doth with their death bury their parents' strife.
The fearful passage of their death-mark'd love,
   And the continuance of their parents' rage,
Which, but their children's end, nought could remove,
   Is now the two hours' traffic of our stage:
The which if you with patient ears attend,
What here shall miss, our toil shall strive to mend

10

ACT I.

Scene I.   *Verona.   A Public Place.*

Enter Sampson *and* Gregory, *of the house of Capulet, with swords and bucklers.*

Sampson. Gregory, on my word, we 'll not carry coals.

Gregory. No, for then we should be colliers.

Sampson. I mean, an we be in choler, we 'll draw.

Gregory. Ay, while you live, draw your neck out o' the collar.

Sampson. I strike quickly, being moved.

Gregory. But thou art not quickly moved to strike.

Sampson. A dog of the house of Montague moves me.

Gregory. To move is to stir, and to be valiant is to stand; therefore, if thou art moved, thou runn'st away.   10

Sampson. A dog of that house shall move me to stand; I will take the wall of any man or maid of Montague's.

Gregory. That shows thee a weak slave; for the weakest goes to the wall.

Sampson. True; and therefore women, being the weaker vessels, are ever thrust to the wall: therefore I will push Montague's men from the wall, and thrust his maids to the wall.

Gregory. The quarrel is between our masters and us their men.   20

Sampson. 'T is all one, I will show myself a tyrant; when I have fought with the men, I will be cruel with the maids, and cut off their heads.

Gregory. Draw thy tool; here comes two of the house of the Montagues.

Sampson. My naked weapon is out; quarrel, I will back thee.

Gregory. How? turn thy back and run?

Sampson. Fear me not.

Gregory. No, marry; I fear thee! ₃₀

Sampson. Let us take the law of our sides; let them begin.

Gregory. I will frown as I pass by, and let them take it as they list.

Sampson. Nay, as they dare. I will bite my thumb at them; which is a disgrace to them, if they bear it.

Enter ABRAM *and* BALTHASAR.

Abram. Do you bite your thumb at us, sir?

Sampson. I do bite my thumb, sir.

Abram. Do you bite your thumb at us, sir?

Sampson. [*Aside to Gregory*] Is the law of our side, if I say ay? ₄₀

Gregory. No.

Sampson. No, sir, I do not bite my thumb at you, sir, but I bite my thumb, sir.

Gregory. Do you quarrel, sir?

Abram. Quarrel, sir! no, sir.

Sampson. If you do, sir, I am for you; I serve as good a man as you.

Abram. No better.

Sampson. Well, sir.

Gregory. [*Aside to Sampson*] Say 'better;' here comes one of my master's kinsmen. ₅₁

Sampson. Yes, better, sir.

Abram. You lie.

Sampson. Draw, if you be men.—Gregory, remember thy swashing blow. [*They fight.*

Enter BENVOLIO.

Benvolio. Part, fools!

Put up your swords; you know not what you do.

[*Beats down their swords.*

Enter TYBALT.

Tybalt. What, art thou drawn among these heartless hinds?
Turn thee, Benvolio, look upon thy death.

Benvolio. I do but keep the peace; put up thy sword,   60
Or manage it to part these men with me.

Tybalt. What, drawn, and talk of peace! I hate the word,
As I hate hell, all Montagues, and thee;
Have at thee, coward!   [*They fight.*

Enter several of both houses who join the fray; then enter
Citizens, *with clubs.*

First Citizen. Clubs, bills, and partisans! strike! beat them
     down!
Down with the Capulets! down with the Montagues!

Enter CAPULET *in his gown, and* LADY CAPULET.

Capulet. What noise is this? Give me my long sword, ho!

Lady Capulet. A crutch, a crutch! why call you for a
     sword?

Capulet. My sword, I say! Old Montague is come,
And flourishes his blade in spite of me.   70

Enter MONTAGUE *and* LADY MONTAGUE.

Montague. Thou villain Capulet!—Hold me not, let me go.

Lady Montague. Thou shalt not stir a foot to seek a foe.

Enter PRINCE, *with his train.*

Prince. Rebellious subjects, enemies to peace,
Profaners of this neighbour-stained steel,—
Will they not hear? What, ho! you men, you beasts,
That quench the fire of your pernicious rage
With purple fountains issuing from your veins,
On pain of torture, from those bloody hands
Throw your mistemper'd weapons to the ground,

And hear the sentence of your moved prince. —   80
Three civil brawls, bred of an airy word,
By thee, old Capulet, and Montague,
Have thrice disturb'd the quiet of our streets,
And made Verona's ancient citizens
Cast by their grave beseeming ornaments,
To wield old partisans, in hands as old,
Canker'd with peace, to part your canker'd hate.
If ever you disturb our streets again,
Your lives shall pay the forfeit of the peace.
For this time, all the rest depart away: 90
You, Capulet, shall go along with me;
And, Montague, come you this afternoon,
To know our further pleasure in this case,
To old Freetown, our common judgment-place.
Once more, on pain of death, all men depart.

  [*Exeunt all but Montague, Lady Montague, and Benvolio*

 Montague. Who set this ancient quarrel new abroach?
Speak, nephew, were you by when it began?

 Benvolio. Here were the servants of your adversary
And yours close fighting ere I did approach.
I drew to part them: in the instant came   100
The fiery Tybalt, with his sword prepar'd;
Which, as he breath'd defiance to my ears,
He swung about his head and cut the winds,
Who, nothing hurt withal, hiss'd him in scorn.
While we were interchanging thrusts and blows,
Came more and more, and fought on part and part,
Till the prince came, who parted either part.

 Lady Montague. O, where is Romeo? saw you him to-day?
Right glad I am he was not at this fray.

 Benvolio. Madam, an hour before the worshipp'd sun   110
Peer'd forth the golden window of the east,
A troubled mind drave me to walk abroad;
Where, underneath the grove of sycamore

That westward rooteth from the city's side,
So early walking did I see your son.
Towards him I made, but he was ware of me
And stole into the covert of the wood ;
I, measuring his affections by my own,
Which then most sought where most might not be found,
Being one too many by my weary self,   120
Pursued my humour not pursuing his,
And gladly shunn'd who gladly fled from me.

    Montague. Many a morning hath he there been seen,
With tears augmenting the fresh morning's dew,
Adding to clouds more clouds with his deep sighs ;
But all so soon as the all-cheering sun
Should in the farthest east begin to draw
The shady curtains from Aurora's bed,
Away from light steals home my heavy son,
And private in his chamber pens himself,   130
Shuts up his windows, locks fair daylight out,
And makes himself an artificial night.
Black and portentous must this humour prove,
Unless good counsel may the cause remove.

    Benvolio. My noble uncle, do you know the cause ?

    Montague. I neither know it nor can learn of him.

    Benvolio. Have you importun'd him by any means ?

    Montague. Both by myself and many other friends ;
But he, his own affections' counsellor,
Is to himself—I will not say how true—   140
But to himself so secret and so close,
So far from sounding and discovery,
As is the bud bit with an envious worm,
Ere he can spread his sweet leaves to the air,
Or dedicate his beauty to the sun.
Could we but learn from whence his sorrows grow,
We would as willingly give cure as know.

Enter ROMEO.

Benvolio. See, where he comes : so please you, step aside ;
I 'll know his grievance, or be much denied.

Montague. I would thou wert so happy by thy stay,   150
To hear true shrift.—Come, madam, let 's away.

                                [*Exeunt Montague and Lady.*

Benvolio. Good morrow, cousin.

Romeo.   Is the day so young ?

Benvolio. But new struck nine.

Romeo.   Ay me ! sad hours seem long.
Was that my father that went hence so fast ?

Benvolio. It was.   What sadness lengthens Romeo's hours ?

Romeo. Not having that which, having, makes them short.

Benvolio. In love ?

Romeo. Out—

Benvolio. Of love ?

Romeo. Out of her favour, where I am in love.   160

Benvolio. Alas, that love, so gentle in his view,
Should be so tyrannous and rough in proof !

Romeo. Alas, that love, whose view is muffled still,
Should without eyes see pathways to his will !
Where shall we dine ?—O me !   What fray was here ?
Yet tell me not, for I have heard it all.
Here 's much to do with hate, but more with love.
Why, then, O brawling love ! O loving hate !
O any thing, of nothing first created !
O heavy lightness ! serious vanity !   170
Misshapen chaos of well-seeming forms !
Feather of lead, bright smoke, cold fire, sick health !
Still-waking sleep, that is not what it is !
This love feel I, that feel no love in this.
Dost thou not laugh ?

Benvolio.   No, coz, I rather weep.

Romeo. Good heart, at what ?

Benvolio.   At thy good heart's oppression.

Romeo. Why, such is love's transgression.
Griefs of mine own lie heavy in my breast,
Which thou wilt propagate, to have it prest
With more of thine; this love that thou hast shown   180
Doth add more grief to too much of mine own.
Love is a smoke rais'd with the fume of sighs;
Being purg'd, a fire sparkling in lovers' eyes;
Being vex'd, a sea nourish'd with lovers' tears:
What is it else? a madness most discreet,
A choking gall, and a preserving sweet.
Farewell, my coz.

Benvolio.   Soft! I will go along;
An if you leave me so, you do me wrong.

Romeo. Tut, I have lost myself; I am not here:
This is not Romeo, he 's some other where.   190

Benvolio. Tell me in sadness, who is that you love.

Romeo. What, shall I groan and tell thee?

Benvolio.   Groan! why, no,
But sadly tell me who.

Romeo. Bid a sick man in sadness make his will;
Ah, word ill urg'd to one that is so ill!
In sadness, cousin, I do love a woman.

Benvolio. I aim'd so near when I suppos'd you lov'd.

Romeo. A right good mark-man! And she 's fair I love.

Benvolio. A right fair mark, fair coz, is soonest hit.

Romeo. Well, in that hit you miss: she 'll not be hit   200
With Cupid's arrow; she hath Dian's wit,
And, in strong proof of chastity well arm'd,
From love's weak childish bow she lives unharm'd.
She will not stay the siege of loving terms,
Nor bide the encounter of assailing eyes,
Nor ope her lap to saint-seducing gold;
O, she is rich in beauty! only poor
That, when she dies, with beauty dies her store.

Benvolio. Then she hath sworn that she will still live
chaste?

Romeo. She hath, and in that sparing makes huge waste;
For beauty starv'd with her severity   211
Cuts beauty off from all posterity.
She is too fair, too wise, wisely too fair,
To merit bliss by making me despair;
She hath forsworn to love, and in that vow
Do I live dead that live to tell it now.

Benvolio. Be rul'd by me, forget to think of her.

Romeo. O, teach me how I should forget to think.

Benvolio. By giving liberty unto thine eyes;
Examine other beauties.

Romeo.   'T is the way   220
To call hers, exquisite, in question more.
These happy masks that kiss fair ladies' brows,
Being black, put us in mind they hide the fair:
He that is strucken blind cannot forget
The precious treasure of his eyesight lost.
Show me a mistress that is passing fair,
What doth her beauty serve but as a note
Where I may read who pass'd that passing fair?
Farewell; thou canst not teach me to forget.

Benvolio. I 'll pay that doctrine, or else die in debt.   230

[*Exeunt.*

SCENE II.   *A Street.*

Enter CAPULET, PARIS, *and* Servant.

Capulet. But Montague is bound as well as I,
In penalty alike; and 't is not hard, I think,
For men so old as we to keep the peace.

Paris. Of honourable reckoning are you both;
And pity 't is you liv'd at odds so long.
But now, my lord, what say you to my suit?

Capulet. But saying o'er what I have said before.
My child is yet a stranger in the world ;
She hath not seen the change of fourteen years :
Let two more summers wither in their pride,   10
Ere we may think her ripe to be a bride.

Paris. Younger than she are happy mothers made.

Capulet. And too soon marr'd are those so early made.
The earth hath swallow'd all my hopes but she,
She is the hopeful lady of my earth :
But woo her, gentle Paris, get her heart,
My will to her consent is but a part ;
An she agree, within her scope of choice
Lies my consent and fair according voice.
This night I hold an old accustom'd feast,   20
Whereto I have invited many a guest,
Such as I love ; and you, among the store,
One more, most welcome, makes my number more.
At my poor house look to behold this night
Earth-treading stars that make dark heaven light :
Such comfort as do lusty young men feel
When well-apparell'd April on the heel
Of limping winter treads, even such delight
Among fresh female buds shall you this night
Inherit at my house ; hear all, all see,   30
And like her most whose merit most shall be :
Which on more view of many, mine being one
May stand in number, though in reckoning none.
Come, go with me.—[*To Servant, giving a paper*] Go, sirrah,
    trudge about
Through fair Verona ; find those persons out
Whose names are written there, and to them say,
My house and welcome on their pleasure stay.

                    [*Exeunt Capulet and Paris.*

Servant. Find them out whose names are written here !
It is written that the shoemaker should meddle with his

yard and the tailor with his last, the fisher with his pencil
and the painter with his nets ; but I am sent to find those
persons whose names are here writ, and can never find what
names the writing person hath here writ. I must to the
learned.—In good time. 44

Enter BENVOLIO *and* ROMEO.

Benvolio. Tut, man, one fire burns out another's burning,
  One pain is lessen'd by another's anguish ;
Turn giddy, and be holp by backward turning ;
  One desperate grief cures with another's languish :
Take thou some new infection to thy eye,
And the rank poison of the old will die. 50

Romeo. Your plantain-leaf is excellent for that.

Benvolio. For what, I pray thee ?

Romeo. For your broken shin.

Benvolio. Why, Romeo, art thou mad ?

Romeo. Not mad, but bound more than a madman is ;
Shut up in prison, kept without my food,
Whipp'd and tormented and—Good-den, good fellow.

Servant. God gi' good-den.—I pray, sir, can you read ?

Romeo. Ay, mine own fortune in my misery.

Servant. Perhaps you have learned it without book ; but,
I pray, can you read any thing you see ? 60

Romeo. Ay, if I know the letters and the language.

Servant. Ye say honestly ; rest you merry !

Romeo. Stay, fellow ; I can read.

[Reads] ' *Signior Martino and his wife and daughters ;
County Anselme and his beauteous sisters ; the lady widow of
Vitruvio ; Signior Placentio and his lovely nieces ; Mercutio and
his brother Valentine ; mine uncle Capulet, his wife, and daughters ; my fair niece Rosaline ; Livia ; Signior Valentio and his
cousin Tybalt ; Lucio and the lively Helena.*'
A fair assembly ; whither should they come ? 70

Servant. Up.

Romeo. Whither?

Servant. To supper; to our house.

Romeo. Whose house?

Servant. My master's.

Romeo. Indeed, I should have ask'd you that before.

Servant. Now I 'll tell you without asking: my master is the great rich Capulet; and if you be not of the house of Montagues, I pray, come and crush a cup of wine. Rest you merry! *[Exit.*

Benvolio. At this same ancient feast of Capulet's   81
Sups the fair Rosaline whom thou so lov'st,
With all the admired beauties of Verona.
Go thither, and with unattainted eye
Compare her face with some that I shall show,
And I will make thee think thy swan a crow.

Romeo. When the devout religion of mine eye
    Maintains such falsehood, then turn tears to fires;
And these, who often drown'd could never die,
    Transparent heretics, be burnt for liars!   90
One fairer than my love! the all-seeing sun
Ne'er saw her match since first the world begun.

Benvolio. Tut! you saw her fair, none else being by,
Herself pois'd with herself in either eye;
But in that crystal scales let there be weigh'd
Your lady's love against some other maid
That I will show you shining at this feast,
And she shall scant show well that now shows best.

Romeo. I 'll go along, no such sight to be shown,   99
But to rejoice in splendour of mine own.   *[Exeunt.*

Scene III. *A Room in Capulet's House.*

Enter Lady Capulet *and* Nurse.

Lady Capulet. Nurse, where 's my daughter? call her forth
    to me.

Nurse. Now, by my maidenhead at twelve year old,
I bade her come.—What, lamb ! what, lady-bird !—
God forbid !—Where 's this girl ?—What, Juliet !

Enter JULIET.

Juliet. How now ! who calls ?
Nurse.   Your mother.
Juliet.   Madam, I am here.
What is your will ?
    Lady Capulet. This is the matter : — Nurse, give leave
        awhile,
We must talk in secret.—Nurse, come back again ;
I have remember'd me, thou 's hear our counsel.
Thou know'st my daughter 's of a pretty age.   10
    Nurse. Faith, I can tell her age unto an hour.
    Lady Capulet. She 's not fourteen.
    Nurse.   I 'll lay fourteen of my teeth,—
And yet, to my teen be it spoken, I have but four,—
She is not fourteen.   How long is it now
To Lammas-tide ?
    Lady Capulet.   A fortnight and odd days.
    Nurse. Even or odd, of all days in the year,
Come Lammas-eve at night shall she be fourteen.
Susan and she—God rest all Christian souls !—
Were of an age : well, Susan is with God ;
She was too good for me : but, as I said,
On Lammas-eve at night shall she be fourteen ;
That shall she, marry ; I remember it well.
'T is since the earthquake now eleven years ;
And she was wean'd,—I never shall forget it,—
Of all the days of the year, upon that day :
For I had then laid wormwood to my dug,
Sitting in the sun under the dove-house wall ;
My lord and you were then at Mantua.—
Nay, I do bear a brain :—but, as I said,

When it did taste the wormwood on the nipple   30
Of my dug, and felt it bitter, pretty fool,
To see it tetchy and fall out with the dug !
Shake, quoth the dove-house ; 't was no need, I trow,
To bid me trudge.
And since that time it is eleven years ;
For then she could stand alone ; nay, by the rood,
She could have run and waddled all about.—
God mark thee to his grace !
Thou wast the prettiest babe that e'er I nurs'd ;
An I might live to see thee married once,   40
I have my wish.

    Lady Capulet. Marry, that 'marry' is the very theme
I came to talk of.—Tell me, daughter Juliet,
How stands your disposition to be married ?

    Juliet. It is an honour that I dream not of.

    Nurse. An honour ! were not I thine only nurse,
I would say thou hadst suck'd wisdom from thy teat.

    Lady Capulet. Well, think of marriage now ; younger than
       you
Here in Verona, ladies of esteem,
Are made already mothers : by my count,   50
I was your mother much upon these years
That you are now a maid.   Thus then in brief :
The valiant Paris seeks you for his love.

    Nurse. A man, young lady ! lady, such a man
As all the world—why, he 's a man of wax.

    Lady Capulet. Verona's summer hath not such a flower.

    Nurse. Nay, he 's a flower ; in faith, a very flower.

    Lady Capulet. What say you ? can you love the gentle-
       man ?
This night you shall behold him at our feast ;
Read o'er the volume of young Paris' face,   60
And find delight writ there with beauty's pen ;
Examine every married lineament

And see how one another lends content,
And what obscur'd in this fair volume lies
Find written in the margent of his eyes.
This precious book of love, this unbound lover,
To beautify him, only lacks a cover;
The fish lives in the sea, and 't is much pride
For fair without the fair within to hide.
That book in many's eyes doth share the glory,   70
That in gold clasps locks in the golden story;
So shall you share all that he doth possess,
By having him making yourself no less.
Speak briefly, can you like of Paris' love?

   Juliet. I 'll look to like, if looking liking move;
But no more deep will I endart mine eye
Than your consent gives strength to make it fly.

Enter a Servant.

   Servant. Madam, the guests are come, supper served up, you called, my young lady asked for, the nurse cursed in the pantry, and every thing in extremity. I must hence to wait; I beseech you, follow straight.   81

   Lady Capulet. We follow thee. [*Exit Servant.*] Juliet, the county stays.

   Nurse. Go, girl, seek happy nights to happy days.

                                 [*Exeunt.*

SCENE IV.   *A Street.*

Enter ROMEO, MERCUTIO, BENVOLIO, *with five or six* Maskers, Torch-bearers, *and others.*

   Romeo. What, shall this speech be spoke for our excuse?
Or shall we on without apology?

   Benvolio. The date is out of such prolixity.
We 'll have no Cupid hoodwink'd with a scarf,
Bearing a Tartar's painted bow of lath,

Scaring the ladies like a crow-keeper;
Nor no without-book prologue, faintly spoke
After the prompter, for our entrance:
But let them measure us by what they will,
We 'll measure them a measure, and be gone.   10

    Romeo. Give me a torch; I am not for this ambling:
Being but heavy, I will bear the light.

    Mercutio. Nay, gentle Romeo, we must have you dance.

    Romeo. Not I, believe me. You have dancing shoes
With nimble soles; I have a soul of lead
So stakes me to the ground I cannot move.

    Mercutio. You are a lover; borrow Cupid's wings,
And soar with them above a common bound.

    Romeo. I am too sore enpierced with his shaft
To soar with his light feathers, and, so bound,   20
I cannot bound a pitch above dull woe;
Under love's heavy burden do I sink.

    Mercutio. And, to sink in it, should you burden love;
Too great oppression for a tender thing.

    Romeo. Is love a tender thing? it is too rough,
Too rude, too boisterous, and it pricks like thorn.

    Mercutio. If love be rough with you, be rough with love;
Prick love for pricking, and you beat love down.—
Give me a case to put my visage in;   [*Putting on a mask.*
A visor for a visor! what care I   30
What curious eye doth quote deformities?
Here are the beetle-brows shall blush for me.

    Benvolio. Come, knock and enter; and no sooner in,
But every man betake him to his legs.

    Romeo. A torch for me; let wantons light of heart
Tickle the senseless rushes with their heels,
For I am proverb'd with a grandsire phrase:
I 'll be a candle-holder, and look on.
The game was ne'er so fair, and I am done.

    Mercutio. Tut, dun 's the mouse, the constable's own word;

If thou art Dun, we 'll draw thee from the mire   41
Of this sir-reverence love, wherein thou stick'st
Up to the ears.—Come, we burn daylight, ho !
   Romeo. Nay, that 's not so.
   Mercutio.   I mean, sir, in delay
We waste our lights in vain, like lamps by day.
Take our good meaning, for our judgment sits
Five times in that ere once in our five wits.
   Romeo. And we mean well in going to this mask ;
But 't is no wit to go.
   Mercutio.   Why, may one ask ?
   Romeo. I dreamt a dream to-night.
   Mercutio.   And so did I.   5c
   Romeo. Well, what was yours ?
   Mercutio.   That dreamers often lie.
   Romeo. In bed asleep, while they do dream things true.
   Mercutio. O, then, I see Queen Mab hath been with you.
She is the fairies' midwife, and she comes
In shape no bigger than an agate-stone
On the fore-finger of an alderman,
Drawn with a team of little atomies
Athwart men's noses as they lie asleep ;
Her waggon-spokes made of long spinners' legs,
The cover of the wings of grasshoppers,   6o
The traces of the smallest spider's web,
The collars of the moonshine's watery beams,
Her whip of cricket's bone, the lash of film,
Her waggoner a small grey-coated gnat,
Not half so big as a round little worm
Prick'd from the lazy finger of a maid ;
Her chariot is an empty hazel-nut
Made by the joiner squirrel or old grub,
Time out o' mind the fairies' coachmakers.
And in this state she gallops night by night   70
Through lovers' brains, and then they dream of love ;

O'er courtiers' knees, that dream on court'sies straight;
O'er lawyers' fingers, who straight dream on fees;
O'er ladies' lips, who straight on kisses dream,
Which oft the angry Mab with blisters plagues,
Because their breaths with sweetmeats tainted are.
Sometime she gallops o'er a courtier's nose,
And then dreams he of smelling out a suit;
And sometime comes she with a tithe-pig's tail
Tickling a parson's nose as a' lies asleep,   80
Then dreams he of another benefice.
Sometime she driveth o'er a soldier's neck,
And then dreams he of cutting foreign throats,
Of breaches, ambuscadoes, Spanish blades,
Of healths five-fathom deep; and then anon
Drums in his ear, at which he starts and wakes,
And being thus frighted swears a prayer or two
And sleeps again.   This is that very Mab
That plats the manes of horses in the night,
And bakes the elf-locks in foul sluttish hairs,   90
Which once untangled much misfortune bodes.
This is she—
   Romeo.   Peace, peace, Mercutio, peace!
Thou talk'st of nothing.
   Mercutio.   True, I talk of dreams,
Which are the children of an idle brain,
Begot of nothing but vain fantasy,
Which is as thin of substance as the air,
And more inconstant than the wind, who wooes
Even now the frozen bosom of the North,
And, being anger'd, puffs away from thence,
Turning his face to the dew-dropping South.   100
   Benvolio. This wind you talk of blows us from ourselves;
Supper is done, and we shall come too late.
   Romeo. I fear, too early; for my mind misgives
Some consequence, yet hanging in the stars,

Shall bitterly begin his fearful date
With this night's revels, and expire the term
Of a despised life clos'd in my breast
By some vile forfeit of untimely death.
But He that hath the steerage of my course
Direct my sail!—On, lusty gentlemen.   110
   Benvolio. Strike, drum.   [*Exeunt.*

SCENE V.   *A Hall in Capulet's House.*

Musicians *waiting.   Enter* Servingmen, *with napkins.*

   1 *Servingman.* Where 's Potpan, that he helps not to take
away?   He shift a trencher! he scrape a trencher!

   2 *Servingman.* When good manners shall lie all in one or
two men's hands and they unwashed too, 't is a foul thing.

   1 *Servingman.* Away with the joint-stools, remove the
court-cupboard, look to the plate.—Good thou, save me a
piece of marchpane; and, as thou lovest me, let the porter
let in Susan Grindstone and Nell.—Antony! and Potpan!

   2 *Servingman.* Ay, boy, ready.

   1 *Servingman.* You are looked for and called for, asked
for and sought for, in the great chamber.   11

   2 *Servingman.* We cannot be here and there too.—Cheerly, boys; be brisk awhile, and the longer liver take all.

Enter CAPULET, *with* JULIET *and others of his house, meeting
the* Guests *and* Maskers.

   Capulet. Welcome, gentlemen! ladies that have their toes
Unplagu'd with corns will have a bout with you.—
Ah ha, my mistresses! which of you all
Will now deny to dance? she that makes dainty,
She, I 'll swear, hath corns; am I come near ye now?—
Welcome, gentlemen! I have seen the day
That I have worn a visor, and could tell   20
A whispering tale in a fair lady's ear,

Such as would please ; 't is gone, 't is gone, 't is gone :—
You are welcome, gentlemen !—Come, musicians, play.—
A hall, a hall! give room ! and foot it, girls.—

                         [*Music plays, and they dance.*

More light, you knaves ; and turn the tables up,
And quench the fire, the room is grown too hot.—
Ah, sirrah, this unlook'd-for sport comes well.—
Nay, sit, nay, sit, good cousin Capulet ;
For you and I are past our dancing days :
How long is 't now since last yourself and I   30
Were in a mask ?

   2 Capulet.   By 'r lady, thirty years.

   Capulet. What, man ! 't is not so much, 't is not so much :
'T is since the nuptial of Lucentio,
Come Pentecost as quickly as it will,
Some five and twenty years ; and then we mask'd.

   2 Capulet. 'T is more, 't is more : his son is elder, sir ;
His son is thirty.

   Capulet.   Will you tell me that ?
His son was but a ward two years ago.

   Romeo. [*To a Servingman*] What lady is that, which doth
      enrich the hand
Of yonder knight ?   40

   Servingman. I know not, sir.

   Romeo. O, she doth teach the torches to burn bright !
Her beauty hangs upon the cheek of night
Like a rich jewel in an Ethiope's ear ;
Beauty too rich for use, for earth too dear !
So shows a snowy dove trooping with crows,
As yonder lady o'er her fellows shows.
The measure done, I 'll watch her place of stand,
And, touching hers, make blessed my rude hand.
Did my heart love till now? forswear it, sight !   50
For I ne'er saw true beauty till this night.

   Tybalt. This, by his voice, should be a Montague.—

Fetch me my rapier, boy.—What dares the slave
Come hither, cover'd with an antic face,
To fleer and scorn at our solemnity?
Now, by the stock and honour of my kin,
To strike him dead I hold it not a sin.

  Capulet. Why, how now, kinsman! wherefore storm you
   so?

  Tybalt. Uncle, this is a Montague, our foe,
A villain that is hither come in spite,   60
To scorn at our solemnity this night.

  Capulet. Young Romeo is it?

  Tybalt.   'T is he, that villain Romeo.

  Capulet. Content thee, gentle coz, let him alone :
He bears him like a portly gentleman ;
And, to say truth, Verona brags of him
To be a virtuous and well-govern'd youth.
I would not for the wealth of all the town
Here in my house do him disparagement ;
Therefore be patient, take no note of him :
It is my will, the which if thou respect,   70
Show a fair presence and put off these frowns,
An ill-beseeming semblance for a feast.

  Tybalt. It fits, when such a villain is a guest ;
I 'll not endure him.

  Capulet.   He shall be endur'd :
What, goodman boy! I say, he shall : go to ;
Am I the master here, or you? go to.
You 'll not endure him!—God shall mend my soul!—
You 'll make a mutiny among my guests!
You will set cock-a-hoop! you 'll be the man!

  Tybalt. Why, uncle, 't is a shame.

  Capulet.   Go to, go to ; 80
You are a saucy boy :—is 't so, indeed?—
This trick may chance to scathe you,—I know what.
You must contrary me! marry, 't is time.—

Well said, my hearts!—You are a princox; go:
Be quiet, or—More light, more light!—For shame!
I 'll make you quiet.   What!—Cheerly, my hearts!
  Tybalt. Patience perforce with wilful choler meeting
Makes my flesh tremble in their different greeting.
I will withdraw; but this intrusion shall,
Now seeming sweet, convert to bitter gall.   [*Exit.*
  Romeo. [*To Juliet*] If I profane with my unworthiest hand
  This holy shrine, the gentle fine is this: 92
My lips, two blushing pilgrims, ready stand
  To smooth that rough touch with a tender kiss.
  Juliet. Good pilgrim, you do wrong your hand too much,
  Which mannerly devotion shows in this;
For saints have hands that pilgrims' hands do touch,
  And palm to palm is holy palmers' kiss.
  Romeo. Have not saints lips, and holy palmers too?
  Juliet. Ay, pilgrim, lips that they must use in prayer.
  Romeo. O, then, dear saint, let lips do what hands do; 101
They pray, grant thou, lest faith turn to despair.
  Juliet. Saints do not move, though grant for prayers'
      sake.
  Romeo. Then move not, while my prayer's effect I take.
Thus from my lips by thine my sin is purg'd.   [*Kissing her.*
  Juliet. Then have my lips the sin that they have took.
  Romeo. Sin from my lips?   O trespass sweetly urg'd!
Give me my sin again.
  Juliet.   You kiss by the book.
  Nurse. Madam, your mother craves a word with you.
  Romeo. What is her mother?
  Nurse.   Marry, bachelor,   110
Her mother is the lady of the house,
And a good lady, and a wise, and virtuous.
I nurs'd her daughter, that you talk'd withal;
I tell you, he that can lay hold of her
Shall have the chinks.

Romeo.   Is she a Capulet?
O dear account! my life is my foe's debt.

Benvolio. Away, be gone; the sport is at the best.

Romeo. Ay, so I fear; the more is my unrest.

Capulet. Nay, gentlemen, prepare not to be gone;
We have a trifling foolish banquet towards.— 120
Is it e'en so? why, then, I thank you all:
I thank you, honest gentlemen; good night.—
More torches here!—Come on then, let's to bed.
Ah, sirrah, by my fay, it waxes late;
I 'll to my rest.   [*Exeunt all but Juliet and Nurse.*

Juliet. Come hither, nurse. What is yond gentleman?

Nurse. The son and heir of old Tiberio.

Juliet. What's he that now is going out of door?

Nurse. Marry, that, I think, be young Petruchio.

Juliet. What's he that follows there, that would **not**
dance?

Nurse. I know not. 131

Juliet. Go, ask his name.—If he be married,
My grave is like to be my wedding bed.

Nurse. His name is Romeo, and a Montague,
The only son of your great enemy.

Juliet. My only love sprung from my only hate!
Too early seen unknown, and known too late!
Prodigious birth of love it is to me,
That I must love a loathed enemy.

Nurse. What's this? what's this?

Juliet.   A rhyme I learn'd even now
Of one I danc'd withal. [*One calls within* 'Juliet.'

Nurse.   Anon, anon!—
Come, let's away; the strangers all are gone.

Enter Chorus.

Now old desire doth in his death-bed **lie**,
    And young affection gapes to be his **heir**;

That fair for which love groan'd for and would die,
    With tender Juliet match'd, is now not fair.
Now Romeo is belov'd and loves again,
    Alike bewitched by the charm of looks,
But to his foe suppos'd he must complain,
    And she steal love's sweet bait from fearful hooks.   150
Being held a foe, he may not have access
    To breathe such vows as lovers use to swear ;
And she as much in love, her means much less
    To meet her new-beloved any where.
But passion lends them power, time means, to meet,
Tempering extremities with extreme sweet.   [*Exit*

THE SO-CALLED TOMB OF JULIET AT VERONA.

"Enter NURSE *and* PETER" (ii. 4).

ACT II.

SCENE I.   *A Lane by the wall of Capulet's Orchard.*

Enter ROMEO.

Romeo. Can I go forward when my heart is here?
Turn back, dull earth, and find thy centre out.
    [*He climbs the wall, and leaps down within it.*

Enter BENVOLIO *and* MERCUTIO.

Benvolio. Romeo! my cousin Romeo! Romeo!
Mercutio.   He is wise:
And, on my life, hath stolen him home to bed.

Benvolio. He ran this way, and leap'd this orchard wall ;
Call, good Mercutio.

    Mercutio.   Nay, I 'll conjure too.—
Romeo ! humours ! madman ! passion ! lover !
Appear thou in the likeness of a sigh !
Speak but one rhyme, and I am satisfied ;
Cry but ' Ay me !' pronounce but ' love ' and ' dove ;'   10
Speak to my gossip Venus one fair word,
One nickname for her purblind son and heir,
Young Abraham Cupid, he that shot so trim,
When King Cophetua lov'd the beggar-maid !—
He heareth not, he stirreth not, he moveth not ;
The ape is dead, and I must conjure him.—
I conjure thee by Rosaline's bright eyes,
By her high forehead and her scarlet lip,
That in thy likeness thou appear to us !

    Benvolio. An if he hear thee, thou wilt anger him.   20

    Mercutio. This cannot anger him : 't would anger him
To raise a spirit in his mistress' circle
Of some strange nature, letting it there stand
Till she had laid it and conjur'd it down ;
That were some spite : my invocation
Is fair and honest, and in his mistress' name
I conjure only but to raise up him.

    Benvolio. Come, he hath hid himself among these trees,
To be consorted with the humorous night ;
Blind is his love and best befits the dark.   30

    Mercutio. If love be blind, love cannot hit the mark.—
Romeo, good night.—I 'll to my truckle-bed ;
This field-bed is too cold for me to sleep.
Come, shall we go ?

    Benvolic.   Go, then ; for 't is in vain
To seek him here that means not to be found.   [*Exeunt.*

Scene II.   *Capulet's Orchard.*

Enter Romeo.

Romeo. He jests at scars that never felt a wound.—

                   [*Juliet appears above at a window.*

But, soft ! what light through yonder window breaks ?

It is the east, and Juliet is the sun.—

Arise, fair sun, and kill the envious moon,

Who is already sick and pale with grief,

That thou her maid art far more fair than she.

Be not her maid, since she is envious :

Her vestal livery is but sick and green,

And none but fools do wear it ; cast it off.—

It is my lady, O, it is my love !

O, that she knew she were !—

She speaks, yet she says nothing ; what of that ?

Her eye discourses ; I will answer it.

I am too bold, 't is not to me she speaks.

Two of the fairest stars in all the heaven,

Having some business, do entreat her eyes

To twinkle in their spheres till they return.

What if her eyes were there, they in her head ?

The brightness of her cheek would shame those stars,

As daylight doth a lamp ; her eyes in heaven

Would through the airy region stream so bright

That birds would sing and think it were not night.

See, how she leans her cheek upon her hand !

O, that I were a glove upon that hand,

That I might touch that cheek !

    Juliet.   Ay me !

    Romeo.   She speaks.

O, speak again, bright angel ! for thou art

As glorious to this night, being o'er my head,

As is a winged messenger of heaven

Unto the white-upturned wondering eyes
Of mortals that fall back to gaze on him,   30
When he bestrides the lazy-pacing clouds
And sails upon the bosom of the air.

 Juliet. O Romeo, Romeo! wherefore art thou Romeo?
Deny thy father and refuse thy name;
Or, if thou wilt not, be but sworn my love,
And I 'll no longer be a Capulet.

 Romeo. [*Aside*] Shall I hear more, or shall I speak at this?

 Juliet. 'T is but thy name that is my enemy;
Thou art thyself, though not a Montague.
What 's Montague? it is nor hand, nor foot,   40
Nor arm, nor face, nor any other part
Belonging to a man. [O, be some other name!
What 's in a name? that which we call a rose
By any other name would smell as sweet;
So Romeo would, were he not Romeo call'd,
Retain that dear perfection which he owes
Without that title.—Romeo, doff thy name,
And for that name, which is no part of thee,
Take all myself.

 Romeo.   I take thee at thy word:
Call me but love, and I 'll be·new baptiz'd;   50
Henceforth I never will be Romeo.

 Juliet. What man art thou that thus bescreen'd in night
So stumblest on my counsel?

 Romeo.   By a name
I know not how to tell thee who I am.
My name, dear saint, is hateful to myself,
Because it is an enemy to thee;
Had I it written, I would tear the word.

 Juliet. My ears have yet not drunk a hundred words
Of that tongue's utterance, yet I know the sound.—
Art thou not Romeo, and a Montague?   60

 Romeo. Neither, fair maid, if either thee dislike.

Juliet. How cam'st thou hither, tell me, and wherefore?
The orchard walls are high and hard to climb,
And the place death, considering who thou art,
If any of my kinsmen find thee here.
  Romeo. With love's light wings did I o'er-perch these walls,
For stony limits cannot hold love out,
And what love can do that dares love attempt;
Therefore thy kinsmen are no let to me.
  Juliet. If they do see thee, they will murther thee.
  Romeo. Alack, there lies more peril in thine eye
Than twenty of their swords; look thou but sweet,
And I am proof against their enmity.
  Juliet. I would not for the world they saw thee here.
  Romeo. I have night's cloak to hide me from their eyes;
And but thou love me, let them find me here:
My life were better ended by their hate,
Than death prorogued, wanting of thy love.
  Juliet. By whose direction found'st thou out this place?
  Romeo. By love, that first did prompt me to inquire;
He lent me counsel, and I lent him eyes.
I am no pilot; yet, wert thou as far
As that vast shore wash'd with the farthest sea,
I would adventure for such merchandise.
  Juliet. Thou know'st the mask of night is on my face,
Else would a maiden blush bepaint my cheek
For that which thou hast heard me speak to-night.
Fain would I dwell on form, fain, fain deny
What I have spoke; but farewell compliment!
Dost thou love me? I know thou wilt say ay,
And I will take thy word: yet, if thou swear'st.
Thou mayst prove false; [at lovers' perjuries, Ovid: Ars. am. I, 633.
They say, Jove laughs.] O gentle Romeo,
If thou dost love, pronounce it faithfully:
Or if thou think'st I am too quickly won.
I'll frown and be perverse and say thee nay.

F.

So thou wilt woo; but else, not for the world.
In truth, fair Montague, I am too fond,
And therefore thou mayst think my haviour light;
But trust me, gentleman, I'll prove more true   100
Than those that have more cunning to be strange.
I should have been more strange, I must confess,
But that thou overheard'st, ere I was ware,
My true love's passion; therefore pardon me,
And not impute this yielding to light love,
Which the dark night hath so discovered.

    Romeo. Lady, by yonder blessed moon I swear
That tips with silver all these fruit-tree tops—

    Juliet. O, swear not by the moon, th' inconstant moon,
That monthly changes in her circled orb,   110
Lest that thy love prove likewise variable.

    Romeo. What shall I swear by?

    Juliet.   Do not swear at all:
Or, if thou wilt, swear by thy gracious self,
Which is the god of my idolatry,
And I'll believe thee.

    Romeo.   If my heart's dear love—

    Juliet. Well, do not swear. Although I joy in thee,
I have no joy of this contract to-night;
It is too rash, too unadvis'd, too sudden,
Too like the lightning, which doth cease to be
Ere one can say it lightens. Sweet, good night!   120
This bud of love, by summer's ripening breath,
May prove a beauteous flower when next we meet.
Good night, good night! as sweet repose and rest
Come to thy heart as that within my breast!

    Romeo. O, wilt thou leave me so unsatisfied?

    Juliet. What satisfaction canst thou have to-night?

    Romeo. The exchange of thy love's faithful vow for mine.

    Juliet. I gave thee mine before thou didst request it:
And yet I would it were to give again.

Romeo. Wouldst thou withdraw it? for what purpose, love?

Juliet. But to be frank, and give it thee again.   131
And yet I wish but for the thing I have:
My bounty is as boundless as the sea,
My love as deep; the more I give to thee,
The more I have, for both are infinite.   [*Nurse calls within.*
I hear some noise within; dear love, adieu!—
Anon, good nurse!—Sweet Montague, be true.
Stay but a little, I will come again.   [*Exit.*

Romeo. O blessed, blessed night! I am afeard,
Being in night, all this is but a dream,   140
Too flattering-sweet to be substantial.

Re-enter JULIET, *above.*

Juliet. Three words, dear Romeo, and good night indeed.
If that thy bent of love be honourable,
Thy purpose marriage, send me word to-morrow,
By one that I 'll procure to come to thee,
Where and what time thou wilt perform the rite;
And all my fortunes at thy foot I 'll lay,
And follow thee my lord throughout the world.

Nurse. [*Within*] Madam!

Juliet. I come, anon.—But if thou mean'st not well,   150
I do beseech thee—

Nurse. [*Within*] Madam!

Juliet.   By and by, I come.—
To cease thy suit, and leave me to my grief;
To-morrow will I send.

Romeo.   So thrive my soul—

Juliet. A thousand times good night!   [*Exit.*

Romeo. A thousand times the worse, to want thy light.—
Love goes toward love, as schoolboys from their books,
But love from love, toward school with heavy looks.
                                        [*Retiring slowly.*

Re-enter JULIET, *above.*

Juliet. Hist! Romeo, hist!—O, for a falconer's voice,
To lure this tassel-gentle back again!   160
Bondage is hoarse, and may not speak aloud;
Else would I tear the cave where Echo lies,
And make her airy tongue more hoarse than mine,
With repetition of my Romeo's name.

Romeo. It is my soul that calls upon my name;
How silver-sweet sound lovers' tongues by night,
Like softest music to attending ears!

Juliet. Romeo!

Romeo.   My dear?

Juliet.   At what o'clock to-morrow
Shall I send to thee?

Romeo.   At the hour of nine.

Juliet. I will not fail; 't is twenty years till then.   170
I have forgot why I did call thee back.

Romeo. Let me stand here till thou remember it.

Juliet. I shall forget, to have thee still stand there,
Remembering how I love thy company.

Romeo. And I 'll still stay, to have thee still forget,
Forgetting any other home but this.

Juliet. 'T is almost morning; I would have thee gone,
And yet no farther than a wanton's bird,
Who lets it hop a little from her hand,
Like a poor prisoner in his twisted gyves,   180
And with a silk thread plucks it back again,
So loving-jealous of his liberty.

Romeo. I would I were thy bird.

Juliet.   Sweet, so would I:
Yet I should kill thee with much cherishing.
Good night, good night! parting is such sweet sorrow,
That I shall say good night till it be morrow.   [*Exit, above.*

Romeo. Sleep dwell upon thine eyes, peace in thy breast!

Would I were sleep and peace, so sweet to rest!
Hence will I to my ghostly father's cell,   189
His help to crave, and my dear hap to tell.   [*Exit.*

SCENE III.   *Friar Laurence's Cell.*
Enter FRIAR LAURENCE, *with a basket.*

Friar Laurence. The grey-eyed morn smiles on the frown-
    ing night,
Chequering the eastern clouds with streaks of light,
And flecked darkness like a drunkard reels
From forth day's path and Titan's fiery wheels.
Now, ere the sun advance his burning eye,
The day to cheer and night's dank dew to dry,
I must up-fill this osier cage of ours
With baleful weeds and precious-juiced flowers.
The earth that's nature's mother is her tomb;
What is her burying grave that is her womb,   10
And from her womb children of divers kind
We sucking on her natural bosom find,
Many for many virtues excellent,
None but for some, and yet all different.
O, mickle is the powerful grace that lies
In herbs, plants, stones, and their true qualities!
For nought so vile that on the earth doth live
But to the earth some special good doth give;
Nor aught so good but, strain'd from that fair use.
Revolts from true birth, stumbling on abuse.   20
Virtue itself turns vice, being misapplied,
And vice sometime's by action dignified.
Within the infant rind of this weak flower
Poison hath residence, and medicine power;
For this, being smelt, with that part cheers each part,
Being tasted, slays all senses with the heart.
Two such opposed kings encamp them still

In man as well as herbs,—grace and rude will ;
And where the worser is predominant,
Full soon the canker death eats up that plant.   30

Enter ROMEO.

 Romeo. Good morrow, father.
 Friar Laurence.   Benedicite !
What early tongue so sweet saluteth me ?—
Young son, it argues a distemper'd head
So soon to bid good morrow to thy bed :
Care keeps his watch in every old man's eye,
And where care lodges, sleep will never lie ;
But where unbruised youth with unstuff'd brain
Doth couch his limbs, there golden sleep doth reign.
Therefore thy earliness doth me assure
Thou art up-rous'd with some distemperature ;   40
Or if not so, then here I hit it right,
Our Romeo hath not been in bed to-night.
 Romeo. That last is true ; the sweeter rest was mine.
 Friar Laurence. God pardon sin ! wast thou with Rosa-
  line ?
 Romeo. With Rosaline, my ghostly father ? no ;
I have forgot that name, and that name 's woe.
 Friar Laurence. That 's my good son ; but where hast thou
  been, then ?
 Romeo. I 'll tell thee, ere thou ask it me again.
I have been feasting with mine enemy,
Where on a sudden one hath wounded me,   50
That 's by me wounded ; both our remedies
Within thy help and holy physic lies.
I bear no hatred, blessed man, for, lo,
My intercession likewise steads my foe.
 Friar Laurence. Be plain, good son, and homely in thy
  drift ;
Riddling confession finds but riddling shrift.

Romeo. Then plainly know, my heart's dear love is set
On the fair daughter of rich Capulet :
As mine on hers, so hers is set on mine ;
And all combin'd, save what thou must combine   60
By holy marriage.   When and where and how
We met, we woo'd and made exchange of vow,
I 'll tell thee as we pass ; but this I pray,
That thou consent to marry us to-day.
   Friar Laurence. Holy Saint Francis, what a change is
       here !
Is Rosaline, that thou didst love so dear,
So soon forsaken ? young men's love then lies
Not truly in their hearts, but in their eyes.
Jesu Maria, what a deal of brine
Hath wash'd thy sallow cheeks for Rosaline !   70
How much salt water thrown away in waste,
To season love, that of it doth not taste !
The sun not yet thy sighs from heaven clears,
Thy old groans ring yet in my ancient ears ;
Lo, here upon thy cheek the stain doth sit
Of an old tear that is not wash'd off yet.
If e'er thou wast thyself and these woes thine,
Thou and these woes were all for Rosaline ;
And art thou chang'd ? pronounce this sentence then :
Women may fall, when there 's no strength in men.   80
   Romeo. Thou chidd'st me oft for loving Rosaline.
   Friar Laurence. For doting, not for loving, pupil mine.
   Romeo. And bad'st me bury love.
   Friar Laurence.   Not in a grave,
To lay one in, another out to have.
   Romeo. I pray thee, chide not : she whom I love now
Doth grace for grace and love for love allow ;
The other did not so.
   Friar Laurence.   O, she knew well,
Thy love did read by rote and could not spell.

But come, young waverer, come, go with me,
In one respect I 'll thy assistant be;   90
For this alliance may so happy prove,
To turn your households' rancour to pure love.

    Romeo. O, let us hence! I stand on sudden haste.

    Friar Laurence. Wisely and slow; they stumble that run
      fast.   [*Exeunt.*

SCENE IV. *A Street.*

Enter BENVOLIO *and* MERCUTIO.

    Mercutio. Where the devil should this Romeo be?
Came he not home to-night?

    Benvolio. Not to his father's; I spoke with his man.

    Mercutio. Why, that same pale hard-hearted wench, that
      Rosaline,
Torments him so that he will sure run mad.

    Benvolio. Tybalt, the kinsman of old Capulet,
Hath sent a letter to his father's house.

    Mercutio. A challenge, on my life.

    Benvolio. Romeo will answer it.

    Mercutio. Any man that can write may answer a letter. 10

    Benvolio. Nay, he will answer the letter's master, how he
dares, being dared.

    Mercutio. Alas, poor Romeo! he is already dead; stabbed
with a white wench's black eye; shot thorough the ear with
a love-song; the very pin of his heart cleft with the blind
bow-boy's butt-shaft: and is he a man to encounter Tybalt?

    Benvolio. Why, what is Tybalt?

    Mercutio. More than prince of cats, I can tell you. O, he
is the courageous captain of compliments. He fights as you
sing prick-song, keeps time, distance, and proportion; rests
me his minim rest, one, two, and the third in your bosom:
.the very butcher of a silk button, a duellist, a duellist; a gentleman of the very first house, of the first and second cause.
Ah, the immortal passado! the punto reverso! the hay! 24

Benvolio. The what?

Mercutio. The pox of such antic, lisping, affecting fantasticoes, these new tuners of accents! 'By Jesu, a very good
blade! a very tall man!'—Why, is not this a lamentable
thing, grandsire, that we should be thus afflicted with these
strange flies, these fashion-mongers, these *pardonnez-mois*,
who stand so much on the new form that they cannot sit at
ease on the old bench? O, their *bons*, their *bons!*   32

Enter ROMEO.

Benvolio. Here comes Romeo, here comes Romeo.

Mercutio. Without his roe, like a dried herring. O flesh,
flesh, how art thou fishified! Now is he for the numbers that
Petrarch flowed in: Laura to his lady was but a kitchen-
wench; marry, she had a better love to be-rhyme her;
Dido a dowdy; Cleopatra a gypsy; Helen and Hero hildings and harlots; Thisbe a grey eye or so, but not to the
purpose.—Signior Romeo, *bon jour!* there's a French salutation to your French slop. You gave us the counterfeit
fairly last night.   42

Romeo. Good morrow to you both. What counterfeit did
I give you?

Mercutio. The slip, sir, the slip; can you not conceive?

Romeo. Pardon, good Mercutio, my business was great;
and in such a case as mine a man may strain courtesy.

Mercutio. That's as much as to say, such a case as yours
constrains a man to bow in the hams.

Romeo. Meaning, to curtsy.   50

Mercutio. Thou hast most kindly hit it.

Romeo. A most courteous exposition.

Mercutio. Nay, I am the very pink of courtesy.

Romeo. Pink for flower.

Mercutio. Right.

Romeo. Why, then is my pump well flowered.

Mercutio. Well said; follow me this jest now till thou hast worn out thy pump, that when the single sole of it is worn, the jest may remain after the wearing sole singular.

Romeo. O single-soled jest, solely singular for the single-ness !   61

Mercutio. Come between us, good Benvolio; my wits fail.

Romeo. Switch and spurs, switch and spurs ; or I'll cry a match.

Mercutio. Nay, if thy wits run the wild-goose chase, I have done, for thou hast more of the wild-goose in one of thy wits than, I am sure, I have in my whole five. Was I with you there for the goose?

Romeo. Thou wast never with me for any thing when thou was not there for the goose.   70

Mercutio. I will bite thee by the ear for that jest.

Romeo. Nay, good goose, bite not.

Mercutio. Thy wit is a very bitter sweeting ; it is a most sharp sauce.

Romeo. And is it not well served in to a sweet goose?

Mercutio. O, here's a wit of cheveril, that stretches from an inch narrow to an ell broad !

Romeo. I stretch it out for that word 'broad ;' which added to the goose, proves thee far and wide a broad goose.

Mercutio. Why, is not this better now than groaning for love? now art thou sociable, now art thou Romeo ; now art thou what thou art, by art as well as by nature : for this driv-elling love is like a great natural,—   83

Benvolio. Stop there, stop there.

Romeo. Here's goodly gear!

Enter Nurse *and* PETER.

Mercutio. A sail, a sail !

Benvolio. Two, two ; a shirt and a smock.

Nurse. Peter !

Peter. Anon !

Nurse. My fan, Peter.   90

Mercutio. Good Peter, to hide her face ; for her fan 's the fairer of the two.

Nurse. God ye good morrow, gentlemen.

Mercutio. God ye good den, fair gentlewoman.

Nurse. Is it good den ?

Mercutio. 'T is no less, I tell you, for the hand of the dial is now upon the prick of noon.

Nurse. Out upon you ! what a man are you !

Romeo. One, gentlewoman, that God hath made for himself to mar.   100

Nurse. By my troth, it is well said; 'for himself to mar,' quoth a'?—Gentlemen, can any of you tell me where I may find the young Romeo ?

Romeo. I can tell you ; but young Romeo will be older when you have found him than he was when you sought him.   I am the youngest of that name, for fault of a worse.

Nurse. You say well.

Mercutio. Yea, is the worst well ? very well took, i' faith ; wisely, wisely.

Nurse. If you be he, sir, I desire some confidence with you.   111

Benvolio. She will indite him to some supper.

Mercutio. So ho !

Romeo. What hast thou found ?

Mercutio. No hare, sir ; unless a hare, sir, in a lenten pie, that is something stale and hoar ere it be spent.—Romeo, will you come to your father's? we 'll to dinner, thither.

Romeo. I will follow you.

Mercutio. Farewell, ancient lady ; farewell, [*singing*] 'lady, lady, lady.'   [*Exeunt Mercutio and Benvolio.*

Nurse. Marry, farewell !—I pray you, sir, what saucy merchant was this, that was so full of his ropery?   122

Romeo. A gentleman, nurse, that loves to hear himself talk, and will speak more in a minute than he will stand to in a month.

Nurse. An a' speak any thing against me, I 'll take him down, an a' were lustier than he is, and twenty such Jacks; and if I cannot, I 'll find those that shall. Scurvy knave! I am none of his flirt-gills; I am none of his skains-mates.— And thou must stand by too, and suffer every knave to use me at his pleasure?　　　　　131

Peter. I saw no man use you at his pleasure; if I had, my weapon should quickly have been out, I warrant you. I dare draw as soon as another man, if I see occasion in a good quarrel, and the law on my side.

Nurse. Now, afore God, I am so vexed, that every part about me quivers. Scurvy knave!—Pray you, sir, a word: and as I told you, my young lady bade me inquire you out; what she bade me say, I will keep to myself: but first let me tell ye, if ye should lead her in a fool's paradise, as they say, it were a very gross kind of behaviour, as they say; for the gentlewoman is young, and, therefore, if you should deal double with her, truly it were an ill thing to be offered to any gentlewoman, and very weak dealing.　　　　　144

Romeo. Nurse, commend me to thy lady and mistress. I protest unto thee—

Nurse. Good heart, and, i' faith, I will tell her as much. Lord, Lord, she will be a joyful woman.

Romeo. What wilt thou tell her, nurse? thou dost not mark me.　　　　　150

Nurse. I will tell her, sir, that you do protest; which, as I take it, is a gentlemanlike offer.

Romeo. Bid her devise some means to come to shrift
This afternoon;
And there she shall at Friar Laurence' cell
Be shriv'd and married. Here is for thy pains.

Nurse. No, truly, sir; not a penny.

Romeo. Go to; I say you shall.

Nurse. This afternoon, sir? well, she shall be there.

Romeo. And stay, good nurse; behind the abbey wall　　160

Within this hour my man shall be with thee,
And bring thee cords made like a tackled stair ;
Which to the high top-gallant of my joy
Must be my convoy in the secret night.
Farewell ; be trusty, and I 'll quit thy pains ;
Farewell ; commend me to thy mistress.

 Nurse. Now God in heaven bless thee ! Hark you, sir.
 Romeo. What say'st thou, my dear nurse ?
 Nurse. Is your man secret ? Did you ne'er hear say,
Two may keep counsel, putting one away ?   170
 Romeo. I warrant thee, my man 's as true as steel.
 Nurse. Well, sir ; my mistress is the sweetest lady—Lord,
Lord ! when 't was a little prating thing—O, there is a noble-
man in town, one Paris, that would fain lay knife aboard ;
but she, good soul, had as lieve see a toad, a very toad, as
see him. I anger her sometimes, and tell her that Paris is
the properer man ; but, I 'll warrant you, when I say so, she
looks as pale as any clout in the versal world. Doth not
rosemary and Romeo begin both with a letter ?
 Romeo. Ay, nurse ; what of that ? both with an R. 180
 Nurse. Ah, mocker ! that 's the dog's name ; R is for the—
No, I know it begins with some other letter—and she hath
the prettiest sententious of it, of you and rosemary, that it
would do you good to hear it.
 Romeo. Commend me to thy lady.
 Nurse. Ay, a thousand times.—[*Exit Romeo.*] Peter !
 Peter. Anon !
 Nurse. Before, and apace.   [*Exeunt*

Scene V. *Capulet's Orchard.*

Enter Juliet.

 Juliet. The clock struck nine when I did send the nurse ;
In half an hour she promis'd to return.
Perchance she cannot meet him ; that 's not so.

O, she is lame! love's heralds should be thoughts,
Which ten times faster glide than the sun's beams
Driving back shadows over lowering hills;
Therefore do nimble-pinion'd doves draw love,
And therefore hath the wind-swift Cupid wings.
Now is the sun upon the highmost hill
Of this day's journey, and from nine till twelve   10
Is three long hours, yet she is not come.
Had she affections and warm youthful blood,
She would be as swift in motion as a ball;
My words would bandy her to my sweet love,
And his to me:
But old folks, many feign as they were dead;
Unwieldy, slow, heavy and pale as lead.—

Enter Nurse *and* PETER.

O God, she comes!—O honey nurse, what news?
Hast thou met with him? Send thy man away.
   Nurse. Peter, stay at the gate.   [*Exit Peter*.
   Juliet. Now, good sweet nurse,—O Lord, why look'st thou
     sad?   21
Though news be sad, yet tell them merrily;
If good, thou sham'st the music of sweet news
By playing it to me with so sour a face.
   Nurse. I am aweary, give me leave awhile.
Fie, how my bones ache! what a jaunt have I had!
   Juliet. I would thou hadst my bones, and I thy news.
Nay, come, I pray thee, speak; good, good nurse, speak.
   Nurse. Jesu, what haste? can you not stay awhile?
Do you not see that I am out of breath?   30
   Juliet. How art thou out of breath, when thou hast breath
To say to me that thou art out of breath?
The excuse that thou dost make in this delay
Is longer than the tale thou dost excuse.
Is thy news good, or bad? answer to that;

Say either, and I 'll stay the circumstance.
Let me be satisfied, is 't good or bad?   37

Nurse. Well, you have made a simple choice; you know
not how to choose a man.   Romeo! no, not he; though his
face be better than any man's, yet his leg excels all men's;
and for a hand, and a foot, and a body, though they be not
to be talked on, yet they are past compare: he is not the
flower of courtesy, but, I 'll warrant him, as gentle as a lamb.
Go thy ways, wench; serve God.   What, have you dined at
home?

Juliet. No, no; but all this did I know before.
What says he of our marriage? what of that?

Nurse. Lord, how my head aches! what a head have I!
It beats as it would fall in twenty pieces.
My back o' t' other side,—O, my back, my back!   50
Beshrew your heart for sending me about,
To catch my death with jaunting up and down!

Juliet. I' faith, I am sorry that thou art not well.
Sweet, sweet, sweet nurse, tell me, what says my love?

Nurse. Your love says, like an honest gentleman,
And a courteous, and a kind, and a handsome,
And, I warrant, a virtuous,—Where is your mother?

Juliet. Where is my mother! why, she is within;
Where should she be?   How oddly thou repliest!
'Your love says, like an honest gentleman,   60
Where is your mother?'

Nurse.   O God's lady dear!
Are you so hot? marry, come up, I trow;
Is this the poultice for my aching bones?
Henceforward do your messages yourself.

Juliet. Here 's such a coil!—come, what says Romeo?

Nurse. Have you got leave to go to shrift to-day?

Juliet. I have.

Nurse. Then hie you hence to Friar Laurence' cell;
There stays a husband to make you a wife.

Now comes the wanton blood up in your cheeks,   70
They 'll be in scarlet straight at any news.
Hie you to church ; I must another way,
To fetch a ladder, by the which your love
Must climb a bird's nest soon when it is dark :
I am the drudge, and toil in your delight.
Go ; I 'll to dinner : hie you to the cell.
    Juliet. Hie to high fortune !—Honest nurse, farewell.

                              [*Exeunt.*

Scene VI. *Friar Laurence's Cell.*

Enter Friar Laurence *and* Romeo.

    Friar Laurence. So smile the heavens upon this holy act
That after hours with sorrow chide us not !
    Romeo. Amen, amen ! but come what sorrow can,
It cannot countervail the exchange of joy
That one short minute gives me in her sight.
Do thou but close our hands with holy words,
Then love-devouring death do what he dare,
It is enough I may but call her mine.
    Friar Laurence. These violent delights have violent ends,
And in their triumph die, like fire and powder,   10
Which as they kiss consume : the sweetest honey
Is loathsome in his own deliciousness,
And in the taste confounds the appetite.
Therefore love moderately ; long love doth so :
Too swift arrives as tardy as too slow.

Enter Juliet.

Here comes the lady.   O, so light a foot
Will ne'er wear out the everlasting flint !
A lover may bestride the gossamer
That idles in the wanton summer air,
And yet not fall ; so light is vanity.   20
    Juliet. Good even to my ghostly confessor.

Friar Laurence. Romeo shall thank thee, daughter, for us
    both.

Juliet. As much to him, else is his thanks too much.

Romeo. Ah, Juliet, if the measure of thy joy
Be heap'd like mine and that thy skill be more
To blazon it, then sweeten with thy breath
This neighbour air, and let rich music's tongue
Unfold the imagin'd happiness that both
Receive in either by this dear encounter.

Juliet. Conceit, more rich in matter than in words, 30
Brags of his substance, not of ornament.
They are but beggars that can count their worth;
But my true love is grown to such excess
I cannot sum up half my sum of wealth.

Friar Laurence. Come, come with me, and we will make
    short work;
For, by your leaves, you shall not stay alone
Till holy church incorporate two in one. *[Exeunt.*

F

"look, love, what envious streaks
Do lace the severing clouds in yonder east!" (iii. 5. 7).

ACT III.

SCENE I. *A Public Place.*

Enter MERCUTIO, BENVOLIO, Page, *and* Servants.

Benvolio. I pray thee, good Mercutio, let's retire:
The day is hot, the Capulets abroad,
And if we meet we shall not scape a brawl;
For now, these hot days, is the mad blood stirring.

Mercutio. Thou art like one of those fellows that when he
enters the confines of a tavern claps me his sword upon the
table, and says 'God send me no need of thee!' and by the
operation of the second cup draws him on the drawer, when
indeed there is no need.

Benvolio. Am I like such a fellow? 10

Mercutio. Come, come, thou art as hot a Jack in thy mood as any in Italy, and as soon moved to be moody, and as soon moody to be moved.

Benvolio. And what to?

Mercutio. Nay, an there were two such, we should have none shortly, for one would kill the other. Thou! why, thou wilt quarrel with a man that hath a hair more, or a hair less, in his beard than thou hast. Thou wilt quarrel with a man for cracking nuts, having no other reason but because thou hast hazel eyes; what eye but such an eye would spy out such a quarrel? Thy head is as full of quarrels as an egg is full of meat, and yet thy head hath been beaten as addle as an egg for quarrelling. Thou hast quarrelled with a man for coughing in the street, because he hath wakened thy dog that hath lain asleep in the sun. Didst thou not fall out with a tailor for wearing his new doublet before Easter? with another, for tying his new shoes with old riband? and yet thou wilt tutor me from quarrelling! 28

Benvolio. An I were so apt to quarrel as thou art, any man should buy the fee-simple of my life for an hour and a quarter.

Mercutio. The fee-simple! O simple!

Benvolio. By my head, here come the Capulets.

Mercutio. By my heel, I care not.

Enter TYBALT *and others.*

Tybalt. Follow me close, for I will speak to them.— Gentlemen, good den; a word with one of you.

Mercutio. And but one word with one of us? couple it with something; make it a word and a blow.

Tybalt. You shall find me apt enough to that, sir, an you will give me occasion. 40

Mercutio. Could you not take some occasion without giving?

Tybalt. Mercutio, thou consort'st with Romeo,—

Mercutio. Consort! what, dost thou make us minstrels? an thou make minstrels of us, look to hear nothing but discords: here 's my fiddlestick; here 's that shall make you dance. Zounds, consort!

Benvolio. We talk here in the public haunt of men.
Either withdraw unto some private place,
Or reason coldly of your grievances,   50
Or else depart; here all eyes gaze on us.

Mercutio. Men's eyes were made to look, and let them
    gaze;
I will not budge for no man's pleasure, I.

Enter ROMEO.

Tybalt. Well, peace be with you, sir; here comes my man

Mercutio. But I 'll be hang'd, sir, if he wear your livery.
Marry, go before to field, he 'll be your follower;
Your worship in that sense may call him man.

Tybalt. Romeo, the hate I bear thee can afford
No better term than this,—thou art a villain.

Romeo. Tybalt, the reason that I have to love thee   60
Doth much excuse the appertaining rage
To such a greeting. Villain am I none;
Therefore farewell: I see thou know'st me not.

Tybalt. Boy, this shall not excuse the injuries
That thou hast done me; therefore turn and draw.

Romeo. I do protest, I never injur'd thee,
But love thee better than thou canst devise,
Till thou shalt know the reason of my love;
And so, good Capulet,—which name I tender
As dearly as my own,—be satisfied.   70

Mercutio. O calm, dishonourable, vile submission!
A la stoccata carries it away.   [*Draws.*
Tybalt, you rat-catcher, will you walk?

Tybalt. What wouldst thou have with me?

Mercutio. Good king of cats, nothing but one of your nine lives ; that I mean to make bold withal, and, as you shall use me hereafter, dry-beat the rest of the eight. Will you pluck your sword out of his pilcher by the ears ? make haste, lest mine be about your ears ere it be out.

Tybalt. I am for you.   [*Drawing.*

Romeo. Gentle Mercutio, put thy rapier up.   81

Mercutio. Come, sir, your passado.   [*They fight.*

Romeo. Draw, Benvolio ; beat down their weapons.—
Gentlemen, for shame, forbear this outrage !
Tybalt, Mercutio, the prince expressly hath
Forbid this bandying in Verona streets.
Hold, Tybalt ! good Mercutio !

        [*Exeunt Tybalt and his partisans.*

Mercutio.   I am hurt.
A plague o' both your houses ! I am sped.
Is he gone, and hath nothing ?

Benvolio.   What, art thou hurt ?   89

Mercutio. Ay, ay, a scratch, a scratch ; marry, 't is enough.—
Where is my page ? Go, villain, fetch a surgeon.

        [*Exit Page.*

Romeo. Courage, man ; the hurt cannot be much.

Mercutio. No, 't is not so deep as a well, nor so wide as a church-door ; but 't is enough, 't will serve : ask for me to-morrow, and you shall find me a grave man. I am peppered, I warrant, for this world.—A plague o' both your houses !—Zounds, a dog, a rat, a mouse, a cat, to scratch a man to death ! a braggart, a rogue, a villain, that fights by the book of arithmetic !—Why the devil came you between us ? I was hurt under your arm.   100

Romeo. I thought all for the best.

Mercutio. Help me into some house, Benvolio,
Or I shall faint.—A plague o' both your houses !
They have made worms' meat of me. I have it,
And soundly too ; your houses !

        [*Exeunt Mercutio and Benvolio.*

Romeo. This gentleman, the prince's near ally,
My very friend, hath got his mortal hurt
In my behalf; my reputation stain'd
With Tybalt's slander,—Tybalt, that an hour
Hath been my cousin!—O sweet Juliet,   110
Thy beauty hath made me effeminate,
And in my temper soften'd valour's steel!

Re-enter BENVOLIO.

Benvolio. O Romeo, Romeo, brave Mercutio's dead!
That gallant spirit hath aspir'd the clouds,
Which too untimely here did scorn the earth.
Romeo. This day's black fate on more days doth depend :
This but begins the woe others must end.
Benvolio. Here comes the furious Tybalt back again.

Re-enter TYBALT.

Romeo. Alive, in triumph! and Mercutio slain!
Away to heaven, respective lenity,   120
And fire-eyed fury be my conduct now!—
Now, Tybalt, take the villain back again
That late thou gavest me! for Mercutio's soul
Is but a little way above our heads,
Staying for thine to keep him company;
Either thou, or I, or both, must go with him.
Tybalt. Thou, wretched boy, that didst consort him here,
Shalt with him hence.
Romeo.   This shall determine that.
                    [*They fight; Tybalt falls.*

Benvolio. Romeo, away, be gone!
The citizens are up, and Tybalt slain.   130
Stand not amaz'd; the prince will doom thee death,
If thou art taken.   Hence, be gone, away!
Romeo. O, I am fortune's fool!
Benvolio.   Why dost thou stay?
                    [*Exit Romeo*

Enter Citizens, *etc.*

1 *Citizen.* Which way ran he that kill'd Mercutio?
Tybalt, that murtherer, which way ran he?

Benvolio. There lies that Tybalt.

1 *Citizen.*   Up, sir, go with me;
I charge thee in the prince's name, obey.

Enter Prince, *attended;* MONTAGUE, CAPULET, *their* Wives,
and others.

Prince. Where are the vile beginners of this fray?

Benvolio. O noble prince, I can discover all
The unlucky manage of this fatal brawl.   140
There lies the man, slain by young Romeo,
That slew thy kinsman, brave Mercutio.

Lady Capulet. Tybalt, my cousin! O my brother's child!
O prince! O cousin! husband! O, the blood is spilt
Of my dear kinsman!—Prince, as thou art true,
For blood of ours, shed blood of Montague.
O cousin, cousin!

Prince. Benvolio, who began this bloody fray?

Benvolio. Tybalt, here slain, whom Romeo's hand did slay;
Romeo that spoke him fair, bade him bethink   150
How nice the quarrel was, and urg'd withal
Your high displeasure: all this, uttered
With gentle breath, calm look, knees humbly bow'd,
Could not take truce with the unruly spleen
Of Tybalt deaf to peace, but that he tilts
With piercing steel at bold Mercutio's breast,
Who, all as hot, turns deadly point to point,
And, with a martial scorn, with one hand beats
Cold death aside, and with the other sends
It back to Tybalt, whose dexterity   160
Retorts it.   Romeo he cries aloud,
' Hold, friends! friends, part!' and swifter than his tongue,

His agile arm beats down their fatal points,
And 'twixt them rushes ; underneath whose arm
An envious thrust from Tybalt hit the life
Of stout Mercutio, and then Tybalt fled ;
But by and by comes back to Romeo,
Who had but newly entertain'd revenge,
And to 't they go like lightning, for, ere I
Could draw to part them, was stout Tybalt slain,   170
And, as he fell, did Romeo turn and fly.
This is the truth, or let Benvolio die.

 Lady Capulet. He is a kinsman to the Montague ;
Affection makes him false, he speaks not true :
Some twenty of them fought in this black strife,
And all those twenty could but kill one life.
I beg for justice, which thou, prince, must give ;
Romeo slew Tybalt, Romeo must not live.

 Prince. Romeo slew him, he slew Mercutio ;
Who now the price of his dear blood doth owe ?   180

 Montague. Not Romeo, prince, he was Mercutio's friend ;
His fault concludes but what the law should end,
The life of Tybalt.

 Prince.   And for that offence
Immediately we do exile him hence.
I have an interest in your hate's proceeding,
My blood for your rude brawls doth lie a-bleeding ;
But I 'll amerce you with so strong a fine
That you shall all repent the loss of mine.
I will be deaf to pleading and excuses ;
Nor tears nor prayers shall purchase out abuses :   190
Therefore use none ; let Romeo hence in haste,
Else, when he 's found, that hour is his last.
Bear hence this body and attend our will ;
Mercy but murthers, pardoning those that kill.   [*Exeunt.*

SCENE II. *Capulet's Orchard.*

Enter JULIET.

Juliet. Gallop apace, you fiery-footed steeds,
Towards Phœbus' lodging ; such a waggoner
As Phaethon would whip you to the west,
And bring in cloudy night immediately.—
Spread thy close curtain, love-performing night,
That runaways' eyes may wink, and Romeo
Leap to these arms, untalk'd of and unseen.—
Lovers can see to do their amorous rites
By their own beauties ; or, if love be blind,
It best agrees with night.—Come, civil night,   10
Thou sober-suited matron, all in black,
And learn me how to lose a winning match,
Play'd for a pair of stainless maidenhoods.
Hood my unmann'd blood, bating in my cheeks,
With thy black mantle, till strange love grown bold
Think true love acted simple modesty.
Come, night, come, Romeo, come, thou day in night ;
For thou wilt lie upon the wings of night
Whiter than new snow on a raven's back.
Come, gentle night, come, loving, black-brow'd night   20
Give me my Romeo ; and, when he shall die,
Take him and cut him out in little stars,
And he will make the face of heaven so fine
That all the world will be in love with night
And pay no worship to the garish sun.—
O, I have bought the mansion of a love,
But not possess'd it, and, though I am sold,
Not yet enjoy'd.   So tedious is this day
As is the night before some festival
To an impatient child that hath new robes   30
And may not wear them.—O, here comes my nurse,

And she brings news ; and every tongue that speaks
But Romeo's name speaks heavenly eloquence.—

Enter Nurse, *with cords.*

Now, nurse, what news? What hast thou there? the cords
That Romeo bid thee fetch?

    Nurse.   Ay, ay, the cords.

                                                   [Throws them down.

    Juliet. Ay me! what news? why dost thou wring thy
        hands?

    Nurse. Ah, well-a-day! he's dead, he's dead, he's dead!
We are undone, lady, we are undone!
Alack the day! he's gone, he's kill'd, he's dead!

    Juliet. Can heaven be so envious?

    Nurse.   Romeo can,   40
Though heaven cannot.—O Romeo, Romeo!—
Who ever would have thought it?—Romeo!

    Juliet. What devil art thou, that dost torment me thus?
This torture should be roar'd in dismal hell.
Hath Romeo slain himself? say thou but ay,
And that bare vowel *I* shall poison more
Than the death-darting eye of cockatrice:
I am not I, if there be such an *I;*
Or those eyes shut, that make thee answer ay.
If he be slain, say ay ; or if not, no: 50
Brief sounds determine of my weal or woe.

    Nurse. I saw the wound, I saw it with mine eyes—
God save the mark!—here on his manly breast:
A piteous corse, a bloody piteous corse ;
Pale, pale as ashes, all bedaub'd in blood,
All in gore-blood ; I swounded at the sight.

    Juliet. O, break, my heart! poor bankrupt, break at once!
To prison, eyes, ne'er look on liberty!
Vile earth, to earth resign ; end motion here,
And thou and Romeo press one heavy bier!   60

Nurse. O Tybalt, Tybalt, the best friend I had!
O courteous Tybalt! honest gentleman!
That ever I should live to see thee dead!
    Juliet. What storm is this that blows so contrary?
Is Romeo slaughter'd, and is Tybalt dead?
My dear-lov'd cousin, and my dearer lord?
Then, dreadful trumpet, sound the general doom!
For who is living, if those two are gone?
    Nurse. Tybalt is gone, and Romeo banished;
Romeo that kill'd him, he is banished.   70
    Juliet. O God! did Romeo's hand shed Tybalt's blood?
    Nurse. It did, it did; alas the day, it did!
    Juliet. O serpent heart, hid with a flowering face!
Did ever dragon keep so fair a cave?
Beautiful tyrant! fiend angelical!
Dove-feather'd raven! wolvish-ravening lamb!
Despised substance of divinest show!
Just opposite to what thou justly seem'st,
A damned saint, an honourable villain!
O nature, what hadst thou to do in hell,   80
When thou didst bower the spirit of a fiend
In mortal paradise of such sweet flesh?
Was ever book containing such vile matter
So fairly bound? O, that deceit should dwell
In such a gorgeous palace!
    Nurse.   There's no trust,
No faith, no honesty in men; all perjur'd,
All forsworn, all naught, all dissemblers.—
Ah, where's my man? give me some aqua vitæ.—
These griefs, these woes, these sorrows, make me old.
Shame come to Romeo!
    Juliet.   Blister'd be thy tongue   90
For such a wish! he was not born to shame:
Upon his brow shame is asham'd to sit;
For 't is a throne where ~~~~~~ ~~nour may be crown'd

Sole monarch of the universal earth.
O, what a beast was I to chide at him!

    Nurse. Will you speak well of him that kill'd your cousin?

    Juliet. Shall I speak ill of him that is my husband?—
Ah, poor my lord, what tongue shall smooth thy name,
When I, thy three-hours wife, have mangled it?
But, wherefore, villain, didst thou kill my cousin?   100
That villain cousin would have kill'd my husband.
Back, foolish tears, back to your native spring;
Your tributary drops belong to woe,
Which you mistaking offer up to joy.
My husband lives, that Tybalt would have slain;
And Tybalt 's dead, that would have slain my husband:
All this is comfort; wherefore weep I then?
Some word there was, worser than Tybalt's death,
That murther'd me. I would forget it fain;
But, O, it presses to my memory,   110
Like damned guilty deeds to sinners' minds:
'Tybalt is dead, and Romeo—banished!'
That 'banished,' that one word 'banished,'
Hath slain ten thousand Tybalts. Tybalt's death
Was woe enough, if it had ended there;
Or, if sour woe delights in fellowship
And needly will be rank'd with other griefs,
Why follow'd not, when she said Tybalt 's dead,
Thy father, or thy mother, nay, or both,
Which modern lamentation might have mov'd?   120
But with a rearward following Tybalt's death,
Romeo is banished!—to speak that word,
Is father, mother, Tybalt, Romeo, Juliet,
All slain, all dead. Romeo is banished!
There is no end, no limit, measure, bound,
In that word's death; no words can that woe sound.—
Where is my father, and my mother, nurse?

    Nurse. Weeping and wailing over Tybalt's corse.
Will you go to them? I will bring you thither.

Juliet. Wash they his wounds with tears; mine shall be
    spent,   130
When theirs are dry, for Romeo's banishment.
Take up those cords.—Poor ropes, you are beguil'd,
Both you and I; for Romeo is exil'd:
He made you for a highway to my bed;
But I, a maid, die maiden-widowed.
    Nurse. Hie to your chamber: I 'll find Romeo
To comfort you; I wot well where he is.
Hark ye, your Romeo will be here at night:
I 'll to him; he is hid at Laurence' cell.
    Juliet. O, find him! give this ring to my true knight, 140
And bid him come to take his last farewell.   [*Exeunt.*

SCENE III.   *Friar Laurence's Cell.*

Enter FRIAR LAURENCE.

Friar Laurence. Romeo, come forth; come forth, thou fear-
    ful man:
Affliction is enamour'd of thy parts,
And thou art wedded to calamity.

Enter ROMEO.

    Romeo. Father, what news? what is the prince's doom?
What sorrow craves acquaintance at my hand,
That I yet know not?
    Friar Laurence.   Too familiar
Is my dear son with such sour company;
I bring thee tidings of the prince's doom.
    Romeo. What less than doomsday is the prince's doom?
    Friar Laurence. A gentler judgment vanish'd from his lips,
Not body's death, but body's banishment.   11
    Romeo. Ha, banishment! be merciful, say death;
For exile hath more terror in his look,
Much more than death: do not say banishment.

Friar Laurence. Hence from Verona art thou banished;
Be patient, for the world is broad and wide.
Romeo. There is no world without Verona walls,
But purgatory, torture, hell itself.
Hence banished is banish'd from the world,
And world's exile is death : then banished   20
Is death misterm'd; calling death banishment
Thou cutt'st my head off with a golden axe,
And smil'st upon the stroke that murthers me.
Friar Laurence. O deadly sin !   O rude unthankfulness !
Thy fault our law calls death ; but the kind prince,
Taking thy part, hath rush'd aside the law,
And turn'd that black word death to banishment :
This is dear mercy, and thou seest it not.
Romeo. 'T is torture, and not mercy : heaven is here,
Where Juliet lives ; and every cat and dog   3c
And little mouse, every unworthy thing,
Live here in heaven and may look on her,
But Romeo may not.   More validity,
More honourable state, more courtship lives
In carrion-flies than Romeo : they may seize
On the white wonder of dear Juliet's hand
And steal immortal blessing from her lips,
Who, even in pure and vestal modesty,
Still blush, as thinking their own kisses sin;
But Romeo may not ; he is banished.   40
This may flies do, when I from this must fly ;
They are free men, but I am banished.
And say'st thou yet that exile is not death ?
Hadst thou no poison mix'd, no sharp-ground knife,
No sudden mean of death, though ne'er so mean,
But 'banished' to kill me ?—Banished !
O friar, the damned use that word in hell ;
Howling attends it : how hast thou the heart,
Being a divine, a ghostly confessor,

A sin-absolver, and my friend profess'd,   50
To mangle me with that word ' banished?'
    Friar Laurence. Thou fond mad man, hear me but speak
        a word.
    Romeo. O, thou wilt speak again of banishment.
    Friar Laurence. I 'll give thee armour to keep off that
        word ;
Adversity's sweet milk, philosophy,
To comfort thee, though thou art banished.
    Romeo. Yet banished? Hang up philosophy!
Unless philosophy can make a Juliet,
Displant a town, reverse a prince's doom,
It helps not, it prevails not ; talk no more.   60
    Friar Laurence. O, then I see that madmen have no ears.
    Romeo. How should they, when that wise men have no
        eyes?
    Friar Laurence. Let me dispute with thee of thy estate.
    Romeo. Thou canst not speak of that thou dost not feel.
Wert thou as young as I, Juliet thy love,
An hour but married, Tybalt murthered,
Doting like me and like me banished,
Then mightst thou speak, then mightst thou tear thy hair,
And fall upon the ground, as I do now,
Taking the measure of an unmade grave. [*Knocking within.*
    Friar Laurence. Arise ; one knocks : good Romeo, hide
        thyself.   71
    Romeo. Not I ; unless the breath of heart-sick groans
Mist-like infold me from the search of eyes. [*Knocking.*
    Friar Laurence. Hark, how they knock!—Who 's there?—
        Romeo, arise ;
Thou wilt be taken.—Stay awhile!—Stand up ; [*Knocking.*
Run to my study.—By and by!—God's will,
What simpleness is this!—I come, I come! [*Knocking.*
Who knocks so hard? whence come you? what 's your
        will?

Nurse. [*Within*] Let me come in, and you shall know my
   errand ;
I come from Lady Juliet.
   Friar Laurence.   Welcome, then.   80

Enter Nurse.

Nurse. O holy friar, O, tell me, holy friar,
Where is my lady's lord, where 's Romeo ?
   Friar Laurence. There on the ground, with his own tears
   made drunk.
   Nurse. O, he is even in my mistress' case,
Just in her case !
   Friar Laurence. O woful sympathy !
Piteous predicament !
   Nurse.   Even so lies she,
Blubbering and weeping, weeping and blubbering.—
Stand up, stand up ; stand, an you be a man :
For Juliet's sake, for her sake, rise and stand.
Why should you fall into so deep an O ?   90
   Romeo. Nurse !
   Nurse. Ah sir ! ah sir ! Well, death 's the end of all.
   Romeo. Spak'st thou of Juliet ? how is it with her ?
Doth she not think me an old murtherer,
Now I have stain'd the childhood of our joy
With blood remov'd but little from her own ?
Where is she ? and how doth she ? and what says
My conceal'd lady to our cancell'd love ?
   Nurse. O, she says nothing, sir, but weeps and weeps ;
And now falls on her bed ; and then starts up,   100
And Tybalt calls ; and then on Romeo cries,
And then down falls again.
   Romeo.   As if that name,
Shot from the deadly level of a gun,
Did murther her ; as that name's cursed hand
Murther'd her kinsman.—O, tell me, friar, tell me,

In what vile part of this anatomy
Doth my name lodge? tell me, that I may sack
The hateful mansion.   [*Drawing his sword.*
　Friar Laurence.　　　Hold thy desperate hand!
Art thou a man? thy form cries out thou art:
Thy tears are womanish; thy wild acts denote　　　110
The unreasonable fury of a beast:
Unseemly woman in a seeming man!
Or ill-beseeming beast in seeming both!
Thou hast amaz'd me; by my holy order,
I thought thy disposition better temper'd.
Hast thou slain Tybalt? wilt thou slay thyself?
And slay thy lady too that lives in thee,
By doing damned hate upon thyself?
Why rail'st thou on thy birth, the heaven, and earth?
Since birth and heaven and earth, all three do meet　　120
In thee at once, which thou at once wouldst lose.
Fie, fie, thou sham'st thy shape, thy love, thy wit,
Which, like a usurer, abound'st in all,
And usest none in that true use indeed
Which should bedeck thy shape, thy love, thy wit.
Thy noble shape is but a form of wax,
Digressing from the valour of a man;
Thy dear love sworn, but hollow perjury,
Killing that love which thou hast vow'd to cherish;
Thy wit, that ornament to shape and love,　　　130
Misshapen in the conduct of them both,
Like powder in a skilless soldier's flask,
Is set a-fire by thine own ignorance,
And thou dismember'd with thine own defence.
What, rouse thee, man! thy Juliet is alive,
For whose dear sake thou wast but lately dead;
There art thou happy: Tybalt would kill thee,
But thou slew'st Tybalt; there art thou happy too:
The law that threaten'd death becomes thy friend
G

And turns it to exile; there art thou happy: 140
A pack of blessings lights upon 'thy back;
Happiness courts thee in her best array;
But, like a misbehav'd and sullen wench,
Thou pout'st upon thy fortune and thy love.
Take heed, take heed, for such die miserable.
Go, get thee to thy love, as was decreed,
Ascend her chamber, hence and comfort her:
But look thou stay not till the watch be set,
For then thou canst not pass to Mantua;
Where thou shalt live, till we can find a time   150
To blaze your marriage, reconcile your friends,
Beg pardon of the prince, and call thee back
With twenty hundred thousand times more joy
Than thou went'st forth in lamentation.—
Go before, nurse; commend me to thy lady,
And bid her hasten all the house to bed,
Which heavy sorrow makes them apt unto:
Romeo is coming.

    Nurse. O Lord, I could have stay'd here all the night
To hear good counsel; O, what learning is!—   160
My lord, I 'll tell my lady you will come.

    Romeo. Do so, and bid my sweet prepare to chide.

    Nurse. Here, sir, a ring she bid me give you, sir;
Hie you, make haste, for it grows very late.   [*Exit.*

    Romeo. How well my comfort is reviv'd by this!

    Friar Laurence. Go hence; good night; and here stands
        all your state:
Either be gone before the watch be set,
Or by the break of day disguis'd from hence.
Sojourn in Mantua; I 'll find out your man,
And he shall signify from time to time   170
Every good hap to you that chances here.
Give me thy hand; 't is late: farewell; good night.

    Romeo. But that a joy past joy calls out on me,

It were a grief, so brief to part with thee.
Farewell.   [*Exeunt.*

SCENE IV. *A Room in Capulet's House.*
Enter CAPULET, LADY CAPULET, *and* PARIS.

Capulet. Things have fallen out, sir, so unluckily,
That we have had no time to move our daughter.
Look you, she lov'd her kinsman Tybalt dearly,
And so did I.—Well, we were born to die.—
'T is very late, she 'll not come down to-night ;
I promise you, but for your company,
I would have been a-bed an hour ago.
Paris. These times of woe afford no time to woo.
Madam, good night ; commend me to your daughter.
Lady Capulet. I will, and know her mind early to-morrow ;
To-night she 's mew'd up to her heaviness.   11
Capulet. Sir Paris, I will make a desperate tender
Of my child's love : I think she will be rul'd
In all respects by me ; nay, more, I doubt it not.—
Wife, go you to her ere you go to bed ;
Acquaint her here of my son Paris' love,
And bid her, mark you me, on Wednesday next—
But, soft ! what day is this?
Paris.   Monday, my lord.
Capulet. Monday ! ha, ha ! Well, Wednesday is too soon :
O' Thursday let it be : o' Thursday, tell her,   20
She shall be married to this noble earl.
Will you be ready? do you like this haste?
We 'll keep no great ado,—a friend or two ;
For, hark you, Tybalt being slain so late,
It may be thought we held him carelessly,
Being our kinsman, if we revel much :
Therefore we 'll have some half a dozen friends,
And there an end.   But what say you to Thursday?

Paris. My lord, I would that Thursday were to-morrow.

Capulet.   Well, get you gone ; o' Thursday be it then.   30
Go you to Juliet ere you go to bed,
Prepare her, wife, against this wedding-day.—
Farewell, my lord.—Light to my chamber, ho !
Afore me, it is so very late, that we
May call it early by and by.—Good night.   [*Exeunt.*

SCENE V.   *Juliet's Chamber.*

Enter ROMEO *and* JULIET.

Juliet. Wilt thou be gone? it is not yet near day :
It was the nightingale, and not the lark,
That pierc'd the fearful hollow of thine ear ;
Nightly she sings on yon pomegranate-tree.
Believe me, love, it was the nightingale.

Romeo. It was the lark, the herald of the morn,
No nightingale ; look, love, what envious streaks
Do lace the severing clouds in yonder east.
Night's candles are burnt out, and jocund day
Stands tiptoe on the misty mountain tops.   10
I must be gone and live, or stay and die.

Juliet. Yon light is not day-light, I know it, I ;
It is some meteor that the sun exhales,
To be to thee this night a torch-bearer,
And light thee on thy way to Mantua :
Therefore stay yet, thou need'st not to be gone.

Romeo. Let me be ta'en, let me be put to death ;
I am content, so thou wilt have it so.
I 'll say yon grey is not the morning's eye,
'T is but the pale reflex of Cynthia's brow ;   20
Nor that is not the lark, whose notes do beat
The vaulty heaven so high above our heads.
I have more care to stay than will to go ;
Come, death, and welcome ! Juliet wills it so.
How is 't, my soul? let 's talk, it is not day.

Juliet. It is, it is ; hie hence, be gone, away !
It is the lark that sings so out of tune,
Straining harsh discords and unpleasing sharps.
Some say the lark makes sweet division ;
This doth not so, for she divideth us.   30
Some say the lark and loathed toad change eyes ;
O, now I would they had chang'd voices too !
Since arm from arm that voice doth us affray,
Hunting thee hence with hunt's-up to the day.
O, now be gone ; more light and light it grows.

    Romeo. More light and light?—More dark and dark our
      woes !

Enter Nurse.

  Nurse. Madam !
  Juliet. Nurse ?
  Nurse. Your lady mother is coming to your chamber.
The day is broke ; be wary, look about.   [*Exit.*
  Juliet. Then, window, let day in, and let life out.   41
  Romeo. Farewell, farewell ! one kiss, and I 'll descend.
                        [*Romeo descends.*
  Juliet. Art thou gone so ? my lord, my love, my friend !
I must hear from thee every day in the hour,
For in a minute there are many days ;
O, by this count I shall be much in years
Ere I again behold my Romeo !
  Romeo. Farewell ! I will omit no opportunity
That may convey my greetings, love, to thee.
  Juliet. O, think'st thou we shall ever meet again ?   50
  Romeo. I doubt it not ; and all these woes shall serve
For sweet discourses in our time to come.
  Juliet. O God, I have an ill-divining soul !
Methinks I see thee, now thou art below,
As one dead in the bottom of a tomb ;
Either my eyesight fails, or thou look'st pale.

Romeo. And trust me, love, in my eye so do you ;
Dry sorrow drinks our blood.   Adieu, adieu !   [*Exit.*
   Juliet. O fortune, fortune ! all men call thee fickle ;
If thou art fickle, what dost thou with him   60
That is renown'd for faith?   Be fickle, fortune ;
For then, I hope, thou wilt not keep him long,
But send him back.
   Lady Capulet. [*Within*] Ho, daughter ! are you up?
   Juliet. Who is 't that calls? is it my lady mother?
Is she not down so late, or up so early?
What unaccustom'd cause procures her hither?

Enter LADY CAPULET.

   Lady Capulet. Why, how now, Juliet !
   Juliet.   Madam, I am not well.
   Lady Capulet. Evermore weeping for your cousin's death?
What, wilt thou wash him from his grave with tears?
An if thou couldst, thou couldst not make him live ;   70
Therefore, have done : some grief shows much of love,
But much of grief shows still some want of wit.
   Juliet. Yet let me weep for such a feeling loss.
   Lady Capulet. So shall you feel the loss, but not the friend
Which you weep for.
   Juliet.   Feeling so the loss,
I cannot choose but ever weep the friend.
   Lady Capulet. Well, girl, thou weep'st not so much for his
         death
As that the villain lives which slaughter'd him.
   Juliet. What villain madam?
   Lady Capulet.   That same villain, Romeo.
   Juliet. Villain and he be many miles asunder.—   80
God pardon him ! I do, with all my heart ;
And yet no man like he doth grieve my heart.
   Lady Capulet. That is, because the traitor murtherer lives.
   Juliet. Ay, madam, from the reach of these my hands.
Would none but I might venge my cousin's death !

Lady Capulet. We will have vengeance 'for it, fear thou
   not ;
Then weep no more.   I 'll send to one in Mantua,
Where that same banish'd runagate doth live,
Shall give him such an unaccustom'd dram,
That he shall soon keep Tybalt company ;   90
And then, I hope, thou wilt be satisfied.
   Juliet. Indeed, I never shall be satisfied
With Romeo, till I behold him—dead—
Is my poor heart so for a kinsman vex'd.—
Madam, if you could find out but a man
To bear a poison, I would temper it,
That Romeo should, upon receipt thereof,
Soon sleep in quiet.   O, how my heart abhors
To hear him nam'd, and cannot come to him,
To wreak the love I bore my cousin   100
Upon his body that hath slaughter'd him !
   Lady Capulet. Find thou the means, and I 'll find such a
   man.
But now I 'll tell thee joyful tidings, girl.
   Juliet. And joy comes well in such a needy time.
What are they, I beseech your ladyship ?
   Lady Capulet. Well, well, thou hast a careful father, child ;
One who, to put thee from thy heaviness,
Hath sorted out a sudden day of joy,
That thou expect'st not, nor I look'd not for.
   Juliet. Madam, in happy time, what day is that ?   110
   Lady Capulet. Marry, my child, early next Thursday morn,
The gallant, young, and noble gentleman,
The County Paris, at Saint Peter's Church,
Shall happily make thee there a joyful bride.
   Juliet. Now, by Saint Peter's Church and Peter too,
He shall not make me there a joyful bride.
I wonder at this haste ; that I must wed
Ere he that should be husband comes to woo.

I pray you, tell my lord and father, madam,
I will not marry yet ; and, when I do, I swear,   120
It shall be Romeo, whom you know I hate,
Rather than Paris.   These are news indeed !
    Lady Capulet. Here comes your father ; tell him so your-
        self,
And see how he will take it at your hands.

      Enter CAPULET *and* Nurse.

    Capulet. When the sun sets, the air doth drizzle dew ;
But for the sunset of my brother's son
It rains downright.—
How now ! a conduit, girl ? what, still in tears ?
Evermore showering ?   In one little body
Thou counterfeit'st a bark, a sea, a wind :   130
For still thy eyes, which I may call the sea,
Do ebb and flow with tears ; the bark thy body is,
Sailing in this salt flood ; the winds, thy sighs ;
Who, raging with thy tears, and they with them,
Without a sudden calm, will overset
Thy tempest-tossed body.—How now, wife !
Have you deliver'd to her our decree ?
    Lady Capulet. Ay, sir ; but she will none, she gives you
        thanks.
I would the fool were married to her grave !
    Capulet. Soft ! take me with you, take me with you, wife.
How ! will she none ? doth she not give us thanks ?   141
Is she not proud ? doth she not count her blest,
Unworthy as she is, that we have wrought
So worthy a gentleman to be her bridegroom ?
    Juliet. Not proud you have, but thankful that you have :
Proud can I never be of what I hate ;
But thankful even for hate that is meant love.
    Capulet. How now, how now, chop-logic !   What is this ?
' Proud ' and ' I thank you ' and ' I thank you not,'

And yet 'not proud!' Mistress minion, you,⠀⠀⠀⠀⠀⠀150
Thank me no thankings, nor proud me no prouds,
But fettle your fine joints 'gainst Thursday next,
To go with Paris to Saint Peter's Church,
Or I will drag thee on a hurdle thither.
Out, you green-sickness carrion! out, you baggage!
You tallow-face!

⠀⠀*Lady Capulet.*⠀⠀Fie, fie! what, are you mad?

⠀⠀*Juliet.*⠀⠀Good father, I beseech you on my knees,
Hear me with patience but to speak a word.

⠀⠀*Capulet.*⠀⠀Hang thee, young baggage! disobedient wretch!
I tell thee what: get thee to church o' Thursday,⠀⠀⠀160
Or never after look me in the face.
Speak not, reply not, do not answer me;
My fingers itch.—Wife, we scarce thought us blest
That God had lent us but this only child;
But now I see this one is one too much,
And that we have a curse in having her:
Out on her, hilding!

⠀⠀*Nurse.*⠀⠀⠀⠀⠀⠀God in heaven bless her!
You are to blame, my lord, to rate her so.

⠀⠀*Capulet.*⠀⠀And why, my lady wisdom? hold your tongue,
Good prudence; smatter with your gossips, go.⠀⠀⠀170

⠀⠀*Nurse.*⠀⠀I speak no treason.

⠀⠀*Capulet.*⠀⠀⠀⠀⠀⠀O, God ye god-den.

⠀⠀*Nurse.*⠀⠀May not one speak?

⠀⠀*Capulet.*⠀⠀⠀⠀⠀⠀Peace, you mumbling fool!
Utter your gravity o'er a gossip's bowl;
For here we need it not.

⠀⠀*Lady Capulet.*⠀⠀You are too hot.

⠀⠀*Capulet.*⠀⠀God's bread! it makes me mad: day, night, late,
⠀⠀⠀⠀early,
At home, abroad, alone, in company,
Waking, or sleeping, still my care hath been
To have her match'd; and having now provided

A gentleman of noble parentage,
Of fair demesnes, youthful, and nobly train'd,   180
Stuff'd, as they say, with honourable parts,
Proportion'd as one's thought would wish a man,—
And then to have a wretched puling fool,
A whining mammet, in her fortune's tender,
To answer 'I 'll not wed ; I cannot love,
I am too young ; I pray you, pardon me.'—
But, an you will not wed, I 'll pardon you ;
Graze where you will, you shall not house with me :
Look to 't, think on 't, I do not use to jest.
Thursday is near ; lay hand on heart, advise.   190
An you be mine, I 'll give you to my friend ;
An you be not, hang, beg, starve, die in the streets,
For, by my soul, I 'll ne'er acknowledge thee,
Nor what is mine shall never do thee good.
Trust to 't, bethink you ; I 'll not be forsworn.   [*Exit.*

     Juliet. Is there no pity sitting in the clouds,
That sees into the bottom of my grief ?
O, sweet my mother, cast me not away !
Delay this marriage for a month, a week ;
Or, if you do not, make the bridal bed   200
In that dim monument where Tybalt lies.

     Lady Capulet. Talk not to me, for I 'll not speak a word ;
Do as thou wilt, for I have done with thee.   [*Exit.*

     Juliet. O God !—O nurse, how shall this be prevented ?
My husband is on earth, my faith in heaven ;
How shall that faith return again to earth,
Unless that husband send it me from heaven
By leaving earth ? comfort me, counsel me.—
Alack, alack, that heaven should practise stratagems
Upon so soft a subject as myself !—   210
What say'st thou ? hast thou not a word of joy ?
Some comfort, nurse.

     Nurse.   Faith, here 't is.   Romeo

Is banished, and all the world to nothing,
That he dares ne'er come back to challenge you;
Or, if he do, it needs must be by stealth.
Then, since the case so stands as now it doth,
I think it best you married with the county.
O, he's a lovely gentleman!
Romeo's a dishclout to him; an eagle, madam,
Hath not so green, so quick, so fair an eye   220
As Paris hath.   Beshrew my very heart,
I think you are happy in this second match,
For it excels your first; or if it did not,
Your first is dead, or 't were as good he were,
As living here and you no use of him.

   Juliet. Speakest thou from thy heart?

   Nurse.   And from my soul too;
Or else beshrew them both.

   Juliet.   Amen!

   Nurse.   What?

   Juliet. Well, thou hast comforted me marvellous much.
Go in, and tell my lady I am gone,
Having displeas'd my father, to Laurence' cell,   230
To make confession and to be absolv'd.

   Nurse. Marry, I will; and this is wisely done.   [*Exit.*

   Juliet. Ancient damnation! O most wicked fiend!
Is it more sin to wish me thus forsworn,
Or to dispraise my lord with that same tongue
Which she hath prais'd him with above compare
So many thousand times?—Go, counsellor;
Thou and my bosom henceforth shall be twain.—
I'll to the friar, to know his remedy;
If all else fail, myself have power to die.   [*Exit.*

FRIAR LAURENCE'S CELL.

ACT IV.

Scene I. *Friar Laurence's Cell.*

Enter Friar Laurence *and* Paris.

Friar Laurence. On Thursday, sir? the time is very short.

Paris. My father Capulet will have it so;
And I am nothing slow to slack his haste.

Friar Laurence. You say you do not know the lady's mind;
Uneven is the course, I like it not.

Paris. Immoderately she weeps for Tybalt's death,

And therefore have I little talk'd of love ;
For Venus smiles not in a house of tears.
Now, sir, her father counts it dangerous
That she doth give her sorrow so much sway,   10
And in his wisdom hastes our marriage,
To stop the inundation of her tears,
Which, too much minded by herself alone,
May be put from her by society.
Now do you know the reason of this haste.

    Friar Laurence. [*Aside*] I would I knew not why it should
        be slow'd.

Look, sir, here comes the lady towards my cell.

Enter JULIET.

    Paris. Happily met, my lady and my wife!
    Juliet. That may be, sir, when I may be a wife.
    Paris. That may be must be, love, on Thursday next.   20
    Juliet. What must be shall be.
    Friar Laurence.   That 's a certain text.
    Paris. Come you to make confession to this father?
    Juliet. To answer that, I should confess to you.
    Paris. Do not deny to him that you love me.
    Juliet. I will confess to you that I love him.
    Paris. So will you, I am sure, that you love me.
    Juliet. If I do so, it will be of more price,
Being spoke behind your back, than to your face.
    Paris. Poor soul, thy face is much abus'd with tears.
    Juliet. The tears have got small victory by that ;   30
For it was bad enough before their spite.
    Paris. Thou wrong'st it more than tears with that report.
    Juliet. That is no slander, sir, which is a truth ;
And what I spake, I spake it to my face.
    Paris. Thy face is mine, and thou hast slander'd it.
    Juliet. It may be so, for it is not mine own.—
Are you at leisure, holy father, now ;
Or shall I come to you at evening mass?

Friar Laurence. **My** leisure serves me, pensive daughter,
   now.—

My lord, we must entreat the time alone.   40

   Paris. God shield I should disturb devotion!—

Juliet, on Thursday early will I rouse ye:

Till then, adieu, and keep this holy kiss.   *[Exit.*

   Juliet. O, shut the door! and when thou hast done so,

Come weep with me; past hope, past cure, past help!

   Friar Laurence. Ah, Juliet, I already know thy grief;

It strains me past the compass of my wits:

I hear thou must, and nothing may prorogue it,

On Thursday next be married to this county.

   Juliet. Tell me not, friar, that thou hear'st of this,   50

Unless thou tell me how I may prevent it;

If in thy wisdom thou canst give no help,

Do thou but call my resolution wise,

And with this knife I 'll help it presently.

God join'd my heart and Romeo's, thou our hands;

And ere this hand, by thee to Romeo seal'd,

Shall be the label to another deed,

Or my true heart with treacherous revolt

Turn to another, this shall slay them both:

Therefore, out of thy long-experienc'd time,   60

Give me some present counsel, or, behold,

'Twixt my extremes and me this bloody knife

Shall play the umpire, arbitrating that

Which the commission of thy years and art

Could to no issue of true honour bring.

Be not so long to speak; I long to die,

If what thou speak'st speak not of remedy.

   Friar Laurence. Hold, daughter! I do spy a kind of hope,

Which craves as desperate an execution

As that is desperate which we would prevent.   70

If, rather than to marry County Paris,

Thou hast the strength of will to slay thyself,

Then is it likely thou wilt undertake
A thing like death to chide away this shame,
That cop'st with death himself to scape from it;
And, if thou dar'st, I 'll give thee remedy.

 Juliet. O, bid me leap, rather than marry Paris,
From off the battlements of yonder tower;
Or walk in thievish ways; or bid me lurk
Where serpents are; chain me with roaring bears;   80
Or shut me nightly in a charnel-house,
O'er-cover'd quite with dead men's rattling bones,
With reeky shanks and yellow chapless skulls;
Or bid me go into a new-made grave
And hide me with a dead man in his shroud;
Things that, to hear them told, have made me tremble;
And I will do it without fear or doubt,
To live an unstain'd wife to my sweet love.

 Friar Laurence. Hold, then; go home, be merry, **giv**e consent
To marry Paris. Wednesday is to-morrow: 90
To-morrow night look that thou lie alone;
Let not thy nurse lie with thee in thy chamber.
Take thou this vial, being then in bed,
And this distilled liquor drink thou off;
When presently through all thy veins shall run
A cold and drowsy humour, for no pulse
Shall keep his native progress, but surcease.
No warmth, no breath, shall testify thou livest;
The roses in thy lips and cheeks shall fade
To paly ashes, thy eyes' windows fall,   100
Like death, when he shuts up the day of life;
Each part, depriv'd of supple government,
Shall, stiff and stark and cold, appear like death:
And in this borrow'd likeness of shrunk death
Thou shalt continue two and forty hours,
And then awake as from a pleasant sleep.

Now, when the bridegroom in the morning comes
To rouse thee from thy bed, there art thou dead :
Then, as the manner of our country is,
In thy best robes uncover'd on the bier   110
Thou shalt be borne to that same ancient vault
Where all the kindred of the Capulets lie.
In the mean time, against thou shalt awake,
Shall Romeo by my letters know our drift,
And hither shall he come ; and he and I
Will watch thy waking, and that very night
Shall Romeo bear thee hence to Mantua.
And this shall free thee from this present shame,
If no inconstant toy nor womanish fear
Abate thy valour in the acting it.   120

   Juliet. Give me, give me! O, tell not me of fear !
   Friar Laurence. Hold ; get you gone, be strong and pros-
        perous
In this resolve : I 'll send a friar with speed
To Mantua, with my letters to thy lord.
   Juliet. Love give me strength ! and strength shall help
        afford.
Farewell, dear father !   [*Exeunt.*

SCENE II.   *Hall in Capulet's House.*

Enter CAPULET, LADY CAPULET, Nurse, *and two* Servingmen.

   Capulet. So many guests invite as here are writ.—
                                              [*Exit Servant.*
Sirrah, go hire me twenty cunning cooks.
   2 Servant. You shall have none ill, sir, for I 'll try if they
can lick their fingers.
   Capulet. How canst thou try them so ?
   2 Servant. Marry, sir, 't is an ill cook that cannot lick his
own fingers ; therefore he that cannot lick his fingers goes
not with me.

Capulet. Go, be gone.—   [*Exit Servant.*
We shall be much unfurnish'd for this time.   10
What, is my daughter gone to Friar Laurence?
Nurse. Ay, forsooth.
Capulet. Well, he may chance to do some good on her;
A peevish self-will'd harlotry it is.
Nurse. See where she comes from shrift with merry look.

Enter JULIET.

Capulet. How now, my headstrong! where have you been
        gadding?
Juliet. Where I have learn'd me to repent the sin
Of disobedient opposition
To you and your behests, and am enjoin'd
By holy Laurence to fall prostrate here,   20
And beg your pardon.   Pardon, I beseech you!
Henceforward I am ever rul'd by you.
Capulet. Send for the county; go tell him of this.
I 'll have this knot knit up to-morrow morning.
Juliet. I met the youthful lord at Laurence' cell;
And gave him what becomed love I might,
Not stepping o'er the bounds of modesty.
Capulet. Why, I am glad on 't; this is well,—stand up:
This is as 't should be.—Let me see the county;
Ay, marry, go, I say, and fetch him hither.—   30
Now, afore God! this reverend holy friar,
All our whole city is much bound to him.
Juliet. Nurse, will you go with me into my closet,
To help me sort such needful ornaments
As you think fit to furnish me to-morrow?
Lady Capulet. No, not till Thursday; there is time enough.
Capulet. Go, nurse, go with her; we 'll to church to-morrow.
                    [*Exeunt Juliet and Nurse*
Lady Capulet. We shall be short in our provision;
'T is now near night.

                    H

Capulet.   Tush, I will stir about,
And all things shall be well, I warrant thee, wife.   40
Go thou to Juliet, help to deck up her:
I 'll not to bed to-night; let me alone;
I 'll play the housewife for this once.—What, ho!—
They are all forth.   Well, I will walk myself
To County Paris, to prepare him up
Against to-morrow.   My heart is wondrous light,
Since this same wayward girl is so reclaim'd.   [*Exeunt.*

SCENE III.   *Juliet's Chamber.*

Enter JULIET *and* Nurse.

Juliet. Ay, those attires are best: but, gentle nurse,
I pray thee, leave me to myself to-night;
For I have need of many orisons
To move the heavens to smile upon my state,
Which, well thou know'st, is cross and full of sin.

Enter LADY CAPULET.

Lady Capulet. What, are you busy, ho? need you my help?
Juliet. No, madam; we have cull'd such necessaries
As are behoveful for our state to-morrow:
So please you, let me now be left alone,
And let the nurse this night sit up with you;   10
For, I am sure, you have your hands full all,
In this so sudden business.
Lady Capulet.   Good night;
Get thee to bed and rest, for thou hast need.
                    [*Exeunt Lady Capulet and Nurse.*
Juliet. Farewell!—God knows when we shall meet again.
I have a faint cold fear thrills through my veins,
That almost freezes up the heat of life;
I 'll call them back again to comfort me.—
Nurse!—What should she do here?

My dismal scene I needs must act alone.—
Come, vial.—   20
What if this mixture do not work at all?
Shall I be married then to-morrow morning?
No, no!—this shall forbid it.—Lie thou there.

[Laying down a dagger

What if it be a poison, which the friar
Subtly hath minister'd to have me dead,
Lest in this marriage he should be dishonour'd,
Because he married me before to Romeo?
I fear it is ; and yet, methinks, it should not,
For he hath still been tried a holy man.
How if, when I am laid into the tomb,   30
I wake before the time that Romeo
Come to redeem me? there's a fearful point!
Shall I not then be stifled in the vault,
To whose foul mouth no healthsome air breathes in,
And there die strangled ere my Romeo comes?
Or, if I live, is it not very like,
The horrible conceit of death and night,
Together with the terror of the place,—
As in a vault, an ancient receptacle,
Where for these many hundred years the bones   40
Of all my buried ancestors are pack'd ;
Where bloody Tybalt, yet but green in earth,
Lies festering in his shroud ; where, as they say,
At some hours in the night spirits resort ;—
Alack, alack, is it not like that I,
So early waking, what with loathsome smells,
And shrieks like mandrakes' torn out of the earth,
That living mortals hearing them run mad ;—
O, if I wake, shall I not be distraught,
Environed with all these hideous fears?   50
And madly play with my forefathers' joints?
And pluck the mangled Tybalt from his shroud?

And, in this rage, with some great kinsman's bone,
As with a club, dash out my desperate brains?—
O, look! methinks I see my cousin's ghost
Seeking out Romeo, that did spit his body
Upon a rapier's point.—Stay, Tybalt, stay!—
Romeo, I come! this do I drink to thee.

[She throws herself on the bed.

SCENE IV.   *Hall in Capulet's House.*

Enter LADY CAPULET *and* Nurse.

Lady Capulet. Hold, take these keys, and fetch more spices,
     nurse.
Nurse. They call for dates and quinces in the pastry.

Enter CAPULET.

Capulet. Come, stir, stir, stir! the second cock hath crow'd,
The curfew-bell hath rung, 't is three o'clock.—
Look to the bak'd meats, good Angelica;
Spare not for cost.
Nurse.   Go, you cot-quean, go,
Get you to bed; faith, you 'll be sick to-morrow
For this night's watching.
Capulet. No, not a whit.   What! I have watch'd ere now
All night for lesser cause, and ne'er been sick.   10
Lady Capulet. Ay, you have been a mouse-hunt in your
     time;
But I will watch you from such watching now.

[Exeunt Lady Capulet and Nurse.

Capulet. A jealous-hood, a jealous-hood!—

Enter three or four Servingmen, *with spits, logs, and baskets.*

Now, fellow,

What 's there?
     1 *Servant.* Things for the cook, sir; but I know not what

Capulet. Make haste, make haste.—[*Exit Servant.*] Sirrah,
  fetch drier logs ;
Call Peter, he will show thee where they are.
  2 *Servant.* I have a head, sir, that will find out logs,
And never trouble Peter for the matter.   [*Exit.*
  Capulet. Mass, and well said ; a merry whoreson, ha ! 20
Thou shalt be logger-head.—Good faith, 't is day :
The county will be here with music straight,
For so he said he would.   I hear him near.—
                                        [*Music within.*
Nurse !—·Wife !—What, ho !—What, nurse, I say !

                    Re-enter Nurse.

Go waken Juliet, go and trim her up ;
I 'll go and chat with Paris.—Hie, make haste,
Make haste ; the bridegroom he is come already :
Make haste, I say.   [*Exeunt.*

      SCENE V.   *Juliet's Chamber.*
            Enter Nurse.

  Nurse. Mistress ! what, mistress ! Juliet ! fast, I warrant
  her, she.—
Why, lamb ! why, lady ! fie, you slug-a-bed !
Why, love, I say ! madam ! sweet-heart ! why, bride !
What, not a word ?—How sound is she asleep !
I needs must wake her.—Madam, madam, madam !
Ay, let the county take you in your bed ;
He 'll fright you up, i' faith.—Will it not be ?
                              [*Undraws the curtains.*
What, dress'd ! and in your clothes ! and down again !
I must needs wake you.   Lady ! lady ! lady !—
Alas, alas !—Help, help ! my lady 's dead !—   10
O, well-a-day, that ever I was born !—
Some aqua vitæ, ho !—My lord ! my lady !

Enter LADY CAPULET.   •

Lady Capulet. What noise is here?

Nurse.   O lamentable day!

Lady Capulet. What is the matter?

Nurse.   Look, look! O heavy day!

Lady Capulet. O me, O me!   My child, my only life,
Revive, look up, or I will die with thee!—
Help, help!   Call help.

Enter CAPULET.

Capulet. For shame, bring Juliet forth; her lord is come.

Nurse. She 's dead, deceas'd, she 's dead; alack the day!

Lady Capulet. Alack the day, she 's dead, she 's dead, she 's
    dead!   20

Capulet. Ha! let me see her.   Out, alas! she 's cold;
Her blood is settled, and her joints are stiff;
Life and these lips have long been separated.
Death lies on her like an untimely frost
Upon the sweetest flower of all the field.

Nurse. O lamentable day!

Lady Capulet.   O woful time!

Capulet. Death, that hath ta'en her hence to make me
    wail,
Ties up my tongue and will not let me speak.

Enter FRIAR LAURENCE *and* PARIS, *with* Musicians.

Friar Laurence. Come, is the bride ready to go to church?

Capulet. Ready to go, but never to return.   30
O son! the night before thy wedding-day
Hath Death lain with thy wife.   See, there she lies,
Flower as she was, deflower'd by him.
Death is my son-in-law, Death is my heir;
My daughter he hath wedded.   I will die,
And leave him all; life, living, all is Death's.

Paris. Have I thought long to see this morning's face,
And doth it give me such a sight as this?
    Lady Capulet. Accurst, unhappy, wretched, hateful day!
Most miserable hour that e'er time saw   40
In lasting labour of his pilgrimage!
But one, poor one, one poor and loving child,
But one thing to rejoice and solace in,
And cruel death hath catch'd it from my sight!
    Nurse. O woe! O woful, woful, woful day!
Most lamentable day, most woful day,
That ever, ever, I did yet behold!
O day! O day! O day! O hateful day!
Never was seen so black a day as this:
O woful day, O woful day!   50
    Paris. Beguil'd, divorced, wronged, spited, slain!
Most detestable death, by thee beguil'd,
By cruel cruel thee quite overthrown!
O love! O life! not life, but love in death!
    Capulet. Despis'd, distressed, hated, martyr'd, kill'd!
Uncomfortable time, why cam'st thou now
To murther, murther our solemnity?—
O child! O child! my soul, and not my child!
Dead art thou! Alack! my child is dead;
And with my child my joys are buried.   60
    Friar Laurence. Peace, ho, for shame! confusion's cure
    lives not
In these confusions. Heaven and yourself
Had part in this fair maid; now heaven hath all,
And all the better is it for the maid:
Your part in her you could not keep from death,
But heaven keeps his part in eternal life.
The most you sought was her promotion,
For 't was your heaven she should be advanc'd;
And weep ye now, seeing she is advanc'd
Above the clouds, as high as heaven itself?   70

O, in this love, you love your child so ill,
That you run mad, seeing that she is well;
She 's not well married that lives married long,
But she 's best married that dies married young.
Dry up your tears, and stick your rosemary
On this fair corse, and, as the custom is,
In all her best array bear her to church;
For though fond nature bids us all lament,
Yet nature's tears are reason's merriment.

 Capulet. All things that we ordained festival, 80
Turn from their office to black funeral:
Our instruments to melancholy bells,
Our wedding cheer to a sad burial feast,
Our solemn hymns to sullen dirges change,
Our bridal flowers serve for a buried corse,
And all things change them to the contrary.

 Friar Laurence. Sir, go you in, — and, madam, go with
  him ;—
And go, Sir Paris ; – every one prepare
To follow this fair corse unto her grave.
The heavens do lower upon you for some ill ; 90
Move them no more by crossing their high will.

   [*Exeunt Capulet, Lady Capulet, Paris, and Friar.*
 1 *Musician.* Faith, we may put up our pipes, and be gone.
 Nurse. Honest good fellows, ah, put up, put up;
For, well you know, this is a pitiful case. [*Exit.*
 1 *Musician.* Ay, by my troth, the case may be amended.

    Enter PETER.

 Peter. Musicians, O, musicians, 'Heart's ease, Heart's ease:'
O, an you will have me live, play 'Heart's ease.'
 1 *Musician.* Why 'Heart's ease?'
 Peter. O, musicians, because my heart itself plays 'My
heart is full of woe:' O, play me some merry dump, to comfort me. 101

1 *Musician.* Not a dump we ; 't is no time to play now.

Peter. You will not, then?

1 *Musician.* No.

Peter. I will then give it you soundly.

1 *Musician.* What will you give us?

Peter. No money, on my faith, but the gleek ; I will give you the minstrel.

1 *Musician.* Then will I give you the serving-creature. 109

Peter. Then will I lay the serving-creature's dagger on your pate. I will carry no crotchets: I 'll re you, I 'll fa you ; do you note me?

1 *Musician.* An you re us and fa us, you note us.

2 *Musician.* Pray you, put up your dagger, and put out your wit.

Peter. Then have at you with my wit! I will dry-beat you with an iron wit, and put up my iron dagger. Answer me like men:

'When griping grief the heart doth wound,
    And doleful dumps the mind oppress, 120
    Then music with her siiver sound '—

why ' silver sound ?' why ' music with her silver sound ?'— What say you, Simon Catling?

1 *Musician.* Marry, sir, because silver hath a sweet sound.

Peter. Pretty!—What say you, Hugh Rebeck?

2 *Musician.* I say ' silver sound,' because musicians sound for silver.

Peter. Pretty too !—What say you, James Soundpost?

3 *Musician.* Faith, I know not what to say. 129

Peter. O, I cry you mercy ; you are the singer : I will say for you. It is ' music with her silver sound,' because musicians have no gold for sounding:

'Then music with her silver sound
    With speedy help doth lend redress.' [*Exit.*

1 *Musician.* What a pestilent knave is this same !

2 *Musician.* Hang him, Jack !—Come, we 'll in here ; tarry for the mourners. and stay dinner. [*Exeunt.*

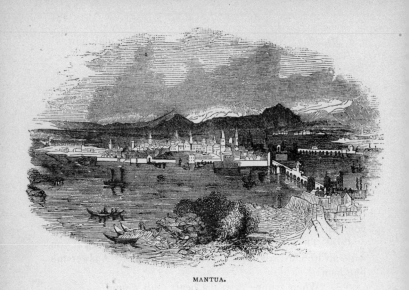

MANTUA.

ACT V.

Scene I. *Mantua. A Street.*

Enter Romeo.

Romeo. If I may trust the flattering truth of sleep,
My dreams presage some joyful news at hand.
My bosom's lord sits lightly in his throne;
And all this day an unaccustom'd spirit
Lifts me above the ground with cheerful thoughts.
I dreamt my lady came and found me dead—
Strange dream, that gives a dead man leave to think !—
And breath'd such life with kisses in my lips,
That I reviv'd, and was an emperor.
Ah me ! how sweet is love itself possess'd,   10
When but love's shadows are so rich in joy !

Enter BALTHASAR.

News from Verona!—-How now, Balthasar!
Dost thou not bring me letters from the friar?
How doth my lady? Is my father well?
How fares my Juliet? that I ask again;
For nothing can be ill, if she be well.

   Balthasar. Then she is well, and nothing can be ill;
Her body sleeps in Capel's monument,
And her immortal part with angels lives.
I saw her laid low in her kindred's vault,   20
And presently took post to tell it you.
O, pardon me for bringing these ill news,
Since you did leave it for my office, sir.

   Romeo. Is it even so? then I defy you, stars!—
Thou know'st my lodging: get me ink and paper,
And hire post-horses; I will hence to-night.

   Balthasar. I do beseech you, sir, have patience;
Your looks are pale and wild, and do import
Some misadventure.

   Romeo.   Tush, thou art deceiv'd;
Leave me, and do the thing I bid thee do.   30
Hast thou no letters to me from the friar?

   Balthasar. No, my good lord.

   Romeo.   No matter: get thee gone,
And hire those horses; I 'll be with thee straight.—

                   [Exit Balthasar.

Well, Juliet, I will lie with thee to-night.
Let 's see for means.—O mischief, thou art swift
To enter in the thoughts of desperate men!
I do remember an apothecary,—
And hereabouts he dwells,—which late I noted
In tatter'd weeds, with overwhelming brows,
Culling of simples; meagre were his looks,   40
Sharp misery had worn him to the bones:

And in his needy shop a tortoise hung,
An alligator stuff'd, and other skins
Of ill-shap'd fishes ; and about his shelves
A beggarly account of empty boxes,
Green earthen pots, bladders and musty seeds,
Remnants of packthread and old cakes of roses,
Were thinly scatter'd, to make up a show.
Noting this penury, to myself I said,
An if a man did need a poison now, 50
Whose sale is present death in Mantua,
Here lives a caitiff wretch would sell it him.
O, this same thought did but forerun my need,
And this same needy man must sell it me!
As I remember, this should be the house.
Being holiday, the beggar's shop is shut.—
What, ho! apothecary!

Enter Apothecary.

Apothecary.   Who calls so loud?
Romeo. Come hither, man.   I see that thou art poor :
Hold, there is forty ducats ; let me have
A dram of poison, such soon-speeding gear 60
As will disperse itself through all the veins
That the life-weary taker may fall dead,
And that the trunk may be discharg'd of breath
As violently as hasty powder fir'd
Doth hurry from the fatal cannon's womb.
Apothecary. Such mortal drugs I have ; but Mantua's
     law
Is death to any he that utters them.
Romeo. Art thou so bare and full of wretchedness,
And fear'st to die? famine is in thy cheeks,
Need and oppression starveth in thine eyes, 70
Contempt and beggary hangs upon thy back,
The world is not thy friend, nor the world's law :

The world affords no law to make thee rich;
Then be not poor, but break it, and take this.

Apothecary. My poverty, but not my will, consents.

Romeo. I pay thy poverty, and not thy will.

Apothecary. Put this in any liquid thing you will,
And drink it off; and, if you had the strength
Of twenty men, it would dispatch you straight.

Romeo. There is thy gold, worse poison to men's souls, 80
Doing more murthers in this loathsome world
Than these poor compounds that thou mayst not sell
I sell thee poison, thou hast sold me none.
Farewell; buy food, and get thyself in flesh.—
Come, cordial and not poison, go with me
To Juliet's grave; for there must I use thee.   [*Exeunt.*

SCENE II.   *Friar Laurence's Cell.*
Enter FRIAR JOHN.

Friar John. Holy Franciscan friar! brother, ho!

Enter FRIAR LAURENCE.

Friar Laurence. This same should be the voice of Friar
     John.—
Welcome from Mantua; what says Romeo?
Or, if his mind be writ, give me his letter.

Friar John. Going to find a barefoot brother out,
One of our order, to associate me,
Here in this city visiting the sick,
And finding him, the searchers of the town,
Suspecting that we both were in a house
Where the infectious pestilence did reign,
Seal'd up the doors, and would not let us forth; 10
So that my speed to Mantua there was stay'd.

Friar Laurence. Who bare my letter, then, to Romeo?

Friar John. I could not send it,—here it is again,—

Nor get a messenger to bring it thee,
So fearful were they of infection.

    Friar Laurence. Unhappy fortune! by my brotherhood,
The letter was not nice, but full of charge
Of dear import, and the neglecting it
May do much danger.   Friar John, go hence;   2c
Get me an iron crow, and bring it straight
Unto my cell.

    Friar John. Brother, I 'll go and bring it thee.   [*Exit.*

    Friar Laurence. Now must I to the monument alone;
Within this three hours will fair Juliet wake.
She will beshrew me much that Romeo
Hath had no notice of these accidents;
But I will write again to Mantua,
And keep her at my cell till Romeo come:
Poor living corse, clos'd in a dead man's tomb!   [*Exit*

SCENE III. *A Churchyard; in it a Tomb belonging to the Capulets.*

    Enter PARIS, *and his* Page *bearing flowers and a torch.*

    Paris. Give me thy torch, boy; hence, and stand aloof:
Yet put it out, for I would not be seen.
Under yond yew-trees lay thee all along,
Holding thine ear close to the hollow ground;
So shall no foot upon the churchyard tread,
Being loose, unfirm, with digging up of graves,
But thou shalt hear it: whistle then to me,
As signal that thou hear'st something approach.
Give me those flowers.   Do as I bid thee, go.

    Page. [*Aside*] I am almost afraid to stand alone   10
Here in the churchyard; yet I will adventure.   [*Retires.*

    Paris. Sweet flower, with flowers thy bridal bed I strew.
    O woe! thy canopy is dust and stones,
Which with sweet water nightly I will dew,
    Or, wanting that, with tears distill'd by moans;

The obsequies that I for thee will keep
Nightly shall be to strew thy grave and weep.

> [*The Page whistles.*

The boy gives warning something doth approach.
What cursed foot wanders this way to-night,
To cross my obsequies and true love's rite?   20
What, with a torch!—Muffle me, night, awhile.   [*Retires.*

Enter ROMEO *and* BALTHASAR, *with a torch, mattock, etc.*

Romeo. Give me that mattock and the wrenching iron.
Hold, take this letter; early in the morning
See thou deliver it to my lord and father.
Give me the light.   Upon thy life, I charge thee,
Whate'er thou hear'st or seest, stand all aloof,
And do not interrupt me in my course.
Why I descend into this bed of death
Is partly to behold my lady's face,
But chiefly to take thence from her dead finger   30
A precious ring, a ring that I must use
In dear employment.   Therefore hence, be gone;
But if thou, jealous, dost return to pry
In what I further shall intend to do,
By heaven, I will tear thee joint by joint
And strew this hungry churchyard with thy limbs.
The time and my intents are savage-wild,
More fierce and more inexorable far
Than empty tigers or the roaring sea.
  Balthasar. I will be gone, sir, and not trouble you.   40
  Romeo. So shalt thou show me friendship.   Take thou
      that:
Live, and be prosperous; and farewell, good fellow.
  Balthasar. [*Aside*] For all this same, I 'll hide me here-
      about;
His looks I fear, and his intents I doubt.   [*Retires.*
  Romeo. Thou detestable maw, thou womb of death.

Gorg'd with the dearest morsel of the earth,
Thus I enforce thy rotten jaws to open,
And, in despite, I 'll cram thee with more food !

[Opens the tomb.

   Paris. This is that banish'd haughty Montague,
That murther'd my love's cousin,—with which grief,   50
It is supposed, the fair creature died,—
And here is come to do some villanous shame
To the dead bodies ; I will apprehend him.—   *[Advances.*
Stop thy unhallow'd toil, vile Montague !
Can vengeance be pursued further than death ?
Condemned villain, I do apprehend thee :
Obey, and go with me ; for thou must die.

   Romeo. I must indeed, and therefore came I hither.
Good gentle youth, tempt not a desperate man ;
Fly hence, and leave me : think upon these gone ;   60
Let them affright thee. I beseech thee, youth,
Put not another sin upon my head,
By urging me to fury ; O, be gone !
By heaven, I love thee better than myself ;
For I come hither arm'd against myself.
Stay not, be gone ; live, and hereafter say,
A madman's mercy bade thee run away.

   Paris. I do defy thy conjurations,
And apprehend thee for a felon here.

   Romeo. Wilt thou provoke me ? then have at thee, boy !   70

[They fight.

   Page. O Lord, they fight ! I will go call the watch.   *[Exit.*

   Paris. O, I am slain !—[*Falls*] If thou be merciful,
Open the tomb, lay me with Juliet.   *[Dies.*

   Romeo. In faith, I will.—Let me peruse this face.
Mercutio's kinsman, noble County Paris !
What said my man, when my betossed soul
Did not attend him as we rode ? I think
He told me Paris should have married Juliet ;

Said he not so? or did I dream it so?
Or am I mad, hearing him talk of Juliet,　　　85
To think it was so?—O, give me thy hand,
One writ with me in sour misfortune's book!
I 'll bury thee in a triumphant grave,—
A grave? O, no! a lantern, slaughter'd youth;
For here lies Juliet, and her beauty makes
This vault a feasting presence full of light.
Death, lie thou there, by a dead man interr'd.—

　　　　　　　　　[Laying Paris in the tomb.

How oft when men are at the point of death
Have they been merry! which their keepers call
A lightning before death; O, how may I　　　90
Call this a lightning?—O my love! my wife!
Death, that hath suck'd the honey of thy breath,
Hath had no power yet upon thy beauty:
Thou art not conquer'd; beauty's ensign yet
Is crimson in thy lips and in thy cheeks,
And death's pale flag is not advanced there.—
Tybalt, liest thou there in thy bloody sheet?
O, what more favour can I do to thee
Than with that hand that cut thy youth in twain
To sunder his that was thine enemy?　　　100
Forgive me, cousin!—Ah, dear Juliet,
Why art thou yet so fair? shall I believe
That unsubstantial Death is amorous,
And that the lean abhorred monster keeps
Thee here in dark to be his paramour?
For fear of that, I still will stay with thee;
And never from this palace of dim night
Depart again: here, here will I remain
With worms that are thy chamber-maids; O, here
Will I set up my everlasting rest,　　　110
And shake the yoke of inauspicious stars
From this world-wearied flesh.—Eyes, look your last!

I

Arms, take your last embrace! and, lips, O you
The doors of breath, seal with a righteous kiss
A dateless bargain to engrossing death!
Come, bitter conduct, come, unsavoury guide!
Thou desperate pilot, now at once run on
The dashing rocks thy sea-sick weary bark!
Here's to my love! [*Drinks.*]—O true apothecary!   119
Thy drugs are quick.—Thus with a kiss I die.   [*Dies.*

Enter, at the other end of the churchyard, FRIAR LAURENCE,
with a lantern, crow, and spade.

    Friar Laurence. Saint Francis be my speed! how oft to-
       night
Have my old feet stumbled at graves!—Who's there?
    Balthasar. Here's one, a friend, and one that knows you
       well.
    Friar Laurence. Bliss be upon you! Tell me, good my
       friend,
What torch is yond, that vainly lends his light
To grubs and eyeless skulls? as I discern,
It burneth in the Capels' monument.
    Balthasar. It doth so, holy sir; and there's my master,
One that you love.
    Friar Laurence.   Who is it?
    Balthasar.   Romeo.   129
    Friar Laurence. How long hath he been there?
    Balthasar.   Full half an hour.
    Friar Laurence. Go with me to the vault.
    Balthasar.   ·   I dare not, sir:
My master knows not but I am gone hence;
And fearfully did menace me with death,
If I did stay to look on his intents.
    Friar Laurence. Stay, then; I'll go alone.--Fear comes
       upon me;
O, much I fear some ill unlucky thing!

Balthasar. As I did sleep under this yew-tree here,
I dreamt my master and another fought,
And that my master slew him.   [*Exit.*

   Friar Laurence.   Romeo!   [*Advances.*
Alack, alack, what blood is this, which stains   140
The stony entrance of this sepulchre?—
What mean these masterless and gory swords
To lie discolour'd by this place of peace?   [*Enters the tomb.*
Romeo! O, pale!—Who else? what, Paris too?
And steep'd in blood?—Ah, what an unkind hour
Is guilty of this lamentable chance!—
The lady stirs.   [*Juliet wakes.*

   Juliet. O comfortable friar! where is my lord?—
I do remember well where I should be,   149
And there I am.—Where is my Romeo?   [*Noise within.*

   Friar Laurence. I hear some noise.—Lady, come from that
     nest
Of death, contagion, and unnatural sleep;
A greater power than we can contradict
Hath thwarted our intents. Come, come away.
Thy husband in thy bosom there lies dead;
And Paris too. Come, I'll dispose of thee
Among a sisterhood of holy nuns:
Stay not to question, for the watch is coming;
Come, go, good Juliet. [*Noise again.*]—I dare no longer stay.

   Juliet. Go, get thee hence, for I will not away.—   160
                           [*Exit Friar Laurence.*
What's here? a cup, clos'd in my true love's hand?
Poison, I see, hath been his timeless end.—
O churl! drunk all, and left no friendly drop
To help me after?—I will kiss thy lips;
Haply some poison yet doth hang on them,
To make me die with a restorative.   [*Kisses him.*
Thy lips are warm.

   1 *Watch.* [*Within*] Lead, boy; which way?

Juliet. Yea, noise? then I 'll be brief.—O happy dagger!
　　　　　　　　　　　　[*Snatching Romeo's dagger.*
This is thy sheath [*Stabs herself*]; there rest, and let me die.
　　　　　　　　　　　[*Falls on Romeo's body, and dies.*

Enter Watch, *with the* Page *of* PARIS.

Page. This is the place; there, where the torch doth burn.
1 *Watch.* The ground is bloody; search about the church-
　　yard.　　　　　　　　　　　　　　　　172
Go, some of you, whoe'er you find attach.—　　[*Exeunt some.*
Pitiful sight! here lies the county slain;
And Juliet bleeding, warm, and newly dead,
Who here hath lain these two days buried.—
Go, tell the prince;—run to the Capulets;—
Raise up the Montagues;—some others search.—
　　　　　　　　　　　[*Exeunt other Watchmen.*
We see the ground whereon these woes do lie;
But the true ground of all these piteous woes　　　180
We cannot without circumstance descry.

Re-enter some of the Watch, *with* BALTHASAR.

2 *Watch.* Here 's Romeo's man; we found him in the
　　churchyard.
1 *Watch.* Hold him in safety, till the prince come hither.

Re-enter others of the Watch, *with* FRIAR LAURENCE.

3 *Watch.* Here is a friar, that trembles, sighs, and weeps:
We took this mattock and this spade from him,
As he was coming from this churchyard side.
1 *Watch.* A great suspicion; stay the friar too.

Enter the PRINCE *and* Attendants.

Prince. What misadventure is so early up,
That calls our person from our morning's rest?

Enter CAPULET, LADY CAPULET, *and others.*

Capulet. What should it be, that they so shriek abroad?

Lady Capulet. The people in the street cry Romeo,   191
Some Juliet, and some Paris, and all run
With open outcry toward our monument.

Prince. What fear is this which startles in our ears?

1 *Watch.* Sovereign, here lies the County Paris slain;
And Romeo dead; and Juliet, dead before,
Warm and new kill'd.

Prince. Search, seek, and know how this foul murther
      comes.

1 *Watch.* Here is a friar, and slaughter'd Romeo's man,
With instruments upon them fit to open   200
These dead men's tombs.

Capulet. O heaven!—O wife, look how our daughter
      bleeds!
This dagger hath mista'en,—for, lo, his house
Is empty on the back of Montague,—
And is mis-sheathed in my daughter's bosom!

Lady Capulet. O me! this sight of death is as a bell,
That warns my old age to a sepulchre.

Enter MONTAGUE *and others.*

Prince. Come, Montague; for thou art early up,
To see thy son and heir more early down.

Montague. Alas, my liege, my wife is dead to-night;   210
Grief of my son's exile hath stopp'd her breath.
What further woe conspires against mine age?

Prince. Look, and thou shalt see.

Montague. O thou untaught! what manners is in this,
To press before thy father to a grave?

Prince. Seal up the mouth of outrage for a while,
Till we can clear these ambiguities,
And know their spring, their head, their true descent;

And then will I be general of your woes,
And lead you even to death : meantime forbear,   220
And let mischance be slave to patience.—
Bring forth the parties of suspicion.

    Friar Laurence. I am the greatest, able to do least,
Yet most suspected, as the time and place
Doth make against me, of this direful murther ;
And here I stand, both to impeach and purge
Myself condemned and myself excus'd.

    Prince. Then say at once what thou dost know in this.

    Friar Laurence. I will be brief, for my short date of breath
Is not so long as is a tedious tale.   230
Romeo, there dead, was husband to that Juliet ;
And she, there dead, that Romeo's faithful wife.
I married them ; and their stolen marriage-day
Was Tybalt's doomsday, whose untimely death
Banish'd the new-made bridegroom from this city,
For whom, and not for Tybalt, Juliet pin'd.
You, to remove that siege of grief from her,
Betroth'd and would have married her perforce
To County Paris ; then comes she to me,
And with wild looks bid me devise some means   240
To rid her from this second marriage,
Or in my cell there would she kill herself.
Then gave I her, so tutor'd by my art,
A sleeping potion ; which so took effect
As I intended, for it wrought on her
The form of death : meantime I writ to Romeo,
That he should hither come as this dire night,
To help to take her from her borrow'd grave,
Being the time the potion's force should cease.
But he which bore my letter, Friar John,   250
Was stay'd by accident, and yesternight
Return'd my letter back.   Then all alone,
At the prefixed hour of her waking,

Came I to take her from her kindred's vault,
Meaning to keep her closely at my cell
Till I conveniently could send to Romeo;
But when I came, some minute ere the time
Of her awaking, here untimely lay
The noble Paris and true Romeo dead.
She wakes, and I entreated her come forth,   260
And bear this work of heaven with patience;
But then a noise did scare me from the tomb,
And she too desperate would not go with me,
But, as it seems, did violence on herself.
All this I know; and to the marriage
Her nurse is privy: and, if aught in this
Miscarried by my fault, let my old life
Be sacrific'd some hour before his time
Unto the rigour of severest law.

   Prince. We still have known thee for a holy man.—   270
Where's Romeo's man? what can he say in this?

   Balthasar. I brought my master news of Juliet's death,
And then in post he came from Mantua
To this same place, to this same monument.
This letter he early bid me give his father,
And threaten'd me with death, going in the vault,
If I departed not and left him there.

   Prince. Give me the letter; I will look on it.—
Where is the county's page, that rais'd the watch?—
Sirrah, what made your master in this place?   280

   Page. He came with flowers to strew his lady's grave;
And bid me stand aloof, and so I did.
Anon comes one with light to ope the tomb,
And by and by my master drew on him;
And then I ran away to call the watch.

   Prince. This letter doth make good the friar's words,
Their course of love, the tidings of her death;
And here he writes that he did buy a poison

Of a poor pothecary, and therewithal
Came to this vault to die and lie with Juliet.—   290
Where be these enemies?—Capulet!—Montague!
See, what a scourge is laid upon your hate,
That heaven finds means to kill your joys with love!
And I, for winking at your discords too,
Have lost a brace of kinsmen; all are punish'd.

   Capulet. O brother Montague, give me thy hand;
This is my daughter's jointure, for no more
Can I demand.

   Montague.   But I can give thee more;
For I will raise her statue in pure gold,
That while Verona by that name is known   300
There shall no figure at such rate be set
As that of true and faithful Juliet.

   Capulet. As rich shall Romeo by his lady lie;
Poor sacrifices of our enmity!

   Prince. A glooming peace this morning with it brings;
The sun for sorrow will not show his head.
Go hence, to have more talk of these sad things;
   Some shall be pardon'd, and some punished:
For never was a story of more woe
Than this of Juliet and her Romeo.   *[Exeunt.*

NOTES.

ABBREVIATIONS USED IN THE NOTES.

Abbott (or Gr.), Abbott's *Shakespearian Grammar* (third edition).
A. S., Anglo-Saxon.
A. V., Authorized Version of the Bible (1611).
B. and F., Beaumont and Fletcher.
B. J., Ben Jonson.
Camb. ed., "Cambridge edition" of *Shakespeare*, edited by Clark and Wright.
Cf. (*confer*), compare.
Coll., Collier (second edition).
Coll. MS., Manuscript Corrections of Second Folio, edited by Collier.
D., Dyce (second edition).
Daniel, P. A. Daniel's revised ed. of Quarto of 1599 (New Shakspere Society, 1875).
F., Furness's "New Variorum" ed. of *Romeo and Juliet* (Philadelphia, 1871).
H., Hudson (first edition).
Id. (*idem*), the same.
K., Knight (second edition).
Nares, *Glossary*, edited by Halliwell and Wright (London, 1859).
Prol., Prologue.
S., Shakespeare.
Schmidt, A. Schmidt's *Shakespeare-Lexicon* (Berlin, 1874).
Sr., Singer.
St., Staunton.
Theo., Theobald.
V., Verplanck.
W., White.
Walker, Wm. Sidney Walker's *Critical Examination of the Text of Shakespeare*
(London, 1860).
Warb., Warburton.
Wb., Webster's Dictionary (revised quarto edition of 1864).
Worc., Worcester's Dictionary (quarto edition).

The abbreviations of the names of Shakespeare's Plays will be readily understood; as
T. N. for *Twelfth Night*, *Cor.* for *Coriolanus*, *3 Hen. VI.* for *The Third Part of King
Henry the Sixth*, etc. *P. P.* refers to *The Passionate Pilgrim; V. and A.* to *Venus
and Adonis; L. C.* to *Lover's Complaint;* and *Sonn.* to the *Sonnets.*

When the abbreviation of the name of a play is followed by a reference to *page*,
Rolfe's edition of the play is meant.

The numbers of the lines (except for *Romeo and Juliet*) are those of the ' Globe'
ed. or Crowell's reprint of that ed.

NOTES.

THE FUNERAL OF JULIET.

PROLOGUE.

Enter Chorus. As Malone suggests, this probably meant only that the prologue was to be spoken by the same actor that personated the Chorus at the end of act i. The prologue is omitted in the folio, and Ulrici believes it was not written by S. See on i. 4. 7 below.

2. *Fair Verona*. The city is thus described in the opening lines of Brooke's poem :*

> "There is beyonde the Alps, a towne of auncient fame
> Whose bright renoune yet shineth cleare, Verona men it name :
> Bylt in an happy time, bylt on a fertile soyle :
> Maynteined by the heauenly fates, and by the townish toyle.
> The fruitefull hilles aboue, the pleasant vales belowe,
> The siluer streame with chanell depe, that through the towne doth flow :
> The store of springes that serue for vse, and eke for ease :
> And other moe commodities, which profite may and please ;
> Eke many certaine signes of thinges betyde of olde,
> To fyll the houngry eyes of those that curiously beholde :
> Doe make this towne to be preferde aboue the rest
> Of Lumbard townes, or at the least compared with the best."

6. *Star-cross'd*. For the astrological allusion, cf. i. 4. 104, v. 1. 24, and v. 3. 111 below. The title of one of Richard Braithwaite's works, published in 1615, is "Love's Labyrinth : or the True Lover's Knot, including the disastrous falls of two Star-crost lovers Pyramus and Thisbe."

8. *Doth*. The reading of the quartos, changed by the modern editors (except Ulrici and St.) to "Do." Ulrici (cf. Gr. 334) considers it the old third person plural in *-th*. He adds that S. mostly uses it only where it has the force of the singular, namely, where the sense is collective, as in *overthrows* here. Cf. v. 1. 70 below.

12. *Two hours*. Cf. *Hen. VIII.* prol. 13 : "may see away their shilling Richly in two short hours."

ACT. I.

SCENE I.—1. *Carry coals*. "Endure affronts" (Johnson). According to Nares, the phrase got this meaning from the fact that the carriers of wood and coals were esteemed the very lowest of menials, the *servi servorum*. Cf. *Hen. V.* iii. 2. 49, where there is a play upon the expression. Steevens quotes Nash, *Have With You*, etc. : "We will bear no coles, I warrant you ;" Marston, *Antonio and Mellida*, part ii. : "He has had wrongs ; and if I were he I would bear no coles," etc. D. cites Cotgrave, *Fr. Dict.* : "*Il a du feu en la teste.* Hee is very chollericke, furious, or couragious ; he will carrie no coales." He might have added from Sherwood's English-French supplement to Cotgrave (ed. 1632) : "That will carrie no coales, *Brave*."

2. *Colliers*. The preceding note explains how *colliers* came to be a term of abuse. Steevens compares *T. N.* iii. 4. 130 : "hang him, foul collier !"

22. *Cruel*. The reading of the 4th quarto ; the other early eds. have "ciuil," "ciuill," or "civill." K. reads "civil."

24. *Comes two of*. The early eds. (except the 1st quarto) have "comes of," which is preferred by K. and St. Delius (*apud* F.) considers that "the omission of the nominative is characteristic of the careless familiar

---

* The entire poem is reprinted in the *Variorum* of 1821, in Collier's *Shakespeare's Library*, in Halliwell's folio ed. of Shakespeare, and by the New Shakspere Society (edited by P. A. Daniel) in 1875. We have followed Daniel's ed.

talk of servants : Here comes (something) of the house of Montague ;" and Ulrici adds "especially as this indefiniteness has a tone of contempt."

Halliwell remarks that the partisans of the Montagues wore a token in their hats to distinguish them from the Capulets ; hence throughout the play they are known at a distance. Cf. Gascoigne, *Devise of a Masque, written for Viscount Montacute*, 1575 :

> "And for a further proofe, he shewed in hys hat
> Thys token which the *Mountacutes* did beare alwaies, for that
> They covet to be knowne from *Capels*, where they pass,
> For ancient grutch whych long ago 'tweene these two houses was."

34. *I will bite my thumb at them.* Steevens makes this equivalent to *making the fig or fico* (for which see Douce's *Illustrations of Shakespeare*) ; but according to St. it was a different sort of insult, expressed by biting the thumb-nail. Cf. Cotgrave, *Fr. Dict.* (ed. 1632) : " *Nique, faire la nique,* to threaten or defie, by putting the thumbe naile into the mouth, and with a ierke (from th' upper teeth) make it to knocke." Malone quotes Dekker, *The Dead Term*, 1608 : "what byting of thumbs, to beget quarrels ?"

39. *Of our side.* On our side. See Gr. 175.

50. *Here comes one*, etc. "Gregory may mean Tybalt, who enters directly after Benvolio, but on a different part of the stage. The eyes of the servant may be directed the way he sees Tybalt coming, and in the mean time Benvolio enters on the opposite side" (Steevens).

54. *Swashing blow.* A dashing or smashing blow (Schmidt). Steevens quotes B. J., *Staple of News :* "I do confess a swashing blow." Baret (*Alvearie*, 1580) says that "*to swash* is to make a noise with swordes against tergats ;" and Coles (*Dict.* 1677) has "To swash, *clango, gladiis concrepo*." Cf. the use of *swash* = bully, bluster ; as in *A. Y. L.* i. 3. 122 : "I 'll have a martial and a swashing outside." The 2d and 3d quartos and the folios have "washing blow," which, curiously enough, occurs in Harvey's *Plaine Percevall*, 1589 (quoted by Daniel) : "A washing blow of this is as good as a Laundresse, it will wash for the names sake ; it can wipe a fellow ouer the thumbs, wring a man in the withers, and must needs dry beate a skoundrell, if it be artificially managed."

58. *Art thou drawn?* Cf. *Temp.* ii. 1. 308 : "Why are you drawn ?" Gr. 374. In 62, just below, the quartos have "drawne," the folios "draw."

64. *Have at thee.* See *Hen. V.* p. 170 or *Hen. VIII.* p. 174.

65. *Clubs.* As K. remarks, the cry of *Clubs!* in a street affray is as thoroughly of English origin as the *bite my thumb* is of Italian. See *A. Y. L.* p. 194 or *Hen. VIII.* p. 204. *Bills* were the pikes or halberds formerly carried by the English infantry and afterwards by watchmen. See *Much Ado*, p. 145. The *partisan* "may be described as a sharp two-edged sword placed on the summit of a staff for the defence of foot-soldiers against cavalry" (Fairholt). Cf. *Ham.* i. 1. 140 : "Shall I strike at it with my partisan ?"

67. *Long sword.* The weapon used in active warfare ; a lighter and shorter one being worn for ornament (see *A. W.* ii. 1. 32 : "no sword worn But one to dance with "). Cf. *M. W.* ii. 1. 236 : "with my long sword I would have made you four tall fellows skip like rats."

70. *In spite of me.* To my mortification (Schmidt). Cf. *M. N. D.* iii.

2. 194 : "To fashion this false sport in spite of me," etc. We should be inclined to make it = in defiance of me ; as Schmidt explains *in despite of me* (3 *Hen. VI.* i. 1. 158) and *in my despite* (*T. A.* i. 1. 361 and *Cymb.* iv. 1. 16).

74. *Steel.* Daniel suggests that this may be a misprint for "soil."

79. *Mistemper'd.* Tempered to an ill end (Schmidt). Steevens explains it as = angry. The word occurs again in *K. John*, v. 1. 12 : "This inundation of mistemper'd humour."

80. *Moved.* That is, "mov'd to wrath" (*T. A.* i. 1. 419). Cf. *L. L. L.* v. 2. 694, *J. C.* iv. 3. 58, etc.

84. *Ancient.* Not of necessity old in years, but long settled there and accustomed to peace and order (Delius).*

85. *Grave beseeming.* Grave and becoming. Cf. *Ham.* iv. 7. 79 :

> "for youth no less becomes
> The light and careless livery that it wears,
> Than settled age his sables and his weeds,
> Importing health and graveness."

Walker would print "grave-beseeming."

87. *Canker'd with peace*, etc. "Rust, through long years of peace, has eaten into the partisans, just as hate has into the hearts of the rival factions " (Delius).

94. *Freetown.* S. takes the name from Brooke's poem. See p. 15 above.

96. S. uses *set abroach* only in a bad sense. Cf. 2 *Hen. IV.* iv. 2. 14 : "Alack, what mischiefs might he set abroach ;" and *Rich. III.* i. 3. 325 : "The secret mischiefs that I set abroach."

104. *Nothing hurt withal.* Nowise harmed by it. See Gr. 55 and 196 ; and for *who*, Gr. 264.

105. *While we*, etc. This line, with the change of *we* to *they*, is found in the 1st quarto in iii. 1, where Benvolio describes the brawl in which Mercutio and Tybalt are slain (Daniel).

108. *Saw you him to-day?* This use of the past tense is not allowable now, but was common in Elizabethan English. Cf. *Cymb.* iv. 2. 66 : "I saw him not these many years," etc. Gr. 347.

110. *The worshipp'd sun.* Cf. iii. 2. 25 below : "And pay no worship to the garish sun." See also *Lear*, i. 1. 111 : "the sacred radiance of the sun ;" and *Cymb.* iv. 4. 41 : "the holy sun." It is remarkable that no German commentator has tried to make S. a Parsee.

Holt White quotes *Summa Totalis*, 1607 :

> "Now heavens bright eye (awake by Vespers sheene)
> Peepes through the purple windowes of the East."

111. *Forth.* Cf. *M. N. D.* i. 1. 164 : "Steal forth thy father's house," etc. Gr. 156.

112. *Drave.* The 2d quarto has "driue," and Mommsen reads "drive," which is used as a past tense by Spenser (*F. Q.* iii. 4. 37, vi. 9. 32, etc.), and

---

* For the quotations from Delius and other German editors I am generally indebted to Furness.

by Gill in his *Logonomia Anglica*, 1621 ; also, as Daniel notes, by B. J. in his *Grammar*, chap. xix.

113. *Sycamore.* According to Beisly, the *Acer pseudo-platanus*, which grows wild in Italy. It had been introduced into England before the time of S. K. takes it to be the Oriental plane-tree (*Platanus orientalis*) ; and Delius and Schmidt, the wild fig-tree of the East (*Ficus sycomorus*). S. mentions it also in *L. L. L.* v. 2. 89 and *Oth.* iv. 3. 41.

114. *Rooteth.* Cf. *W. T.* i. 1. 25 : "there rooted betwixt them such an affection," etc.

116. *Ware.* Aware ; but not to be printed as a contraction of that word. Cf. ii. 2. 103 below.

118. *Affections.* Feelings, inclinations. Cf. *Ham.* iii. 1. 170 : "Love ! his affections do not that way tend," etc.

119. *Which then*, etc. "The plain meaning seems to be that Benvo-lio, like Romeo, was indisposed for society, and sought to be most where most people were not to be found, being one too many, even when by himself" (Coll.). K., D., and St. follow Pope in reading (from 1st quar-to) "That most are busied when they 're most alone." Prof. George Allen (F. p. 431) suggests "where more might not be found." S., he says, "was not the man (in *R. and J.* at least) to let slip the chance of running through the degrees of comparison, *many, more, most.*"

120. *Humour.* Misprinted "honour" in the early eds. except the 2d, 4th, and 5th quartos.

126. *All.* Often used in this "intensive" way. Gr. 28.

129. *Heavy.* S. is fond of playing on *heavy* and *light.* Cf. *R. of L.* 1574, *T. G. of V.* i. 2. 84, *M. of V.* v. 1. 130, etc. See also *Much Ado*, p. 149, note on *Light.*

137. *Importun'd.* Accented on the second syllable, as regularly in S. See *Ham.* p. 190.

138. *Other friends.* The folio has "others Friends," and K. reads "others, friends."

143. *With.* By. See Gr. 193.

145. *Sun.* The early eds. all have "same." The emendation is due to Theo. and is almost universally adopted. Daniel remarks : "It should however be observed that instances of this flat lawyer's-clerk-like diction are frequent in the works of Shakespeare's predecessors and contempo-raries ;" and quotes as an instance Greene's *Alphonsus* :

"that which every one doth know for truth
Needs no examples to confirm the same."

151. *To hear.* For the omission of *as*, see Gr. 281.

152. *Is the day so young ?* Is it not yet noon? *Good morrow* or *gooa day* was considered proper only before noon, after which *good den* was the usual salutation. See on i. 2. 56 below.

153. *New.* Often used by S. in this adverbial way=just, lately. Cf. v. 3. 197 below : "new kill'd," etc.

161. *Alas that love*, etc. Alas "that love, though blind, should discover pathways to his will, and yet cannot avail himself of them—should per-ceive the road which he is forbidden to take" (Steevens) ; or, perhaps, alas that he "should blindly and recklessly think he can surmount all

obstacles to his will" (Sr.). St. would read "set pathways to our will ;" that is, "make us walk in any direction he chooses to appoint." The 1st quarto reads: "Should without lawes giue pathwaies to our will ;" that is, "being lawless itself, prescribes laws to others."

View. Appearance ; as in *M. of V.* iii. 2. 132 : "You that choose not by the view." *Proof*=experience ; as in *Ham.* iii. 2. 179 : "What my love is, proof hath made you know ;" *Id.* iv. 7. 113 : "passages of proof," etc.

167. *Here's much,* etc. "Romeo is speaking in the riddling mood now upon him. He means that the fray has much to do with the hate between the rival houses, yet affects him more, inasmuch as his Rosaline is of the Capulet family ; that what has just passed has had reference to the animosity which divides the two factions, and has also shown him the anxious affection felt on his account by his father and Benvolio. To the latter he refers where he says, 'This love that thou hast shown,' etc." (Clarke).

168. *O brawling love!* etc. See p. 23 above.

169. *Created.* Some eds. prefer the "create" of the 1st quarto, which "introduces improperly a couplet amidst the blank verse" (K).

171. *Well-seeming.* The 2d and 3d quartos and the 1st folio have "welseeing."

180. *This love.* The first quarto has "this griefe," which Daniel considers "probably the better reading."

182. *Rais'd.* The reading of the 1st quarto, adopted by Pope, K., Coll., St., W., F., and others. The other early eds. have "made."

183. *Purg'd.* That is, ⌐om smoke (Schmidt). Johnson suggested "urg'd," that is, "excited and enforced." The Coll. MS. has "puff'd."

184. *Being vex'd,* etc. The 1st quarto has "Being vext, a sea raging with a louers tears."

186. *Preserving.* Ulrici strangely makes this="preserved." Love is compared to a preserved sweet, he thinks, "because, although against our will, it is kept and cherished."

190. *Some other where.* Cf. *C. of E.* iv. 1. 30 : "How if your husband start some other where?"

191. *Sadness.* Seriousness. Cf. *A. W.* iv. 3. 230 : "In good sadness, I do not know," etc. For *sad*=serious, see *A. Y. L.* p. 175 or *Much Ado,* p. 121. So *sadly* just below=seriously, as in *Much Ado,* ii. 3. 229. For *who is that* Pope substituted "who she is," and Sr. reads "who 't is that." The 1st quarto has "whome she is."

194. *Bid,* etc. The reading of 1st, 4th, and 5th quartos. The other quartos and 1st folio have "A sicke man in sadnesse makes his will ;" and the other folios insert "good" before "sadnesse."

198. *Mark-man.* The 3d and 4th folios have "marks-man." S. uses the word nowhere else.

201. *Wit.* "Sentiments" (Schmidt).

202. *Proof.* Used technically of armour. Cf. *Rich. II.* i. 3. 73 : "Add proof unto mine armour with thy prayers ;" and see note in our ed. p. 162. See also *Ham.* p. 235.

Steevens remarks here : "As this play was written in the reign of

Queen Elizabeth, I cannot help regarding these speeches of Romeo as an oblique compliment to her majesty, who was not liable to be displeased at hearing her chastity praised after she was suspected to have lost it, or her beauty commended in the 67th year of her age, though she never possessed any when she was young."

203. *Unharm'd.* The reading of the 1st quarto ; the other early eds. have " vncharmd." The Coll. MS. has " encharm'd," which H. adopts.

204. *The siege*, etc. Cf. *V. and A.* 423 :

> " Remove your siege from my unyielding heart ;
> To love's alarm it will not ope the gate."

See also *R. of L.* 221, *A. W.* iii. 7. 18, *Cymb.* iii. 4. 137, etc.

208. *That when she dies*, etc. " *She is rich in beauty*, and *only poor* in being subject to the lot of humanity, that *her store*, or riches, *can be destroyed by death*, who shall, by the same blow, put an end to beauty " (Johnson) ; or, as Mason puts it, " she is poor because she leaves no part of her store behind her." Theo. would read " with her dies beauty's store."

211. *Starv'd.* The early eds. (except the 4th folio) have " sterv'd," the old form of the word, found in several other passages in the folio (*M. of V.* iv. 1. 138, *Cor.* iv. 2. 51, etc.) and rhyming with *deserve* in *Cor.* ii. 3. 120. Cf. Spenser, *F. Q.* iv. 1. 4 :

> " Untill such time as noble Britomart
> Released her, that else was like to sterve
> Through cruell knife that her deare heart did kerve."

There it means to die, as in *Hen. VIII.* v. 3. 132 ; and Sr. (who reads " sterv'd ") thinks it has that sense in the present passage.

221. *To call hers, exquisite.* " That is, to call hers, which is exquisite, the more into my remembrance and contemplation " (Heath) ; or " to make her unparalleled beauty more the subject of thought and conversation " (Malone). For *question* = conversation, cf. *A. Y. L.* iii. 4. 39, v. 4. 167, etc. Keightley says that " to *call in question* in S. always means to express a doubt of ;" but cf. *J. C.* iv. 3. 165 : " call in question our necessities " (that is, consider or discuss them).

222. *These happy masks.* Steevens took this to refer to " the masks worn by female spectators of the play ;" but it is probably = the masks worn nowadays. They are called *happy* as " being privileged to touch the sweet countenances beneath " (Clarke).

223. *Put.* The 2d, 3d, and 4th quartos and 1st and 2d folios have " puts," which may be what S. wrote. *Being black* may have been regarded as the subject. Cf. *Ham.* iii. 1. 182 :

> " Whereon his brains still beating puts him thus
> From fashion of himself ;"

and see note in our ed. p. 220, or Gr. 337.

224. *Strucken.* The early eds. have " strucken " or " strooken." See Gr. 344.

226. *Passing.* Often used adverbially, but only before adjectives and adverbs (Schmidt). Cf. *L. L. L.* iv. 3. 103, *Much Ado*, ii. 1. 84, etc.

230. *Pay that doctrine.* Give that instruction. Cf. *L. L. L.* iv. 3. 350 : "From women's eyes this doctrine I derive;" *A. and C.* v. 2. 31 :

> "I hourly learn
> A doctrine of obedience," etc.

SCENE II.—4. *Reckoning.* Estimation, reputation.

9. *Fourteen years.* In Brooke's poem her father says, "Scarce saw she yet full xvi. yeres;" and in Paynter's novel "as yet shee is not attayned to the age of xviii. yeares."

13. *Made.* The 1st quarto has "maried," which is followed by Sr., Coll., H., and W. The antithesis of *make* and *mar* is a very common one in S. Cf. ii. 4. 110 below : "that God hath made for himself to mar." See also *L. L. L.* iv. 3. 191, *M. N. D.* i. 2. 39, *A. Y. L.* i. 1. 34, *T. of S.* iv. 3. 97, *Macb.* ii. 3. 36, *Oth.* v. 1. 4, etc. On the other hand, Steevens quotes an example of the opposition of *married* and *marred* from Puttenham, *Art of Poesie :* "The maid that soon married is, **soon** marred is;" and Sr. adds from Flecknoe's *Epigrams :*

> "You're to be marr'd or marryed, **as** they say,
> To-day or to-morrow, to-morrow or to-day."

See also *A. W.* ii. 3. 315 : "A young man married is a man that's marr'd."

14. *The earth.* The reading of the 4th and 5th quartos; the earlier quartos and the 1st folio omit *The,* and the later folios have "Earth up."

15. *My earth.* Steevens and Schmidt make this=my lands, my landed property; Mason explains it as "my corporal part." It seems better, with Ulrici, to understand it as "my world, my life." It was apparently suggested by the *earth* of the preceding line.

17. *My will,* etc. "My will is only a part of her consent, belongs to her consent" (Delius). The old man talks very differently in iii. 5 below.

23. *Makes.* Capell conjectured "make;" but it is probably an example of what Abbott (Gr. 412) calls "confusion of proximity."

25. *Dark heaven.* Warb. thought "this nonsense should be reformed" by reading "dark even;" but *dark heaven* obviously means the dark sky of evening or night. As K. notes, passages in the masquerade scene seem to indicate that the banqueting-room opened into a garden. See i. 5. 43 below.

26. *Young men.* Johnson conjectured "yeomen," which Daniel endorses. Malone compares *Sonn.* 98. 2 :

> "When proud-pied April dress'd in all his trim
> Hath put a spirit of youth in every thing."

28. *Limping.* The 1st quarto has "lumping," which Daniel adopts "as conveying a more picturesque notion of dull, heavy, boorish winter than *limping.*"

29. *Female.* The quartos (except the 1st) and 1st folio have the curious misprint "fennell."

30. *Inherit.* Possess; as in *Temp.* iv. 1. 154, *Rich. II.* ii. 1. 83, *Cymb.* iii. 2. 63, etc.

32. *Which on more view,* etc. A perplexing and much disputed line.

The 2d and 3d quartos and the folios read "Which one more view, of many, mine being one" ("veiw" in 3d quarto and 1st folio) ; the 4th and 5th quartos, as in the text ; the 1st quarto, "Such amongst view of many myne being one." Of the many emendations suggested, Mason's "Whilst on more view of many, mine being one" (adopted by D. in his 2d ed.) is the only one that seems to us worth mentioning. With the reading in the text the meaning seems to be : *which one* (referring to *her of most merit*), after your further inspection of the many, my daughter (who is one of the number) may prove to be,—one in number, though one is no number. The quibble at the end alludes to the old proverb that "one is no number." Cf. *Sonn.* 136. 8 : "Among a number one is reckon'd none." Malone quotes Dekker, *H. W. :* "For one no number is ;" and *Hero and Leander* : "One is no number." Delius takes *which* to be used in a "loose relative connection ;" apparently the same as Abbott illustrates in Gr. 272. However these minor questions of *construction* are decided, they do not affect the general sense of the passage. Capulet says in substance : Come to my house to-night, and decide whom you like best of the beauties gathered there ; if Juliet be the one, well and good. He has already told Paris that she shall be his if he can gain her love, but discreetly suggests that he look more carefully at the "fresh female buds" of Verona before plucking one to wear on his heart.

36. *Written there.* See the extract from Malone, p. 15 above. The passage in Brooke reads thus :

> "No Lady fayre or fowle was in Verona towne :
> No knight or gentleman of high or lowe renowne :
> But Capilet himselfe hath byd vnto his feast :
> Or by his name in paper sent, appoynted as a geast."

45. *One fire,* etc. Alluding to the old proverb that "fire drives out fire." Cf. *J. C.* iii. 1. 171 : "As fire drives out fire, so pity pity ;" *Cor.* iv. 7. 54 : "One fire drives out one fire ; one nail, one nail," etc.

47. *Holp.* Used by S. oftener than *helped*, for both the past tense and the participle. See *Much Ado*, p. 119.

48. *Cures with.* Is cured by. S. does not elsewhere use *cure* intransitively. *Languish* occurs again as a noun in *A. and C.* v. 2. 42 : "That rids our dogs of languish."

Steevens remarks : "*Veterem amorem novo, quasi clavum clavo repellere* is a morsel of very ancient device ; and Ovid also has assured us that 'Alterius vires subtrahit alter amor,' or 'successore novo truditur omnis amor.'" Cf. Brooke's poem :

> "Ere long the townishe dames together will resort :
> Some one of bewty, fauour, shape, and of so louely porte·
> With so fast fixed eye, perhaps thou mayst beholde :
> That thou shalt quite forget thy loue, and passions past of olde.
>
> ⁙   *   *   *
>
> The prouerbe saith vnminded oft are they that are vnseene.
> And as out of a planke a nayle a nayle doth driue :
> So nouell loue out of the minde the auncient loue doth riue."

51. *Your plantain leaf.* The common plantain (*Plantago major*), which still holds a place in the domestic *materia medica*. For its use in healing bruises, cf. *L. L. L.* iii. 1. 74 :

" *Moth.* A wonder, master! here 's a costard broken in a shin.
        *   *   *   *   *   *

    Costard. O sir, plantain, a plain plantain! . . . no salve, sir, but a plantain!"

Steevens quotes *Albumazar :* " Bring a fresh plantain leaf, I 've broke me shin." Ulrici misunderstands the meaning of *broken* here. He says (as quoted by F.) : " Romeo means, Thy remedy is as excellent for my complaint as a plantain leaf is for a broken shin. Plantain was used to stop the blood, but not for a fracture of a bone, to which such a remedy obviously cannot apply. Hence when Costard in *L. L. L.* calls for a plantain leaf for his broken shin, or a fellow in Ben Jonson's *The Case is Altered* wants it for a broken head, it is, I think, in the same ironical sense as here. If Romeo, as the English commentators suppose, really considered plantain a good remedy for a broken bone, his words would have no sense." Schmidt understands the English idiom better, for he defines *to break the head* as =" to crack the skin of the head, so that the blood comes." Cf. *M. W.* i. 1. 125, *T. N.* v. 1. 178, etc., where Ulrici would of course see a fractured skull instead of a " bloody coxcomb."

The plantain was supposed to have other virtues. Halliwell quotes Withals, *Little Dictionarie for Children,* 1586 : " The tode being smitten of the spyder in fighte, and made to swell with hir poyson, recovereth himselfe with plantaine."

53. *Not mad, but bound,* etc. For the allusion to the old-time treatment of the insane, cf. *A. Y. L.* iii. 2. 420 : " Love is merely a madness, and, I tell you, deserves as well a dark house and a whip as madmen do ;" and see note in our ed. p. 178.

56. *Good-den.* Printed " godden" and " gooden" in the early eds., and a corruption of *good e'en,* or *good evening.* See *Hen. V.* p. 164, note on *God-den. God gi' good-den* in the next line is printed " Godgigoden" in the quartos and first three folios, " God gi' Good-e'en" in the 4th folio. " This salutation was used by our ancestors as soon as noon was past, after which time *good morrow* or *good day* was esteemed improper " (Nares). See on i. 1. 152 above, and cf. ii. 4. 95 below.

62. *Rest you merry!* For the full form, *God rest you merry!* (= God keep you merry), cf. *A. Y. L.* v. 1. 65, and see note in our ed. p. 193. It was a common form of salutation at meeting, and oftener at parting. Here the servant is about to leave, thinking that Romeo is merely jesting with him. Cf. 79 below.

64. *Signior Martino,* etc. Capell pointed out that this list of names is nearly perfect blank verse, and suggested reading " Anselmo " and " gentle Livia " to complete the measure. Dyce (2d ed.) and Daniel print it as verse, reading " and Livia " from 1st quarto.

66. *Mercutio.* " It is noteworthy that Mercutio here figures among the invited guests, although we find him always associating with the young men of the Montague family. He is the prince's 'kinsman,' and it may be supposed is on terms of acquaintance with both the rival houses, although evidently having greater intimacy with the Montagues than the Capulets " (Clarke).

68. *Rosaline.* This shows that Rosaline is a Capulet (Clarke).

73. *To supper.* In all the early eds. these words are joined to the

preceding speech. The correction was made by Theo. and is generally adopted.

79. *Crush a cup*, etc. A common expression in the old plays. We still say "crack a bottle" (Steevens).

82. *Lov'st.* The reading of the later folios; the quartos (except the 5th) and the 1st folio have "loves," which Walker defends as a grammatical license of the time. Cf. Gr. 340.

84. *Unattainted.* Unprejudiced, impartial.

88. *Fires.* The early eds. have "fire," which W. retains. He remarks: "The mere difference of a final *s* seems not to have been regarded in rhyme in Shakespeare's day, and the reading *fires* tends to impoverish a line not over-rich." To us "fire" seems the more commonplace reading.

89. *Who, often drown'd*, etc. Alluding to the old notion that if a witch were thrown into the water she would not sink. King James, in his *Dæmonology*, says : "It appeares that God hath appointed for a supernatural signe of the monstrous impietie of witches, that the water shall refuse to receive them in her bosom that have shaken off them the sacred water of baptism, and wilfully refused the benefit thereof."

93. *Tut.* Repeated in the 2d folio, and also by Coll. and D.

95. *That crystal scales.* The reading of the early eds. Rowe changed *that* to "those ;" but, as Malone remarks, *scales* may be used for the entire machine. D. says it was often so used by writers of the time.

96. *Lady's love.* Theo. substituted "lady-love," and is followed by D. S. does not use *lady-love* elsewhere. W. doubts whether the compound is as old as his time, but D. cites Wilson, *Coblers Prophesie*, 1594 : "then downe came I my lady loue to finde."

98. *Scant.* Not elsewhere used adverbially by S. *Scantly* occurs only in *A. and C.* iii. 4. 6. The 1st folio reads corruptly, "And she shew scant shell, well," etc.

SCENE III.—1. On the character of the Nurse, see extract from Coleridge, p. 20 above. Cf. what Mrs. Jameson says of the same personage :

"She is drawn with the most wonderful power and discrimination. In the prosaic homeliness of the outline, and the magical illusion of the colouring, she reminds us of some of the marvellous Dutch paintings, from which, with all their coarseness, we start back as from a reality. Her low humour, her shallow garrulity, mixed with the dotage and petulance of age—her subserviency, her secrecy, and her total want of elevated principle, or even common honesty—are brought before us like a living and palpable truth. . . .

"Among these harsh and inferior spirits is Juliet placed ; her haughty parents, and her plebeian nurse, not only throw into beautiful relief her own native softness and elegance, but are at once the cause and the excuse of her subsequent conduct. She trembles before her stern mother and her violent father, but, like a petted child, alternately cajoles and commands her nurse. It is her old foster-mother who is the confidante of her love. It is the woman who cherished her infancy, who aids and abets her in her clandestine marriage. Do we not perceive how immediately our impression of Juliet's character would have been lowered, if Shakespeare had placed her in connection with any commonplace dramatic waiting-woman?—even with Portia's adroit Nerissa, or Desdemona's Emilia? By giving her the Nurse for her confidante, the sweetness and dignity of Juliet's character are preserved inviolate to the fancy, even in the midst of all the romance and wilfulness of passion."

2. *Maidenhead.* Etymologically the same word as *maidenhood.* So *lustihead*=lustihood (see quotations in *Much Ado*, p. 163) ; *livelihead*= livelihood (as in Spenser, *F. Q.* ii. 2. 2 : " for porcion of thy livelyhed "), etc. Cf. *Godhead*, etc. See Wb. under *Hood.*

4. *God forbid!* " An exquisite touch of nature. The old nurse, in her fond garrulity, uses *lady-bird* as a term of endearment ; but recollecting its application to a female of loose manners, checks herself—*God forbid* her darling should prove such a one !" (St.) D. considers that *God forbid* is " properly an ellipsis of ' God forbid that any accident should keep her away !' but used here merely as an expression of impatience."

7. *Give leave awhile.* Leave us alone ; a courteous form of dismissal. Cf. *T. G. of V.* iii. 1. 1 : " Sir Thurio, give us leave, I pray, awhile ;" *M. W.* ii. 2. 165 : " Give us leave, drawer," etc.

9. *I have remember'd me.* For the reflexive use, cf. 1 *Hen. IV.* ii. 4. 468 : " and now I remember me, his name is Falstaff," etc.

Thou 's. The early eds. have " thou 'se ;" most modern ones substitute " thou shalt," to the injury of the metre. See Gr. 461.

12. *Lay.* Wager. Cf. *L. L. L.* i. 1. 310, *T. and C.* iii. 1. 95, etc.

13. *Teen.* Sorrow ; used here for the play on *fourteen.* Cf. *V. and A.* 808 : " My face is full of shame, my heart of teen ;" *Temp.* i. 2. 64 : " the teen I have turn'd you to ;" *L. L. L.* iv. 3. 164 : " Of sighs and groans, of sorrow and of teen," etc.

15. *Lammas-tide.* The 1st of August. *Tide*=time, as in *even-tide, spring-tide*, etc. Cf. *K. John*, iii. 1. 86 :

> " What hath this day deserv'd? what hath it done,
> That it in golden letters should be set
> Among the high tides in the calendar?"

See also the play upon this word in *T. of A.* i. 2. 57 : " Flow this way! A brave fellow ! he keeps his tides well."

23. *The earthquake.* Tyrwhitt was the first to suggest (see p. 12 above) that this may refer to the earthquake felt in England on the 6th of April, 1580. Malone remarks : " Shakespeare's frequent allusions to the manners and events of his own time have shown me that Tyrwhitt's conjecture is not so improbable as I once thought it. . . . If the earthquake which happened in England in 1580 was in his thoughts and induced him to state the earthquake at Verona as happening on the day when Juliet was *weaned*, and *eleven* years before the commencement of the piece, it has led him into a contradiction ; for, according to the Nurse, Juliet was within a fortnight and odd days of completing her *fourteenth* year ; and yet, according to the computation, she could not well be much more than *twelve* years old. Whether indeed the English earthquake was or was not in his thoughts, the Nurse's account is inconsistent and contradictory. Perhaps Shakespeare was more careful to mark the gar-

rulity than the precision of the old woman ; or perhaps he meant this very incorrectness as a trait of character; or, without having recourse to either of these suppositions, shall we say that he was here, as in some other places, hasty and inattentive ?" For instances of the poet's carelessness in these little matters, see *M. N. D.* p. 122, *Ham.* p. 241, and *Much Ado*, p. 125.

26. *Wormwood.* Halliwell quotes Cawdray, *Treasurie or Storehouse of Similies*, 1600 : " Like as when a mother, willing to weane her child, shall say unto him, night and day, ' My child, it is time to weane thee, thou art growne great inough,' . . . yet he is so fond of the breast that he cannot forsake it : but if the mother put worme-wood or mustard upon the breast, the child sucking it, and feeling the bitternesse, he quite forsaketh it, without sucking any more : Even so, though God's Preachers preach unto us, and exhort us to forsake the corrupt milke of the world and of the flesh, yet we seeme deaf still, and are alwayes backward, untill God put upon these cursed teates the mustard and worme-wood of afflictions to weane us."

27. *Sitting in the sun*, etc. Cf. Dame Quickly's circumstantial reminiscences, 2 *Hen. IV.* ii. 1. 93 fol. : " Thou didst swear to me," etc.

29. *Bear a brain.* Have a brain, that is, a good memory. Reed quotes *The Country Captain*, 1649 : " you beare a braine and memory."

31. *Pretty fool.* On *fool* as a term of endearment or pity, see *A. Y. L.* p. 151 or *M. N. D.* p. 133.

32. *Tetchy.* Cf. *Rich. III.* iv. 4. 168 : " Tetchy and wayward was thy infancy."

33. *Shake, quoth the dove-house.* The reading, except for the comma, of all the early eds. It refers of course to the effects of the earthquake. Daniel suggests that *quoth* may be a misprint for " go'th " or " goeth."

36. *By the rood.* That is, by the cross. See *Ham.* p. 235.

According to the description here, Juliet could not have been much more than a year old at the time. See on 23 above.

38. *Mark.* Appoint, elect. Cf. *T. A.* i. 1. 125 : " To this your son is mark'd, and die he must."

40. *To see thee married once.* Only to see thee married. For peculiar uses of *once* in S. see Gr. 57.

45. *Honour.* From the 1st quarto ; the other early eds. read " houre " or " hour " both here and in the next line.

51. *Much upon these years.* Nearly at the same age. Cf. *M. for M.* iv. 1. 17 : " much upon this time ;" *Rich. III.* v. 3. 70 : " Much about cockshut time," etc. Cf. v. 3. 207, and see note on p. 217 below.

As Juliet is fourteen, Lady Capulet would be about twenty-eight, while her husband, having done masking for some thirty years (see i. 5. 30 fol.) must be at least threescore (St.). K. reads " a mother," but all the early eds. have " your." Besides, Juliet is an only child (iii. 5. 164).

55. *A man of wax.* " As pretty as if he had been modelled in wax " (Schmidt). S. Weston refers to Horace, *Od.* i. 13. 2 :

> " cerea Telephi
> Laudas brachia ;"

but it is doubtful whether *cerea* means " well-shaped, fine-turned," or white as wax.　Steevens quotes *Wily Beguiled:* "Why, he's a man as one should picture him in wax."　W. adds from Lyly, *Euphues and his England:* "so exquisite that for shape he must be framed in wax," and refers to iii. 3. 126 below.　D. cites *Faire Em.:*

> "A sweet face, an exceeding daintie hand:
> A body, were it framed of wax
> By all the cunning artists of the world,
> It could not better be proportioned."

60. *Read o'er the volume,* etc.　Here, as K. notes, one quibble leads to another by the power of association.　"The *volume* of young Paris's face suggests the *beauty's pen,* which hath *writ* there.　Then the obscurities of the fair volume are written in *the margin of his eyes,* as comments of ancient books are always printed in the margin.　Lastly, this *book of love* lacks a *cover;* the *golden story* must be locked with *golden clasps.*"

62. *Married.*　The reading of the 2d quarto: the other early eds. have "severall," which is adopted by K. and W.　*Married* = "closely joined, and hence concordant, harmonious" (Schmidt).　Steevens quotes *T. and C.* i. 3. 100: "The unity and married calm of states;" and *Sonn.* 8. 6:

> "If the true concord of well-tuned sounds,
> By unions married, do offend thine ear."

Cf. Milton, *L'All.* 137: "Married to immortal verse."

65. *Margin.*　Malone quotes *R. of L.* 102:

> "But she that never cop'd with stranger eyes
> Could pick no meaning from their parting looks,
> Nor read the subtle shining secrecies
> Writ in the glassy margent of such books."

See also *M. N. D.* p. 142 and *Ham.* p. 272.

67. *Cover.*　"A quibble on the law phrase for a married woman, who is styled a *femme couverte* [*feme covert*] in law French" (Mason).

68. *Lives in the sea.*　"The speaker means to say, the fish is not yet caught which is to supply this *cover* or *coverture.*　The bride who is to be bound in marriage with Paris has not yet been won" (Clarke).　As Farmer notes, fish-skin was often used for binding books.

70. *Many's.*　Cf. *Sonn.* 93. 7: "In many's looks," etc.

74. *Like of.*　Cf. *Much Ado,* v. 4. 59: "I am your husband, if you like of me;" and see note in our ed. p. 171.

76. *Endart.*　Not elsewhere used by S. and perhaps of his own coining (Delius).　Cf. Gr. 440.

79. *Cursed.*　Because she is not at hand to help (Delius).

80. *In extremity.*　At a desperate pass.　Cf. *M. N. D.* iii. 2. 3, *A. Y. L.* iv. 1. 5, etc.

82. *County.*　Count.　See *Much Ado,* p. 131.

SCENE IV.—1. *Spoke.*　See Gr. 343.
Mercutio is thus described in Brooke's poem:

> "At thone syde of her chayre, her louer Romeo:
> And on the other side there sat one cald Mercutio.
> A courtier that eche where was highly had in pryce:
> For he was coorteous of his speche, and pleasant of deuise.

Euen as a Lyon would emong the lambes be bolde:
Such was emong the bashfull maydes, Mercutio to beholde.
With frendly gripe he ceasd fayre Juliets snowish hand:
A gyft he had that nature gaue him in his swathing band.
That frosen mountayne yse was neuer halfe so cold
As were his handes, though nere so neer the fire he dyd them holde."

In Paynter's *Palace of Pleasure* he is spoken of as "an other Gentle-man called *Mercutio,* which was a courtlyke Gentleman, very well be loued of all men, and by reason of his pleasaunt and curteous behauior was in euery company wel intertayned." His "audacity among Maydens" and his cold hands are also mentioned. Malone suggests that this latter cir-cumstance may have induced S. to represent Mercutio as little sensible to the passion of love and "a jester at wounds he never felt."

3. *The date is out,* etc. That is, such tediousness is now out of fashion. "In *Henry VIII.* where the king introduces himself to the entertainment given by Wolsey [i. 4.] he appears, like Romeo and his companions, in a *mask,* and sends a messenger before to make an apology for his intrusion. This was a custom observed by those who came uninvited, with a desire to conceal themselves for the sake of intrigue, or to enjoy the greater freedom of conversation. Their entry on these occasions was always prefaced by some speech in praise of the beauty of the ladies or the gen-erosity of the entertainer; and to the *prolixity* of such introductions I believe Romeo is made to allude. So in *Histriomastix,* 1610, a man ex-presses his wonder that the maskers enter without any compliment: 'What, come they in so blunt, without device?' In the accounts of many entertainments given in reigns antecedent to that of Elizabeth, I find this custom preserved. Of the same kind of masquerading see a specimen in *T. of A.* [i. 2], where Cupid precedes a troop of ladies with a speech" (Steevens). "S. ridicules a formal prolix introduction, such as that in *L. L. L.* v. 2. 158 fol." (Coll.).

5. *Bow of lath.* The Tartar bows resembled in form the old Roman or Cupid's bow, such as we see on medals and bas-reliefs; while the English bow had the shape of the segment of a circle (Douce).

6. *Crow-keeper.* Originally a boy stationed in a field to drive the birds away (as in *Lear,* iv. 6. 88 : "That fellow handles his bow like a crow-keeper"); afterwards applied, as here, to what we call a *scarecrow.* The latter was often a stuffed figure with a bow in his hand.

7, 8. These lines are found only in the 1st quarto, and were first insert-ed in the text by Pope. W. believes that they were purposely omitted, but only on account of their disparagement of the prologue-speakers on the stage. Prologues and epilogues were often prepared, not by the au-thor of the play, but by some other person; and this was probably the case with some of the prologues and epilogues in S. See *Temp.* p. 145 or *Hen. VIII.* p. 155.

Faintly. "In a weak mechanical way" (Ulrici).

Entrance. Here a trisyllable, as in *Macb.* i. 5. 40. See Gr. 477.

10. *A measure.* A formal courtly dance. Cf. *Much Ado,* ii. 1. 80 : "as a measure, full of state and ancientry;" and for the play on the word, *Id.* ii. 1. 74, *L. L. L.* iv. 3. 384, and *Rich. II.* iii. 4. 7.

11. *A torch.* Maskers were regularly attended by torch-bearers. The

commentators quote illustrations of this from other authors, but do **not** refer to *M. of V.* ii. 4. 5 : " We have not spoke us yet of torch-bearers ;" and in 21 just below :

> " Will you prepare you for this masque to-night?
> I am provided of a torch-bearer."

See also *Id.* ii. 6. 40 fol.

For the contemptuous use of *ambling*, see *Ham.* p. 219.

12. For the poet's frequent playing on the different senses of *light*, see on i. 1. 129 above. Cf. ii. 2. 105 below.

15. *Soul.* For the play on the word, cf. *M. of V.* ii. 4. 68, iv. 1. 123, and *J. C.* i. 1. 15.

16. *So stakes.* For the omission of the relative, see Gr. 244.

19. *Enpierced.* Used by S. nowhere else. Walker would read "empierced." The later folios have "impearced" or "impierced." Gr. 440.

20. *Bound.* For the quibble, Steevens compares Milton, *P. L.* iv. 180 :

> "in contempt
> At one slight bound high overleap'd all bound
> Of hill or highest wall," etc.

31. *Quote.* Note, observe. Cf. *Ham.* ii. 1. 112 :

> " I am sorry that with better heed and judgment
> I had not quoted him ;"

and see note in our ed. p. 201.

35. *Let wantons,* etc. As Steevens remarks, Middleton has borrowed this in his *Blurt Master-Constable,* 1602 :

> " bid him whose heart no sorrow feels
> Tickle the rushes with his wanton heels ;
> I have too much lead at mine."

36. *Rushes.* Before the introduction of carpets floors were strewn with rushes. Cf. 1 *Hen. IV.* iii. 1. 214 : " on the wanton rushes lay you down ;" *Cymb.* ii. 2. 13 :

> " Our Tarquin thus
> Did softly press the rushes," etc.

See also *R. of L.* 318, *T. of S.* iv. 1. 48, and 2 *Hen. IV.* v. 5. 1.

The stage was likewise strewn with rushes. Steevens quotes Dekker, *Guls Hornbook :* " on the very rushes where the comedy is to daunce."

37. *Proverb'd,* etc. The proverb which Romeo means is contained in the next line. *To hold the candle* is a very common phrase for being *an idle spectator.* Among Ray's proverbs is " A good candle-holder proves a good gamester " (Steevens).

39. *The game,* etc. " An allusion to an old proverbial saying which advises to give over when the game is at the fairest " (Ritson).

40. *Dun's the mouse.* Apparently=keep still ; but no one has satisfactorily explained the origin of the phrase or its connection with the *constable.* Malone quotes *Patient Grissel,* 1603 : " yet don is the mouse, lie still ;" and Steevens adds *The Two Merry Milkmaids,* 1620 : " Why then 't is done, and dun 's the mouse and undone all the courtiers."

41. *If thou art Dun,* etc. Douce quotes Chaucer, *C. T.* 16936 :

> " Ther gan our hoste for to jape and play,
> And sayde, 'sires, what? Dun is in the myre.' "

Gifford explains the expression thus : "*Dun in the mire* is a Christmas gambol, at which I have often played. A log of wood is brought into the midst of the room : this is *Dun* (the cart-horse), and a cry is raised that he is *stuck in the mire*. Two of the company advance, either with or without ropes, to draw him out. After repeated attempts, they find themselves unable to do it, and call for more assistance. The game continues till all the company take part in it, when Dun is extricated of course ; and the merriment arises from the awkward and affected efforts of the rustics to lift the log, and from sundry arch contrivances to let the ends of it fall on one another's toes. This will not be thought a very exquisite amusement ; and yet I have seen much honest mirth at it." Halliwell quotes *Westward Hoe*, 1607 : "I see I 'm born still to draw dun out o' th' mire for you ; that wise beast will I be ;" and Butler, *Remains :* " they meant to leave reformation, like Dun in the mire."

42. *Sir-reverence.* A contraction of "save reverence" (*salva reverentia*), used as an apology for saying what might be deemed improper. Taylor the Water-Poet says in one of his epigrams :

> " If to a foule discourse thou hast pretence,
> Before thy foule words name sir-reverence,
> Thy beastly tale most pleasantly will slip,
> And gaine thee praise, when thou deserv'st a whip."

Cf. Warner, *Albions England :* "And all for love (surreverence love) did make her chew the cudde." Here "Mercutio says he will draw Romeo from the *mire of this love*, and uses parenthetically the ordinary form of apology for speaking so profanely of love" (K.). The early eds., except the 1st quarto, have "save your reverence" (or "you"). For the full phrase, see *Much Ado*, iii. 4. 32, *M. of V.* ii. 2. 27, 139, etc. ; and for the contracted form, cf. *C. of E.* iii. 2. 91 : "A very reverent body ; ay, such a one as a man may not speak of without he say sir-reverence."

43. *Burn daylight.* "A proverbial expression used when candles are lighted in the daytime" (Steevens) ; hence, as St. notes, "applied to superfluous actions in general." Here it is = waste time, as the context shows. Cf. *M. W.* ii. 1. 54, where it has the same meaning.

45. *We waste*, etc. The quartos have "We waste our lights in vaine, lights lights by day ;" the folios, "We wast our lights in vaine, lights, by day." The emendation is Capell's. Daniel adopts Nicholson's suggestion, "light lights by day."

47. *Five wits.* Malone's emendation of the "fine wits" of the early eds. Cf. *Much Ado*, i. 1. 66 : "four of his five wits went halting off ;" and see note in our ed. p. 120.

48. *And we mean well*, etc. See extract from Maginn, p. 29 above.

50. *To-night.* That is, last night, as in *M. W.* iii. 3. 171 : "I have dreamed to-night ;" *W. T.* ii. 3. 10 : "He took good rest to-night," etc. See also ii. 4. 2 below.

53. *O, then*, etc. After this line the 1st quarto inserts "*Ben :* Queene Mab whats she ?" which Hunter would retain "as affording a just pretence for the long description of Queen Mab which follows."

Queen Mab. No earlier instance of *Mab* as the name of the fairy-queen has been discovered, but S. no doubt learned it from the folk-lore of his own time (Thoms). Its derivation is uncertain.

54. *The fairies' midwife.* Not midwife *to* the fairies, but the fairy whose department it was to deliver the fancies of sleeping men of their dreams, those *children of an idle brain* (Steevens). T. Warton believes she was so called "because it was her peculiar employment to steal the new-born babe in the night, and to leave another in its place." See *M. N. D.* p. 138, note on *Changeling.*

55. *No bigger*, etc. That is, no bigger than the figures cut in such an agate. Cf. *Much Ado*, iii. 1. 65 : "If low, an agate very vilely cut ;" and see note in our ed. p. 141.

These rings appear to have been sometimes worn on the *thumb.* Steevens quotes Glapthorne, *Wit in a Constable*, 1639 : "and an alderman as I may say to you, he has no more wit than the rest o' the bench ; and that lies in his thumb-ring."

57. *Atomies.* Atoms, or creatures as minute as atoms. Cf. *A. Y. L.* iii. 2. 245 : "to count atomies ;" and *Id.* iii. 5. 13 : "Who shut their coward gates on atomies." See *A. Y. L.* p. 175. In 2 *Hen. IV.* v. 4. 33, Mrs. Quickly confounds the word with *anatomy.* S. uses it only in these four passages, *atom* not at all.

58. *Athwart.* From the 1st quarto ; the other early eds. and some modern ones have "over."

59. *Spinners.* Long-legged spiders, mentioned also in *M. N. D.* ii. 2. 21 : "Hence, you long-legg'd spinners, hence !"

61. *The traces.* From 1st quarto ; the other early eds. have "Her traces" and "Her collars."

63. *Film.* The quartos and 1st folio have "Philome ;" the later folios "filme."

65. *Worm.* Nares says, under *idle worms :* "Worms bred in idleness. It was supposed, and the notion was probably encouraged for the sake of promoting industry, that when maids were idle, worms bred in their fingers ;" and he cites B. and F., *Woman Hater*, iii. 1 :

> "Keep thy hands in thy muff and warm the idle
> Worms in thy fingers' ends."

66. *Maid.* From 1st quarto. The other quartos and 1st folio have "man," the later folios "woman." The Coll. MS. gives "milkmaid."

67–69. *Her chariot . . . coachmakers.* Daniel puts these lines before 59. Lettsom says : "It is preposterous to speak of the parts of a chariot (such as the waggon-spokes and cover) before mentioning the chariot itself." But *chariot* here, as the description shows, means only the *body* of the vehicle, and is therefore one of the "parts." The lines are not in the 1st quarto, and it is of course possible that if added in the margin the printer inserted them in the wrong place.

72. *O'er courtiers' knees.* From 1st quarto ; the other early eds. have "On." For *court'sies* the early eds. have "cursies." See *Much Ado*, p. 129, note on *Curtsy*, and p. 159, note on *Courtesies.*

76. *Sweetmeats.* "That is, kissing-comfits. These artificial aids to perfume the breath are mentioned by Falstaff, in *M. W.* v. 5. 22 " (Malone).

77. *Courtier's.* Pope substituted "lawyer's" (from 1st quarto), Theo. conjectured "taylor's," and the Coll. MS. has "counsellor's." W. is inclined to think that S. wrote "counsellor's," which is certainly the most plausible of the attempts to avoid the repetition.

79. *Sometime.* Used by S. interchangeably with *sometimes.* See *Ham.* pp. 172, 177.

84. *Ambuscadoes.* Ambuscades ; used by S. only here.

Spanish blades. The 1st quarto has "Of breaches ambuscados, countermines." The swords of Toledo were famous for their quality.

85. *Healths,* etc. Malone quotes *Westward Hoe,* 1607 : "troth, sir, my master and sir Goslin are guzzling ; they are dabbling together fathom deep. The knight has drunk so much health to the gentleman yonder, upon his knees, that he hath almost lost the use of his legs." Cf. *2 Hen. IV.* v. 3. 57 :

> "Fill the cup, and let it come ;
> I 'll pledge you a mile to the bottom."

For *of healths* Thirlby suggests "Of delves" (=trenches), and Keightley "Trenches."

89. *Plats the manes,* etc. "This alludes to a very singular superstition not yet forgotten in some parts of the country. It was believed that certain malignant spirits, whose delight was to wander in groves and pleasant places, assumed occasionally the likeness of women clothed in white ; that in this character they sometimes haunted stables in the night-time, carrying in their hands tapers of wax, which they dropped on the horses' manes, thereby plaiting them in inextricable knots, to the great annoyance of the poor animals and vexation of their masters. These hags are mentioned in the works of William of Auvergne, bishop of Paris in the 13th century" (Douce).

90. *Elf-locks.* Hair matted or clotted, either from neglect or, as Warb. thought, from the disease known as the *Plica Polonica.* Cf. *Lear,* ii. 3. 10 : "elf all my hair in knots ;" and Lodge, *Wit's Miserie,* 1596 : "His haires are curld and full of elves locks, and nitty for want of kembing."

91. *Which,* etc. The real subject of *bodes* is *which once untangled*=the untangling of which. Cf. Gr. 337. Daniel reads "entangled," which is in the 3d folio.

97. *Who.* For "*who* personifying irrational antecedents," see Gr. 264. Cf. *2 Hen. IV.* iii. 1. 22 :

> "the winds,
> Who take the ruffian billows by the top."

100. *Face.* From the 1st quarto ; the other early eds. have "side." The Coll. MS. gives "tide."

103. *My mind misgives,* etc. One of many illustrations of Shakespeare's fondness for presentiments. See *Ham.* p. 273, note on *But thou wouldst not think,* etc.

105. *Date.* Duration ; as often in S. Cf. *R. of L.* 935 : "To endless date of never-ending woes ;" *Sonn.* 18. 4 : "And summer's lease hath all too short a date ;" *M. N. D.* iii. 2. 373 : "With league whose date till death shall never end," etc.

106. *Expire.* For the transitive use, see Gr. 291. Cf. Spenser, *F. Q.* iv.

1. 54 : " Till time the tryall of her truth expyred." Malone quotes *Chloris,* etc., 1596 : " When wasting time expires her tragedy."

107. *Clos'd.* Enclosed, shut up. Cf. v. 2. 30 below : " clos'd in a dead man's tomb." See also *R. of L.* 761, *Macb.* iii. 1. 90, etc.

110. *Sail.* From 1st quarto ; "sute " in the other early eds.

111. In the early eds. the stage-direction is " *They march about the Stage, and Seruingmen come forth with* [or *with their*] *Napkins.*" As Coll. remarks, this shows that the scene was supposed to be immediately changed to the hall of Capulet's house.

SCENE V.—2. *Shift a trencher.* "Trenchers were still used by persons of good fashion in our author's time. In the *Household Book of the Earls of Northumberland,* compiled at the beginning of the same century, it appears that they were common to the tables of the first nobility" (Percy). To *shift a trencher* was a technical term (Reed). For *scrape a trencher,* cf. *Temp.* ii. 2. 187 : " Nor scrape trencher, nor wash dish."

5. *Joint-stools.* A kind of folding-chair. Cf. 1 *Hen. IV.* ii. 4. 418, 2 *Hen. IV.* ii. 4. 269, etc.

Court-cupboard. Sideboard. Steevens quotes Chapman, *Monsieur D'Olive,* 1606 : "Here shall stand my court-cupboard, with its furniture of plate ;" and his *May-Day,* 1611 : "Court-cupboards planted with flag-gons, cans, cups, beakers," etc. Cotgrave defines *dressoir* as "a court-cupboord (without box or drawer), onely to set plate on."

6. *Good thou.* For this vocative use of *good,* cf. *Temp.* i. 1. 3, 16, 20, *C. of E.* iv. 4. 22, etc. See Gr. 13.

7. *Marchpane.* A kind of almond-cake, much esteemed in the time of S. Nares gives the following from one of the old English receipt-books, *Delightes for Ladies,* 1608 : " *To make a marchpane.*—Take two poundes of almonds being blanched, and dryed in a sieve over the fire, beate them in a stone mortar, and when they be small mix them with two pounde of sugar beeing finely beaten, adding two or three spoonefuls of rosewater, and that will keep your almonds from oiling : when your paste is beaten fine, drive it thin with a rowling pin, and so lay it on a bottom of wafers, then raise up a little edge on the side, and so bake it, then yce it with rosewater and sugar, then put it in the oven againe, and when you see your yce is risen up and drie, then take it out of the oven and garnish it with pretie conceipts, as birdes and beasts being cast out of standing moldes. Sticke long comfits upright in it, cast bisket and carrowaies in it, and so serve it ; guild it before you serve it : you may also print of this *marchpane* paste in your molds for banqueting dishes. And of this paste our comfit makers at this day make their letters, knots, armes, es-cutcheons, beasts, birds, and other fancies." Castles and other figures were often made of marchpane, to decorate splendid desserts, and were demolished by shooting or throwing sugar-plums at them. Cf. B. and F., *Faithful Friends,* iii. 2 :

> "They barr'd their gates,
> Which we as easily tore unto the earth
> As I this tower of marchpane."

12. *Cheerly*   Cheerily, briskly. Cf. *Temp.* i. 1. 6, 29, etc.

14. *Toes.* Pope thought it necessary to change this to "feet." Malone
remarks that the word "undoubtedly did not appear indelicate to the
audience of Shakespeare's time, though perhaps it would not be endured
at this day." We smile at this when we recollect some of the words that
were endured then ; but it shows how fashions change in these matters.
Cf. *Ham.* p. 241, note on *Guts.*

15. *Will have a bout.* From 1st quarto ; the other early eds. have "will
walke about." Daniel reads "walk a bout," which he thinks is = dance,
and quotes *Much Ado*, ii. 1. 75 : "Lady, will you walk about with your
friend ?" But it is not clear to us that it is there an invitation to dance.

17. *Deny.* Refuse. Cf. *L. L. L.* v. 2. 228 : "If you deny to dance ;"
T. of S. ii. 1. 180 : "If she deny to wed," etc.

Makes dainty. Cf. *K. John*, iii. 4. 138 :

> "And he that stands upon a slippery place
> Makes nice of no vile hold to stay him up."

18. *Am I come near ye now ?* Do I touch you, or hit you, now ? Cf.
1 Hen. IV. i. 2. 14 : "Indeed, you come near me now, Hal." Schmidt is
clearly wrong in giving *T. N.* ii. 5. 29 as another example of the phrase
in this sense. He might have given *T. N.* iii. 4. 71.

19. *Welcome, gentlemen !* Addressed to the masked friends of Romeo
(Delius).

24. *A hall, a hall !* Steevens remarks that this exclamation occurs frequently in the old comedies, and is = make room. Cf. *Doctor Dodypoll*,
1600 : "Room ! room ! a hall ! a hall !" B. J., *Tale of a Tub :* "Then
cry, a hall ! a hall !" Marston, *Sat.* iii. :

> "A hall ! a hall !
> Roome for the spheres, the orbs celestiall
> Will dance Kempe's jigge," etc.

25. *Turn the tables up.* The tables in that day were flat leaves hinged
together and placed on trestles ; when removed they were therefore turned
up (Steevens).

28. *Cousin.* The "uncle Capulet" of i. 2. 67. For the use of *cousin*
in S., see *Ham.* p. 179. Cf. iii. 1. 143 below : "Tybalt, my cousin ! O my
brother's child !"

33. *Nuptial.* The regular form in S. In the folio *Nuptials* occurs
only in *Per.* v. 3. 80. See *Temp.* p. 143, and cf. *J. C.* p. 183, note on *His
funerals.*

39. *What lady's that*, etc. Cf. Brooke's poem :

> "At length he saw a mayd, right fayre of perfect shape:
> Which Theseus, or Paris would haue chosen to their rape.
> Whom erst he neuer sawe, of all she pleasde him most:
> Within himselfe he sayd to her, thou iustly mayst thee boste.
> Of perfit shapes renoune, and Beauties sounding prayse:
> Whose like ne hath, ne shalbe seene, ne liueth in our dayes.
> And whilest he fixd on her his partiall perced eye,
> His former loue, for which of late he ready was to dye.
> Is nowe as quite forgotte, as it had neuer been."

43. *Her beauty hangs.* The reading of the later folios, adopted by K., V.,
Coll., D., and W. The quartos and 1st folio have "It seemes she hangs."

As V. remarks, it is quite probable that the correction was the poet's own, obtained from some other MS. altered during the poet's life ; it is besides confirmed by the repetition of *beauty* in 45.   Delius, who retains *it seems*, thinks that the boldness of the simile led the poet to introduce it in that way ; but it is Romeo who is speaking, and the simile is not over-bold for him.   The commentators often err in looking at the text from the "standpoint" of the critic rather than that of the character.

44. *Ethiope's.*   See *M. N. D.* p. 166.   For the simile, cf. *Sonn.* 27. 11 ; "Which, like a jewel hung in ghastly night," etc.   Holt White quotes Lyly, *Euphues:* "A fair pearl in a Morian's ear."

51. *I ne'er saw,* etc.   Cf. *Hen. VIII.* i. 4. 75 :

> "The fairest hand I ever touch'd! O beauty,
> Till now I never knew thee !"

53. *What dares,* etc.   How dares, or why dares, etc.   The reading is that of all the early eds. except the 5th quarto, which has "What ? dares," etc.   Nearly all the modern eds. print "What ! dares " or "What, dares." Cf. 2 *Hen. IV.* i. 2. 129 : "What tell you me of it ? be it as it is ;" *A. ana C.* v. 2. 316 : "What should I stay ?" etc.   See also Gr. 253.

54. *Antic face.*   Referring to Romeo's mask.   For *antic*, see *Rich. II.* p. 192.

55. *Fleer.*   Sneer, grin.   See *Much Ado,* p. 162.   For *scorn at,* cf. *A. Y. L.* iii. 5. 131, *K. John,* i. 1. 228, etc.   We find *scorn* without the preposition in *L. L. L.* iv. 3. 147 : "How will he scorn !"

Solemnity.   The word here expresses only the idea of ceremony, or formal observance.   Cf. the use of *solemn* = ceremonious, formal ; as in *Macb.* iii. 1. 14 : "To-night we hold a solemn supper, sir ;" *T. of S.* iii. 2. 103 : "our solemn festival," etc.   Hunter quotes Harrington, *Ariosto:*

> "Nor never did young lady brave and bright
> Like dancing better on a solemn day."

60. *In spite.*   In malice ; or, as Schmidt explains it, "only to defy and provoke us."   Cf. i. 1. 70 above.

63. *Content thee.*   "Compose yourself, keep your temper" (Schmidt). Cf. *Much Ado,* v. 1. 87, *T. of S.* i. 1. 90, 203, ii. 1. 343, etc.   So *be contented ;* as in *M. W.* iii. 3. 177, *Lear,* iii. 4. 115, etc.

64. *Portly.*   The word here seems to mean simply "well-behaved, well-bred" (Schmidt), though elsewhere it has the modern sense ; as in *M. W.* i. 3. 69 : "my portly belly ;" 1 *Hen. IV.* ii. 4. 464 : "A goodly portly man, i' faith, and a corpulent," etc.

68. *Do him disparagement.*   Do him injury.   Cf. "do danger" (*J. C.* ii. 1. 17), "do our country loss" (*Hen. V.* iv. 3. 21), "do him shame" (*R. of L.* 597, *Sonn.* 36. 10, *L. L. L.* iv. 3. 204), etc.   See also iii. 3. 118 below.

73. *It fits.*   Cf. *A. W.* ii. 1. 147 : "where hope is coldest, and despair most fits," etc.

77. *God shall mend my soul.*   Cf. *A. Y. L.* iv. 1. 193 : "By my troth, and in good earnest, and so God mend me, and by all pretty oaths that are not dangerous," etc.   See also 1 *Hen. IV.* iii. 1. 255.

79. *Cock-a-hoop.*   Much nonsense (see F.) has been written on the origin of this phrase, which is simply the Fr. *coq à huppe,* as Wb. gives

it. **Coles** (*Lat. Dict.* 1677) appears to have understood it, for one of his translations of " To be Cock-a-hoop" is "*cristas erigere.*"

82. *Scathe.* Injure. S. uses the verb nowhere else; but cf. the noun in *K. John*, ii. 1. 75 : " To do offence and scathe in Christendom ;" *Rich. III.* i. 3. 317 : " To pray for them that have done scathe to us," etc.

83. *Contrary.* Oppose, cross ; the only instance of the verb in S. Steevens quotes Greene, *Tully's Love:* " to contrary her resolution ;" Warner, *Albion's England:* " his countermand should have contraried so," etc. For the accent, see Gr. 490.

84. *Well said.* Well done (Schmidt). Cf. *Oth.* ii. 1. 169, v. 1. 98, etc.

Princox. A pert or impertinent boy ; used by S. only here. Steevens quotes *The Return from Parnassus*, 1606 : " Your proud university prin cox." Cotgrave renders "*un jeune estourdeau superbe*" by " a young princox boy." For the origin of the word, see Wb.

Coleridge remarks here : " How admirable is the old man's impetuosity, at once contrasting, yet harmonized with young Tybalt's quarrelsome violence ! But it would be endless to repeat observations of this sort. Every leaf is different on an oak tree ; but still we can only say, our tongues defrauding our eyes, This is another oak leaf !"

87. *Patience perforce.* Compulsory submission ; a proverbial expression. Nares quotes Ray's *Proverbs:* " Patience perforce is a medicine for a mad dog" (or " a mad horse," as Howell gives it). Cf. Spenser. *F. Q.* ii. 3. 3 :

> " Patience perforce : helplesse what may it boot
> To frett for anger, or for griefe to mone?"

Many other examples might be given.

90. *Convert.* For the intransitive use, cf. *R. of L.* 592, *Much Ado,* i. 1. 123, *Rich. II.* v. 1. 66, v. 3. 64, etc. Lettsom makes *sweet* the object of *convert.*

92. *The gentle fine.* The sweet penance for the offence ; that is, for the rude touch of my hand. For *fine* the early eds. have " sin" or " sinne." The emendation is due to Warb. Ulrici and Delius defend "sin."

101. *Let lips do*, etc. Juliet has said that palm to palm is holy palmers' kiss. She afterwards says that palmers have lips that they must use in prayer. Romeo replies that the prayer of his lips is that they may do what hands do, that is, that they may kiss (Mason).

105. As Malone remarks, kissing in a public assembly was not then thought indecorous. Cf. *Hen. VIII.* i. 4. 28.

W. remarks : " I have never seen a Juliet on the stage who appeared to appreciate the archness of the dialogue with Romeo in this scene. They go through it solemnly, or at best with staid propriety. They reply literally to all Romeo's speeches about saints and palmers. But it should be noticed that, though this is the first interview of the lovers, we do not hear them speak until the close of their dialogue, in which they have arrived at a pretty thorough understanding of their mutual feeling. Juliet makes a feint of parrying Romeo's advances, but does it archly, and knows that he is to have the kiss he sues for. He asks, ' Have not saints lips, and holy palmers too ?' The stage Juliet answers with literal solemnity. But it was not a conventicle at old Capulet's. Juliet was not

holding forth.   **How demure is her real answer** : 'Ay, pilgrim, lips that
they must use—-in prayer !' And when Romeo fairly gets her into the
corner, towards which she has been contriving to be driven, and he says
'Thus from my lips, by thine, my sin is purg'd,' and does put them to
that purgation, how slyly the pretty puss gives him the opportunity to
repeat the penance by replying, 'Then have my lips the sin that they
have took !'"

110. *What.* Who. See *Much Ado*, p. 118 and *Ham.* p. 253. Cf. Gr.
254.

113. *Withal.* See Gr. 196.

116. *My life*, etc. "He means that, as bereft of Juliet he should die,
his existence is at the mercy of his enemy, Capulet " (St.). Cf. Brooke :

> "So hath he learnd her name, ard knowth she is no geast.
> Her father was a Capilet, and master of the feast.
> Thus hath his foe in choyse to geue him lyfe or death :
> That scarsely can his wofull brest keepe in the liuely breath.'

120. *Foolish.* A mere repetition of the apologetic *trifling.*

Banquet. The word sometimes meant a dessert, as here and in *T. of
S.* v. 2. 9 :

> "My banquet is to close our stomachs up,
> After our great good cheer."

Nares quotes Massinger, *Unnatural Combat :*

> "We 'll dine in the great room, but let the music
> And banquet be prepared here ;"

and Taylor, *Pennilesse Pilgrim :* " our first and second course being threescore dishes at one boord, and after that alwayes a banquet."

Towards = ready, at hand (Steevens). So *toward ;* as in *M. N. D.* iii.
1. 81 : " What, a play toward !" See also *Ham.* p. 173.

121. *Is it e'en so ?* The 1st quarto has here the stage-direction : " *They
whisper in his eare ;*" that is, as Delius remarks, whisper the reason of
their departure.

124. *By my fay.* That is, by my faith. See *Ham.* p. 205.

126. *Come hither, nurse,* etc. Cf. Brooke :

> "As carefull was the mayde what way were best deuise
> To learne his name, that intertaind her in so gentle wise.
> Of whome her hart receiued so deepe, so wyde a wound,
> An auncient dame she calde to her, and in her eare gan rounde.*
> This old dame in her youth, had nurst her with her mylke,
> With slender nedle taught her sow, and how to spin with silke.
> What twayne are those (quoth she) which prease vnto the doore,
> Whose pages in theyr hand doe beare, two toorches light before.
> And then as eche of them had of his houshold name,
> So she him namde yet once agayne the yong and wyly dame.
> And tell me who is he with vysor in his hand
> That yender doth in masking weede besyde the window stand.
> His name is Romeus (said shee) a Montegewe :
> Whose fathers pryde first styrd the strife which both your housholdes rewe

128. *What 's he,* etc. See on 110 above.

---

* That is, whisper. See *Hen. VIII.* p. 168, foot-note.

138. *Prodigious.* Monstrous, portentous. Cf. *M. N. D.* v. 1. 419, *K. John*, iii. 1. 46, *Rich. III.* i. 2. 23, etc.

143. *Enter Chorus.* Johnson remarks: "The use of this Chorus is not easily discovered. It conduces nothing to the progress of the play, but relates what is already known, or what the next scene will show; and relates it without adding the improvement of any moral sentiment." Ulrici calls it "one of the *without-book prologues* of i. 4. 7," and believes that S. could not have written it.

144. *Gapes.* Rushton quotes Swinburn, *Briefe Treatise of Testaments and Last Willes*, 1590: "such personnes as do gape for greater bequests;" and again: "It is an impudent part still to gape and crie upon the testator."

145. On the repetition of *for*, cf. *A. W.* i. 2. 29: "But on us both did haggish age steal on;" *Cor.* ii. 1. 18: "In what enormity is Marcius poor in?" etc. Gr. 407.

156. *Extremities.* That is, extreme difficulties or dangers (Schmidt).

ACT II.

Scene I.—2. *Dull earth.* "Romeo's epithet for his small world of man, the earthlier portion of himself" (Clarke).

Thy centre. Delius compares *Sonn.* 146. 1: "Poor soul, the centre of my sinful earth."

5. *Orchard.* That is, garden. See *J. C.* p. 142 or *Much Ado*, p. 126.

6. *Conjure.* For the accent of the word in S., see *M. N. D.* p. 164.

7. *Humours.* Fancies, caprices. Singer reads "Humour's-madman! Passion-lover!" See on 29 below.

10. *Pronounce.* The reading of 1st, 4th, and 5th quartos; the other quartos and 1st folio have "prouaunt" or "Prouant;" the latter folios, "Couply." Steevens thought that "provant" (=provide) might be right.

11. *My gossip Venus.* Cf. *M. of V.* iii. 1. 7: "if my gossip Report be an honest woman of her word."

13. *Young Abraham Cupid.* The 2d and 3d quartos have "Abraham: Cupid;" the other early eds. "Abraham Cupid." Upton conjectured "Adam Cupid," with an allusion to the famous archer, Adam Bell (see *Much Ado*, p. 124), and was followed by Steevens and others. Theo. suggested "auborn," and it has since been shown that *abraham, abram, aborne, aborn, abron, aubrun*, etc., were all forms of the word now written *auburn.* In *Cor.* ii. 3. 21 the 1st, 2d, and 3d folios read: "our heads are some browne, some blacke, some Abram, some bald;" the 4th folio changes "Abram" to "auburn." In *T. G. of V.* iv. 4. 194, the folio has "Her haire is *Aburne*, mine is perfect *Yellow*." These are the only instances of the word in S. "Auburn" is adopted by H. and W. and is explained as="auburn-haired," but that surely is no *nickname.* K. retains "Abraham" and takes it to be="Abraham-man," or cheat. Schmidt understands "Young Abraham Cupid" to be used "in derision of the eternal boyhood of Cupid, though in fact he was at least as old as father Abraham." Cf. *L. L. L.* iii. 1. 182: This "senior-junior, giant-dwarf, Dan Cupid;" and *Id.* v. 2. 10: "For he hath been five thousand years a boy." In *Rich. II.* iv. 1. 104, "good old Abraham" is mentioned, but we find no reference to the "Abraham-man" in S. On the whole, we are inclined to agree with Schmidt; the choice must be between his explanation and Knight's. F. in his Var. ed. gives "Adam," but he now prefers "Abraham"=the young counterfeit, with his sham make-up, pretending to be *purblind* and yet *shooting so trim.* He thinks the allusion to the *beggar-maid* also favours this explanation. D. in his 1st ed. gives "auburn," in the 2d "Adam."

Trim. The reading of 1st quarto; the other early eds. have "true." That the former is the right word is evident from the ballad of *King Cophetua and the Beggar-Maid* (see Percy's *Reliques*), in which we read:

> "The blinded boy that shoots so trim
> From heaven down did hie,
> He drew a dart and shot at him,
> In place where he did lie."

For other allusions to the ballad, see *L. L. L.* iv. 1. 66 and *2 Hen. IV.* v. 3. 106.

16. *Ape.* As Malone notes, *ape,* like *fool* (see on i. 3. 31 above), was sometimes used as a term of endearment or pity. Cf. *2 Hen. IV.* ii. 4. 234: "Alas, poor ape, how thou sweatest!"

22. *Circle.* Alluding to the ring drawn by magicians. Cf. *A. Y. L.* ii. 5. 62: "a Greek invocation, to call fools into a circle. See also *Hen. V.* v. 2. 320.

25. *Spite.* Vexation. Cf. i. 5. 60 above.

29. *Humorous.* "In an ambiguous sense: *moist* and *capricious,* full of such humours as characterize lovers, and as whose personification Mercutio had just conjured Romeo under the collective name *humours*" (Delius). Schmidt recognizes the same quibble in the word.

32. *Truckle-bed.* Trundle-bed; one made to run under a "standing-bed," as it was called. Cf. *M. W.* iv. 5. 7: "his standing-bed and truckle-bed." The former was for the master, the latter for the servant. Mercutio probably uses the term in sport; but K. thinks it is because the truckle-bed is one degree above the *field-bed* or travelling-bed.

SCENE II.—1. *He jests,* etc. Referring to Mercutio, whom he has overheard (Johnson). As St. remarks, the rhyme in *found* and *wound* favours this view. W. does not begin a new scene here. The Camb. editors suggest that in the old arrangement of the scene the wall may have been represented as dividing the stage, so that the audience could see Romeo on one side and Mercutio on the other.

7. *Be not her maid.* Be not a votary to the moon, or Diana (Johnson). Cf. *M. N. D.* i. 1. 73.

8. *Sick.* The 1st quarto has "pale," which is adopted by Sr. (2d. ed.), D., and W. The Coll. MS. has "white." It has been objected that *sick and green* is a strange combination of *colours* in a livery; but it is rather the *effect* of the colours that is meant. Cf. *T. N.* ii. 4. 116: "with a green and yellow melancholy."

31. *Lazy-pacing.* The first quarto has "lasie pacing;" the other early eds. "lazie (or "lazy") puffing." The Coll. MS. gives "lazy passing."

39. *Thou art thyself,* etc. That is, you would be yourself, or what you now are, even if you were not a Montague; just "as a rose is a rose—has all its characteristic sweetness and beauty—though it be not called a rose" (W.). The thought is repeated below in *So Romeo would . . . that title.* Malone pointed the line "Thou art thyself though, not a Montague," and explained it "Thou art, however, a being *sui generis,* amiable and perfect, not tainted by the enmity which your family bears to mine." For sundry foolish attempts at emendation, see the collation in F.

41, 42. For these two lines the 1st quarto has "Nor arme, nor face, nor any other part;" the other early eds. have

> "Nor arme, nor face, ô be some other name
> Belonging to a man."

The reading in the text is due to Malone.

44. *Name.* From 1st quarto, and generally adopted; the other early eds. have "word," which is preferred by St. and Ulrici.

46. *Owes.* Possesses. See *Rich. II.* p. 204, *Macb.* p. 162, or *M. N. D.* p. 152.

47. *Doff.* The 1st quarto has "part," which, on account of the frequent playing upon words in this drama, Daniel thinks may be what S. wrote. He compares *Sonn.* 113. 3 : "Doth part his function."

52. *Bescreen'd.* Used by S. only here. For verbs with the prefix *be-,* see Gr. 438. Cf. *bepaint* in 86 below.

58. *Yet not.* The 1st quarto has "not yet," which is adopted by H., D., St., and others. *Yet not* is common in S. Cf. *Hen. V.* iii. 3. 46 : "his powers are yet not ready ;" *Hen. VIII.* ii. 4. 204 : "full sick, and yet not well ;" *Cor.* i. 5. 18 : "My work hath yet not warm'd me ;" *Cymb.* ii. 3. 80 : "I yet not understand the case myself," etc.

61. *Dislike.* Displease. Cf. *Oth.* ii. 3. 49 : "I 'll do 't; but it dislikes me." So *like*=please ; as in *Ham.* v. 2. 276 : "This likes me well," etc. Cf. Gr. 297.

62. *Wherefore.* For the accent, cf. *M. N. D.* iii. 2. 272 : "Hate me! Wherefore? O me! what news, my love !" See Gr. 490.

66. *O'er-perch.* Used by S. nowhere else.

69. *Let.* Hinderance; as in *R. of L.* 330, 646, and *Hen. V.* v. 2. 65. Cf. the verb in *Ham.* i. 4. 85, etc. *Let* is from the 1st quarto ; the other early eds. and some modern ones have "stop."

78. *Prorogued.* Delayed ; as in iv. 1. 48 below. On *wanting of,* see Gr. 178, and cf. v. 1. 40 below : "Culling of simples."

83. *As that vast shore,* etc. See p. 12, foot-note.

84. *Adventure.* Venture, try the chance. Cf. *Cymb.* iii. 4. 156 :

> "O for such means !
> Though peril to my modesty, not death on 't,
> I would adventure."

89. *Farewell compliment !* Away with formality ! The early eds. have "complement" or "complements," as in ii. 4. 19 below and elsewhere.

93. *At lovers' perjuries*, etc. Douce remarks that S. found this in Ovid's *Art of Love*—perhaps in Marlowe's translation, book i. :

> "For Jove himself sits in the azure skies,
> And laughs below at lovers' perjuries."

Malone suggests that he may have taken it from Greene, *Metamorphosis* : "What ! Eriphila, Jove laughs at the perjurie of lovers."

99. *Haviour.* Not "'haviour," as often printed. See Wb. s. v. The folio has "behaviour."

101. *Cunning.* The reading of 1st quarto ; the other early eds. have "coying" or "coyning."

To be strange. "To put on affected coldness, to appear shy" (Steevens). Cf. Greene, *Mamillia*, 1593 : "Is it the fashion in Padua to be so strange with your friends?" See also iii. 2. 15 below : "strange love" (that is, coy love).

103. *Ware.* See on i. 1. 116 above.

106. *Discovered.* Revealed, betrayed. Cf. iii. 1. 139 below, where it is=tell, explain.

107. *Blessed* is omitted in the folios ; and for *swear* all the early eds. except 1st quarto have "vow."

109. *Th' inconstant moon.* Cf. *M. for M.* iii. 1. 25 :

> "For thy complexion shifts to strange effects,
> After the moon."

See also *L. L. L.* v. 2. 212, *Lear*, v. 3. 19, and *Oth.* iii. 3. 178. Hunter remarks that the comparison was a commonplace one when S. made it, and has become more so since his day. He quotes Wilson, *Retorique*, 1553 : "as in speaking of constancy, to shew the sun who ever keepeth one course ; in speaking of inconstancy, to shew the moon which keepeth no certain course."

113. *Gracious.* W. adopts the "glorious" of the 1st quarto as more suitable to Juliet's mood and to the remainder of her speech.

116. Coleridge remarks here : "With love, pure love, there is always an anxiety for the safety of the object, a disinterestedness by which it is distinguished from the counterfeits of its name. Compare this scene with the *Tempest*, iii. 1. I do not know a more wonderful instance of Shakespeare's mastery in playing a distinctly rememberable variation on the same remembered air than in the transporting love-confessions of Romeo and Juliet and Ferdinand and Miranda. There seems more passion in the one, and more dignity in the other ; yet you feel that the sweet girlish lingering and busy movement of Juliet, and the calmer and more maidenly fondness of Miranda, might easily pass into each other."

117. *Contract.* Accented by S. on either syllable, as suits the measure. See Gr. 490. The verb is always *contráct.*

119. *Like the lightning*, etc. Cf. *M. N. D.* i. 1. 145 :

> "Brief as the lightning in the collied night,
> That, in a spleen, unfolds both heaven and earth,
> And ere a man hath power to say 'Behold !'
> The jaws of darkness do devour it up :
> So quick bright things come to confusion."

124. *As that,* etc. As to that heart, etc.

131. *Frank.* Bountiful (Schmidt). So Delius, who remarks that to this meaning of the word the following *bounty* refers. Cf. *Sonn.* 4. 4 :

> "Nature's bequest gives nothing but doth lend,
> And being frank she lends to those are free ;"

and *Lear,* iii. 4. 20 : "Your old kind father, whose frank heart gave all."

139. *Afeard.* Used by S. interchangeably with *afraid* (v. 3. 10 below).

141. *Substantial.* Metrically a quadrisyllable. Gr. 479.

142. *Three words,* etc. See p. 33 above. Cf. Brooke's poem :

> "In few vnfained woords your hidden mynd vnfolde,
> That as I see your pleasant face, your heart I may beholde.
> For if you doe intende my honor to defile :
> In error shall you wander still, as you haue done this whyle,
> But if your thought be chaste, and haue on vertue ground,
> If wedlocke be the ende and marke which your desire hath found :
> Obedience set aside, vnto my parentes dewe :
> The quarell eke that long agoe betwene our housholdes grewe :
> Both me and myne I will all whole to you betake :
> And following you where so you goe, my fathers house forsake."

143. *Bent.* Inclination ; as in *J. C.* ii. 1. 210 : "I can give his humour the true bent," etc.

151. *Madam!* This forms no part of the verse, and might well enough be separated from it, like the *Juliet* in i. 5. 141 above. The early eds. put the word in the margin, with or without "*Within ;*" but the modern ones follow Capell in inserting it in the text.

By and by. Presently ; as in iii. 1. 167 and iii. 3. 76 below. See *Ham.* p. 231 or *Hen. V.* p. 155.

152. *Suit.* The reading of 4th ("sute") and 5th quartos ; the other early eds. have "strife." The expression "To cease your sute" occurs in Brooke's poem, a few lines below the passage just quoted.

153. *To-morrow.* "Exquisitely has S. made Juliet pause not a moment on the impossible alternative that Romeo *means* otherwise than *well.* The breathless hurry with breathing earnestness in all that Juliet utters during this scene is marvellously true to the pulsing rapture of a young girl's heart on first learning that she loves and is beloved" (Clarke). Cf. what Mrs. Jameson says on this passage : "In the alternative which she places before her lover with such a charming mixture of conscious delicacy and girlish simplicity, there is that jealousy of female honour which precept and education have infused into her mind, without one real doubt of his truth, or the slightest hesitation in her self-abandonment ; for she does not even wait to hear his asseverations."

157. *Toward school,* etc. Cf. *A. Y. L.* ii. 7. 145 :

> "And then the whining schoolboy, with his satchel
> And shining morning face, creeping like snail
> Unwillingly to school."

159. *Tassel-gentle.* The *tassel-gentle* or *tercel-gentle* is the male hawk. D. quotes Cotgrave, *Fr. Dict.* : "Tiercelet. The Tassell or male of any kind of Hawke, so tearmed, because he is, commonly, a third part less than the female ;" and Holmes, *Academy of Armory* : "*Tiercell, Tercell,* or *Tassell* is the general name for the Male of all large Hawks." Cf.

Spenser, *F. Q.* iii. 4. 49: "Having farre off espyde a Tassell gent." We find *tercel* in *T. and C.* iii. 2. 56: "The falcon as the tercel." The word is used figuratively, as here, in Mabbe's translation of *Guzman de Alfarache*, 1623: "When then they came home, they would one while returne with Tassel-gentles [which a marginal note explains as "kinde Louers"], amorous knights, like *Amadis de Gaule*, that would easily be mou'd, and quickly brought to stoope to the Lure; and other whiles with fierce Mastiffes, roaring Boyes, and ruffian-like Swaggerers, such as would sweare and drinke, and throw the house out at the Windowes."

The hawk was trained to know and obey *the falconer's voice.* Cf. *T. of S.* iv. 1. 196:

> "Another way I have to man my haggard,
> To make her come and know her keeper's call."

For *haggard* = wild hawk, see *Much Ado*, p. 140.

160–164. The 1st quarto reads:

> "Bondage is hoarse, and may not crie aloud,
> Els would I teare the Caue where Eccho lies
> And make her airie voice as hoarse as mine
> With repetition of my *Romeos* name."

The 2d and 3d quartos and 1st folio have:

> "Bondage is hoarse and may not speake aloude,
> Else would I teare the Caue where Eccho lies,
> And make her ayrie tongue more hoarse, then
> With repetition of my *Romeo.*"

The 4th and 5th quartos add "mine" (probably from 1st quarto) to the third line. The later folios attempt to supply the deficiency by reading

> "And make her airy tongue more hoarse than with
> The repetition of my *Romeo.*"

On *airy tongue*, cf. Milton, *Comus*, 208: "And airy tongues, that syllable men's names," etc.

165. *Silver-sweet.* Cf. *Per.* v. 1. 111: "As silver-voic'd." See also iv. 5. 131 below: "Then music with her silver sound," etc.

166. *Attending.* Attentive. Cf. *T. A.* v. 3. 82: "To love-sick Dido's sad attending ear."

167. *My dear.* The reading of 4th and 5th quartos. The 1st quarto has "Madame;" the 2d and 3d quartos and 1st folio, "My Neece;" the later folios, "My sweete" (or "sweet").

178. *Who . . . her.* The reading of 1st quarto; the other early eds. have "That . . . his." *Wanton* was sometimes masculine (=an effeminate boy); as in *K. John*, v. 1. 70: "A cocker'd silken wanton." See also *Rich. II.* p. 213, note on *Young wanton.*

180. *Plucks it back.* Cf. *Sonn.* 126. 6: "As thou goest onwards, still will pluck thee back." See also *W. T.* iv. 4. 476, 762 and *A. and C.* i. 2. 131. *Pluck* is a favourite word with S.

181. *Loving-jealous.* For compound adjectives in S., see Gr. 2.

188. *Father's cell.* From 1st quarto; the other early eds. have "Friers close cell" ("Fries" in 1st folio).

189. *Dear hap.* Good fortune. The 1st quarto has "good hap," which occurs in iii. 3. 171 below.

SCENE III.—1. *Grey-eyed.* Delius says that *grey* here and in *Much Ado*, v. 3. 27 is="bright blue," and D. defines it as "blue, azure;" but we see no reason why the word should not have its ordinary meaning. The *grey*, as in *M. N. D.* iii. 2. 419, *J. C.* ii. 1. 103, and iii. 5. 19 below, is the familiar poetic grey of the early morning before sunrise. Whether ascribed, as here, to the eyes of the Morn, or, as in Milton's *Lycidas*, to her sandals, does not matter. With regard to such passages as *V. and A.* 140 ("Mine eyes are grey and bright"), *T. G. of V.* iv. 4. 197 ("Her eyes are grey as glass"), *T. N.* i. 5. 266 ("two grey eyes"), etc., there may be room for question; but even in these we think, with Schmidt, that the word "may well have the modern signification." See p. 192, foot-note.

2. *Chequering the eastern clouds.* Cf. *Much Ado*, v. 3. 27 : "Dapples the drowsy east with spots of grey."

3. *Flecked.* Spotted, dappled; used by S. nowhere else. The early eds. except 1st quarto have "fleckeld," "fleckled," or "fleckel'd."

4. *From forth.* Cf. *M. W.* iv. 4. 53 : "Let them from forth a sawpit rush at once," etc. See also Gr. 156.

For *Titan* as the sun-god, cf. *V. and A.* 177, *T. and C.* v. 10. 25, *Cymb.* iii. 4. 166, etc.

7. *Osier cage.* Basket.

8. *Precious-juiced flowers.* S. here prepares us for the part which the friar is afterwards to sustain. Having thus early found him to be a chemist, we are not surprised at his furnishing the sleeping-draught for Juliet (Steevens). Cf. Brooke's poem :

> "What force the stones, the plants, and metals haue to woorke,
> And diuers other thinges that in the bowels of earth do loorke,
> With care I haue sought out, with payne I did them proue;
> With them eke can I helpe my selfe at times of my behoue," etc.

9. *The earth*, etc. Steevens cites Lucretius, v. 259 : "Omniparens eadem rerum commune sepulcrum ;" and Milton, *P. L.* ii. 911 : "The womb of nature, and perhaps her grave." See also *Per.* ii. 3. 45 :

> "Whereby I see that Time's the king of men,
> He's both their parent, and he is their grave."

15. *Mickle.* Much, great; a word already half obsolete in the time of S. (Ulrici). Cf. *C. of E.* iii. 1. 45 : "The one ne'er got me credit, the other mickle blame," etc.

Powerful grace. "Efficacious virtue" (Johnson).

19. *Strain'd.* Wrenched, forced.

23. *Weak.* So all the early eds. except 1st quarto, which has "small." *Weak* seems the better word as opposed to the following *power* (Daniel).

25. *With that part.* "That is, with its odour" (Sr.). Malone and Clarke take *part* to be=the sense of smell. The Coll. MS. has "with that act."

27. *Encamp them.* For the reflexive use, cf. *Hen. V.* iii. 6. 180 : "we'll encamp ourselves." For *kings* the 1st quarto has "foes."

29. *Worser.* Cf. iii. 2. 108 below : " worser than Tybalt's death." **Gr.** 11.
Predominant. Originally an astrological term. See *Macb.* p. 203.

30. *Canker.* Canker-worm. Cf. *V. and A.* 656 : " The canker that eats
up Love's tender spring ;" *T. G. of V.* i. 1. 43 : " in the sweetest bud The
eating canker dwells," etc. See also *M. N. D.* p. 150.

37. *Unstuff'd.* " Not overcharged " (Schmidt).

40. *With some.* The editors, with the exception of St., adopt " by
some " from the 1st quarto ; but *with=by* is so common in S. (see Gr.
193) that the reading of all the other early eds. may be accepted. See
on i. 1. 143 and i. 2. 48 above.

Distemperature = disorder. Cf. *C. of E.* v. 1. 82 :

> " a huge infectious troop
> Of pale distemperatures and foes to life."

See also *M. N. D.* p. 144.

51. *Both our remedies.* The healing of both of us. Cf. *A. W.* i. 3. 169 :
" both our mothers " = the mother of both of us. See also *Ham.* iii. 1.
42, *Cymb.* ii. 4. 56, etc.

52. *Lies.* Cf. *V. and A.* 1128 :

> " She lifts the coffer-lids that close his eyes,
> Where lo ! two lamps burnt out in darkness lies."

See also *Rich. II.* iii. 3. 168 and *Cymb.* ii. 3. 24. Gr. 333.

54. *Steads.* Benefits, helps. Cf. *Temp.* i. 2. 165 : " Which since have
steaded much ;" *M. of V.* i. 3. 7 : " May you stead me ?" etc.

55. *Homely in thy drift.* Simple in what you have to say.

56. *Riddling.* Cf. *M. N. D.* ii. 2. 53 : " Lysander riddles very prettily ;"
and 1 *Hen. VI.* ii. 3. 57 : " a riddling merchant."

66. *That.* Most of the editors adopt " whom " from the 1st quarto.

72. *To season love.* A favourite metaphor with S. See *Much Ado*, p.
155.

74. *Ancient.* Aged ; as in ii. 4. 119 below. See also *Lear*, ii. 2. 67.
Cymb. v. 3. 15, etc.

85. *Chide not : she whom I*, etc. From 1st quarto ; the other early
eds. have " chide me not, her I loue now."

88. *Did read by rote*, etc. " Consisted of phrases learned by heart, but
knew nothing of the true characters of love " (Schmidt).

92. *To turn.* As to turn. See Gr. 281.

93. *I stand on sudden haste.* I must be in haste. Cf. the impersonal
use of *stand on* or *upon* = it concerns, it is important to ; as in *C. of E.*
iv. 1. 68 : " Consider how it stands upon my credit ;" *Rich. II.* ii. 3. 138 :
" It stands your grace upon to do him right " (that is, it is your duty),
etc.

SCENE IV.—2. *To-night.* Last night. See on i. 4. 50 above.

11. *How he dares.* For the play on *dare* = venture, and *dare* = challenge, cf. 2 *Hen. VI.* iii. 2. 203 (Delius).

14. *Thorough.* Through. See *M. of V.* p. 144, note on *Throughfares*,
or *M. N. D.* p. 136. Gr. 478.

15. *The very pin*, etc. The allusion is to archery. The clout or white

mark at which the arrows were aimed was fastened by a black pin in the centre (Malone). Cf. Marlowe, *Tamburlane*, 1590 :

> " For kings are clouts that every man shoots at,
>   Our crown the pin that thousands seek to cleave."

16. *Butt-shaft.* A kind of arrow used for shooting at butts ; formed without a barb, so as to be easily extracted (Nares).

18. *Prince of cats.* *Tybert* is the name of the cat in *Reynard the Fox* (Warb.). Steevens quotes Dekker, *Satiromastix*, 1602 : " tho' you were Tybert, the long-tail'd prince of cats ;" and *Have with You*, etc. : " not Tibalt, prince of cats." As St. notes, *Tibert*, *Tybert*, and *Tybalt* are forms of the ancient name *Thibault.* Cf. iii. 1. 75 below.

19. *Captain of compliments.* " A complete master of all the laws of ceremony " (Johnson) : " one versed in punctilios " (St.). Cf. *L. L. L.* i. 1. 169 :

> " A man of compliments, whom right and wrong
>   Have chose as umpire of their mutiny."

As Schmidt remarks, the modern distinction of *compliment* and *complement* is unknown to the orthography of the old eds. See on ii. 2. 89 above.

20. *Prick-song.* Music sung from notes (Schmidt) ; so called from the points or dots with which it is expressed. When opposed to *plain song* it meant counter-point as distinguished from mere melody (Nares).

21. *Me.* For the " ethical dative," see Gr. 220.

22. *Button.* Steevens quotes *The Return from Parnassus*, 1606 : "Strikes his poinado at a button's breadth." St. cites George Silver's *Paradoxes of Defence*, 1599 : " Signior Rocco, thou that art thought to be the only cunning man in the world with thy weapons ; thou that takest upon thee to hit anie Englishman with a thrust upon anie button," etc.

A duellist. Duels were frequent in England in the time of S. The matter had been reduced to a science, and its laws laid down in books. The *causes* of quarrel had been duly graded and classified, as Touchstone explains in *A. Y. L.* v. 4. 63 fol. See note in our ed. p. 198.

23. *Of the very first house.* That is, of the first rank among duellists (Steevens) ; or of the best school of fencing (St.).

24. *Passado.* " A motion forwards and thrust in fencing " (Schmidt). Cf. *L. L. L.* i. 2. 184 : " the passado he respects not."

The *punto reverso* was a back-handed stroke. We have *punto* (=thrust) in *M. W.* ii. 3. 26 : " to see thee pass thy punto." Saviolo says : " you maie give him a punta either dritta [that is, direct] or riversa." Halliwell cites Lodge, *Wit's Miserie:* " his hose ungartered, his rapier punto reverso ;" where it appears to refer to the manner of wearing the rapier, with point reversed.

The *hay* was a home-thrust ; from the Italian *hai*=thou hast it (not " he has it," as Schmidt and others explain it). Johnson gives it correctly : " The *hay* is the word *hai*, you *have* it, used when a thrust reaches the antagonist, from which our fencers, on the same occasion, without knowing, I suppose, any reason for it, cry out ha !"

26. *Fantasticoes.* From 1st quarto ; the other early eds. have " phanta-

cies" or "phantasies." Steevens quotes Nash, *Have with You*, etc.
"Follow some of these new-fangled Galiardo's and Signor.Fantastico's;"
and Dekker, *Old Fortunatus:* " I have danced with queens, dallied with
ladies, worn strange attires, seen fantasticoes," etc.

29. *Grandsire.* This appears to be addressed to Benvolio, partly in
raillery of his staid demeanour, partly by way of impersonating him as a
departed progenitor who would be disgusted could he witness the affec-
tations that have sprung up since his time " (Clarke).

30. *Fashion - mongers.* Cf. *Much Ado,* v. 1. 94 : "fashion - monging
boys."

Pardonnez-mois. Fellows who are continually saying *pardonnez-moi.*
The early eds. have "pardon mees," "pardons mees," "pardon-mee's,"
or "pardona' mees." The reading in the text is due to Theo.

31. *Form.* There is a play on the word, as in *L. L. L.* i. 1. 209 : "sitting with her upon the form . . . in manner and form following." Blakeway remarks : " I have heard that during the reign of large breeches it
was necessary to cut away hollow places in the benches in the House
of Commons, to make room for those monstrous protuberances, without
which contrivance they who stood on the new form could not sit at ease
on the old bench."

32. *Bons.* The early eds. have "bones," which is unintelligible. Theo.
says : " Mercutio is here ridiculing those Frenchified fantastical coxcombs
whom he calls *pardonnez-moi's :* and therefore I suspect here he meant
to write French too. 'O, their *bon's !* their *bon's !*' that is, how ridiculous they make themselves in crying out, *good,* and being in ecstasies with
every trifle ; as he had just described them before : 'a very good blade !'
etc." Malone remarks that the emendation of Theo. is confirmed by
Green's Tu Quoque, from which we learn that *bon jour* was the affected
salutation of the fine gentlemen. of the time : " No, I want the *bon jour*
and the *tu quoque,* which yonder gentleman has."

34. *Without his roe.* "That is, he comes but half himself ; he is only
a sigh—*O me !* that is, *me O !* the half of his name " (Seymour). It may
mean without his mistress, whom he has had to leave ; *roe* meaning a
female deer as well as the spawn of a fish. Cf. *L. L. L.* v. 2. 309, where
the Princess says : " Whip to our tents, as roes run over land ;" and *T.
and C.* v. 1. 68 : "a herring without a roe."

37. *Be-rhyme.* Cf. *A. Y. L.* iii. 2. 186 : " I was never so be-rhymed,"
etc.

38. *Hildings.* Base menials ; used of both sexes. Cf. *T. of S.* ii. 1.
26 : " For shame, thou hilding ;" *A. W.* iii. 6. 4 : " If your lordship find
him not a hilding, hold me no more in your respect," etc. See also iii.
5. 167 below. It is used as an adjective in 2 *Hen. IV.* i. 1. 57 and *Hen. V.*
iv. 2. 29.

39. *Grey eye.* Here Malone, D., and Delius make *grey*=blue ; while
Steevens and Ulrici take the ground that it has its ordinary meaning.
The latter quote *Temp.* i. 2. 269 (" This blue-eyed hag ") in proof that
blue eyes were accounted ugly ; but the reference there, as in *A. Y. L.* iii.
2. 393 (" a blue eye and sunken "), seems to be, as Schmidt explains it,
to a bluish circle about the eyes. It is curious that these are the only

allusions to blue eyes in S. In *W. T.* i. 2. 136, some make "welkin eye" =blue eye; but it is more probably=heavenly eye, as Schmidt gives it. In *V. and A.* 482 ("Her two blue windows faintly she upheaveth") the eyelids, not the eyes, are meant, on account of their "blue veins" (*R. of L.* 440). Cf. *Cymb.* ii. 2. 21 :

> "would under-peep her lids,
> To see the enclosed lights, now canopied
> Under these windows, white and azure lac'd
> With blue of heaven's own tinct."

Malone cites both this last passage and *V. and A.* 482 as referring to blue eyes ; but the "azure *lac'd*" ought to settle the question in regard to the former, and "windows" evidently has the same meaning in both. If the "blue windows" *were* blue eyes, Malone would make out his case, for in *V. and A.* 140 the goddess says "Mine eyes are grey and bright." But why should the poet call them *blue* in the one place and *grey* in the other, when the former word would suit the verse equally well in both? In our opinion, when he says *blue* he means blue, and when he says *grey* he means grey. See on ii. 3. 1 above.

"Mercutio means to say that in Romeo's opinion Thisbe to his lady-love was indeed grey-eyed (pretty-eyed) or something of the sort, but on the whole insignificant" (Ulrici).

41. *Slop.* For *slops* (=large loose breeches), see *Much Ado*, p. 143.

Gave us the counterfeit. Played a trick on us. *Counterfeit* is used for the sake of the coming play on *slip*, which sometimes meant a counterfeit coin. Reed cites Greene, *Thieves Falling Out*, etc. : "And therefore he went and got him certain slips which are counterfeit pieces of money, being brasse, and covered over with silver, which the common people call slips ;" and *Magnetick Lady*, iii. 6 :

> "I had like t' have been
> Abus'd i' the business, had the slip slur'd on me,
> A counterfeit."

Steevens adds from *Skialetheia*, 1598 :

> "Is not he fond then which a slip receaves
> For currant money?"

There is also a play upon the word in the only other instance in which S. uses it, *V. and A.* 515 :

> "Which purchase if thou make, for fear of slips
> Set thy seal-manual on my wax-red lips."

51. *Kindly.* The word literally means "naturally, in a manner suited to the character or occasion" (Schmidt) ; hence aptly, pertinently. For the adjective *kindly*=natural, see *Much Ado*, p. 154.

56. *Then is my pump*, etc. The idea seems to be, my shoe or *pump*, being *pinked* or punched with holes, is well *flowered*. There may also be an allusion to wearing "rosettes" of ribbon on shoes (St.). We have *pinked* in this sense in *Hen. VIII.* v. 4. 50 : "her pinked porringer ;" and *unpinked* in *T. of S.* iv. 1. 136 · "And Gabriel's pumps were all unpink'd i' the heel."

57. *Well said.* From 1st quarto; the other early eds. have "Sure wit," which K., St., and W. adopt.

60. *Single-soled.* "With a quibble on *sole* and *soul*=having but one sole, and silly, contemptible" (Schmidt). Steevens gives several examples of *single-soled*=mean, contemptible; and Sr. quotes Cotgrave, *Fr. Dict.:* "a threadbare, coarse-spun, single-soled gentleman."

62. *Wits fail.* So in 1st quarto; the other quartos and 1st folio have "wits faints" ("faint" in 5th quarto).

65. *Wild-goose chase.* A kind of horse-race, resembling the flight of wild-geese. Two horses were started together; and if one got the lead the other was obliged to follow over whatever ground the foremost rider chose to take (Holt White).

67. *My whole five.* See on i. 4. 47 above.

Was I with you, etc. Was I even with you, have I paid you off, etc. Cf. *T. of S.* iv. 1. 170: "What, do you grumble? I 'll be with you straight!" (that is, I 'll pay you for this); *Hen. VIII.* v. 4. 29: "I shall be with you presently, good master puppy," etc. Schmidt gives several other examples of the phrase in this sense, but in all of them (and perhaps in those just quoted) it would seem that the threat might be taken more literally.

71. *I will bite thee by the ear.* A playful expression of endearment, common in the old dramatists.

72. *Good goose, bite not.* A proverbial phrase, found in Ray's *Proverbs.*

73. *Sweeting.* A kind of sweet apple. The word is still used in this sense, at least in New England. Steevens quotes Sumner's *Last Will and Testament,* 1600: "as well crabs as sweetings for his summer fruits." There was also a variety known as the *bitter-sweet.* Cf. *Fair Em.:* "And left me such a bitter sweet to gnaw upon;" and Gower, *Conf. Am.:*

> "For all such tyme of love is lore,
> And like unto the bitter swete;
> For though it thynke a man fyrst swete,
> He shall well felen at laste
> That it is sower," etc.

Coles (*Latin Dict.*) translates "Bitter-sweet" by "*Amarimellum.*"

75. *And is it not well served in,* etc. W. remarks that "the passage illustrates the antiquity of that dish so much esteemed by all boys and many men—goose and apple-sauce."

76. *Cheveril.* Soft leather for gloves (Johnson). Cf. *Henry VIII.* ii. 3. 32:

> "which gifts,
> Saving your mincing, the capacity
> Of your soft cheveril conscience would receive,
> If you might please to stretch it."

See also *T. N.* iii. 1. 13. Steevens quotes Drayton, *The Owl:* "A cheverell conscience."

79. *A broad goose.* No satisfactory explanation of this quibble has been given. The folios have "abroad," and Farmer would read "far and wide abroad, goose." Schmidt defines *broad* here as "plain, evident."

83. *Natural.* Fool, idiot. Cf. *Temp.* iii. 2. 37 and *A. Y. L.* i. 2. 52, 57.

85. *Gear.* Matter, business. Cf. *T. and C.* i. 1. 6: "Will this gear

ne'er be mended?" *2 Hen. VI.* i. 4. 17 : "To this gear the sooner the better," etc.

86. *A sail, a sail!* The 1st quarto gives this to Mercutio; the other early eds. add it to Romeo's speech, and assign the next speech to Mercutio, to whom W. considers it better suited than to "the taciturn, correct, and commonplace Benvolio."

90. *My fan, Peter.* Farmer cites an old pamphlet, *The Serving Man's Comfort,* 1598 : "The mistress must have one to carry her cloake and hood, another her fanne." Cf. *L. L. L.* iv. 1. 147 : "To see him walk before a lady and to bear her fan!"

92. *Fairer of the two.* From 1st quarto; the other early eds. have "fairer face," which is preferred by K., D., St., and W.

93. *God ye good morrow.* That is, God give ye, etc. For *good den,* see on i. 2. 56 above.

97. *Prick of noon.* Point of noon. Cf. *3 Hen. VI.* i. 4. 34 : "at the noontide prick." See also *R. of L.* 781.

99. *For himself.* The early eds., except 1st quarto, omit *for;* but the repetition of the words by the Nurse makes it probable that it was accidentally left out.

110. *Confidence.* Probably meant for *conference.* Cf. *Much Ado,* iii. 5. 3, where Dogberry says "Marry, sir, I would have some confidence with you that decerns you nearly."

112. *Indite.* The 1st quarto and 3d and 4th folios have "invite." If *indite* is correct, it is probably used in ridicule of the Nurse's *confidence.* It may be noted in favour of *indite* that Mrs. Quickly uses the word in the same way in *2 Hen. IV.* ii. 1. 30 : "he is indited to dinner."

113. *So ho!* The cry of the sportsmen when they find a hare.

116. *Hoar.* Like *hoary,* often=mouldy, as things grow white from moulding (Steevens). Cf. *Pierce Pennilesses Supplication to the Devil,* 1595 : "as hoary as Dutch butter." Halliwell cites B. J., *Every Man out of his Humour :* "his grain . . . might rot Within the hoary ricks."

119. *Lady, lady, lady.* From the old ballad of *Susanna,* also quoted in *T. N.* ii. 3. 85 : "There dwelt a man in Babylon, lady, lady!"

121. *Merchant.* Used contemptuously, like *chap,* which is a contraction of *chapman.* Cf. *1 Hen. VI.* ii. 3. 57 : "a riddling merchant." Steevens cites Churchyard's *Chance,* 1580 : "What saucie merchaunt speaketh now, saied Venus in her rage?"

122. *Ropery.* Roguery. Steevens quotes *The Three Ladies of London,* 1584 : "Thou art very pleasant and full of thy roperye." Cf. *rope-tricks* in *T. of S.* i. 2. 112, which Schmidt explains as "tricks deserving the halter." Nares and Douce see the same allusion to the halter in *ropery.*

127. *Jacks.* For the contemptuous use of the word, cf. *M. of V.* iii. 4. 77 : "these bragging Jacks;" *Much Ado,* v. 1. 91 : "Boys, apes, braggarts, Jacks, milksops!" etc. See *Much Ado,* pp. 121 and 164.

129. *Flirt-gills.* That is *flirting Gills,* or women of loose behaviour. *Gill* or *Jill* was a familiar term for a woman, as *Jack* was for a man. Cf. the proverbs, "Every Jack must have his Jill," and "A good Jack makes a good Jill." The word is a contraction of *Gillian* (see *C. of E.* iii. 1. 31), which is a corruption of *Juliana. Gill-flirt* was the more common form.

Nares quotes B. and F., *K. of B. P.* iv. 1 : " You heard him take me up like a flirt-gill " ("gill-flirt" in 2d quarto) ; *Chances*, iii. 1 : " As I had been a maukin, a flurt-gillian ;" and *The World in the Moon :* "a parcel of mad wild gilflirts, that like nothing but boys and beaus, and powder and paint, and fool and feather."

Skains-mates. A puzzle to the commentators. As *skein* is an Irish word for knife (used by Warner, Greene, Chapman, and other writers of the time) Malone and Steevens make *skains-mates*="cut-throat companions " or fencing-school companions. Schmidt defines it as "messmates," and Nares as probably="roaring or swaggering companions." St. thinks it may mean "scape-grace or ne'er-do-well," the word *skain* having been formerly used in Kent in that sense. Douce suggests that it is="*sempstresses*, a word not always used in the most honourable acceptation." D. says that, if not a misprint, its meaning remains to be discovered. Walker conjectured "scurvy-mates." There is probably some corruption in the first part of the compound.

136. *Afore.* Not a mere vulgarism. It is used by Capulet in iii. 4. 34 and iv. 2. 31 below. Cf. *Temp.* iv. 1. 7 :

> " here afore Heaven,
> I ratify this my rich gift," etc.

140. *In a fool's paradise.* Most of the editors adopt " into " from 1st quarto ; but S. often uses *in* with verbs of motion. See Gr. 159.

Malone cites *A Handful of Pleasant Delightes,* 1584 :

> "When they see they may her win,
> They leave then where they did begin ;
> They prate, and make the matter nice,
> And leave her in fooles paradise."

and Barnaby Rich's *Farewell :* " Knowing the fashion of you men to be such, as by praisyng our beautie, you think to bring into a fooles paradize."

144. *Weak.* The Coll. MS. gives "wicked," but to mend the Nurse's talk is to mar it. As Clarke observes, "she intends to use a most forcible expression, and blunders upon a most feeble one."

160. *And stay*, etc. The pointing is White's. Most editors follow the early eds. and read

> " And stay, good nurse, behind the abbey wall :
> Within this hour," etc.

162. *A tackled stair.* That is, a rope-ladder. Cf. "ladder-tackle" in *Per.* iv. 1. 61.

163. *High top-gallant.* Steevens quotes Markham, *English Arcadia*, 1607 : "the high top-gallant of his valour."

165. *Quit.* Requite, reward. See *Rich. II.* p. 208 or *Ham.* p. 269.

170. *Two may keep counsel.* That is, keep a secret. Cf. *T. A.* iv. 2. 144 : "Two may keep counsel when the third's away."

172. *Lord*, etc. Cf. Brooke's poem :

> "A prety babe (quod she) it was when it was yong :
> Lord how it could full pretely haue prated with it tong."

175. *Lieve.* Lief. See *A. Y. L.* p. 139, note on *Had as lief.*

177. *Properer.* Handsomer. See *Much Ado*, p. 139.

178. *Versal.* That is, universal. Most modern eds. print "varsal."

179. *A letter.* One letter. Cf. *Ham.* v. 2. 276 : "These foils have all a length," etc. Gr. 81. For *rosemary* as the symbol of remembrance, see *Ham.* p. 250.

181. *The dog's name.* R was called "the dog's letter." Cf. B. J., *Eng. Gram.* : "R is the dog's letter and hurreth in the sound." Farmer cites Barclay, *Ship of Fools,* 1578 :

> "This man malicious which troubled is with wrath,
> Nought els soundeth but the hoorse letter R.
> Though all be well, yet he none aunswere hath
> Save the dogges letter glowming with nar, nar."

D. remarks : "Even in the days of the Romans, *R* was called *the dog's letter,* from its resemblance in sound to the snarling of a dog. Lucilius alludes to it in a fragment which is quoted with various corruptions by Nonius Marcellus, Charisius, and Donatus on Terence, and which Joseph Scaliger amended thus : ' Irritata canes quod, homo quam, planiu' dicit ' (' canes ' being the nom. sing. fem.) ; and Persius has ' Sonat hic de nare canina Litera.' "

The reading in the text was suggested by Ritson, and is adopted by Delius, the Camb. editors, and F. The early eds. have "R. is for the no, I know," etc. Coll. and W. follow Warb. and Theo. in reading "R is for thee? No ;" and K., H., D., St., Halliwell, and others adopt Tyrwhitt's conjecture of "R is for the dog. No," etc.

188. *Before, and apace.* Go before, and quickly ; the reading of the early eds. except 1st quarto, which has "*Peter,* take my fanne, and goe before." For *apace,* cf. iii. 2. 1 below.

SCENE V.—6. *Back.* The Coll. MS. gives "black."

7. *Love.* That is, Venus. Cf. *Temp.* iv. 1. 94 :

> " I met her deity
> Cutting the clouds towards Paphos, and her son
> Dove-drawn with her ;"

and *V. and A.* 1190 :

> "Thus weary of the world, away she hies,
> And yokes her silver doves."

See also *M. of V.* ii. 6. 5 : "O, ten times faster Venus' pigeons fly," etc.

9. *Highmost.* Cf. *Sonn.* 7. 9 : "But when from highmost pitch, with weary car," etc. We still use *hindmost, topmost,* etc.

16. *Many feign.* The early eds. have "many fain" or "faine." Johnson has "marry, feign," and W. "marry, fare." D. conjectures that the MS. had "moue yfaith" ("move i' faith") which the printer corrupted into "many fain." The Coll. MS. gives the passage thus :

> " And his to me ; but old folks seem as dead ;
> Unwieldy, slow, heavy and dull as lead."

Keightley adopts the "dull," and refers to the "dull lead" of *M. of V.* ii. 7. 8.

18. *Honey nurse.* Cf. *L. L. L.* v. 2. 530 : "my fair, sweet, honey monarch ;" *T. of S.* iv. 3. 52 : "my honey love," etc.

M

22. *Them.* S. makes *news* both singular and plural. See *Much Ado*, p. 125.

25. *Aweary.* See *J. C.* p. 172.

Give me leave. Let me alone, let me rest. See on i. 3. 7 above.

26. *Ache.* Spelt "ake" in the folio both here and in 48 below. See *Much Ado*, p. 150 or *Temp.* p. 119.

36. *Stay the circumstance.* Wait for the particulars. Cf. *A. Y. L.* iii. 2. 221 : "let me stay the growth of his beard," etc. On *circumstance*, cf. v. 3. 181 below ; "without circumstance" (= without further particulars). See also *V. and A.* 844, *Ham.* v. 2. 2, etc.

42. *Past compare.* Cf. iii. 5. 236 below : "above compare," etc. For *on*=of, see Gr. 181.

49. *As.* The *if* is implied in the subjunctive (Gr. 107).

50. *O' t' other.* On the other. Cf. i. 1. 39 above : "of our side." Gr. 175.

51. *Beshrew.* A mild form of imprecation, often used playfully. Cf. iii. 5. 221, 227 below ; and see *M. N. D.* p. 152.

53. *Not well.* The 1st folio misprints "so well," which the 2d attempts to mend by reading "so ill."

55–57. *Your love,* etc. Believed by Walker to be prose, and so printed by the Camb. editors and Daniel.

65. *Coil.* Ado, "fuss." See *Much Ado*, p. 146 or *M. N. D.* p. 168.

71. *Straight at any news.* Hanmer and the Coll. MS. give "straitway at my news ;" and Walker would read "at my next news." Capell explains it, "at such talk (of love and Romeo), *any* talk of that kind."

SCENE VI.—**9.** *These violent delights,* etc. Malone compares *R. of L.* 894 : "These violent vanities can never last." He might have added *Ham.* ii. 1. 102 :

> "This is the very ecstasy of love,
> Whose violent property fordoes itself."

10. *Like fire and powder.* For the simile, cf. iii. 3. 132 and v. 1. 64 below.

12. *His.* Its. Gr. 228.

13. *Confounds.* Destroys, as often. See *Macb.* p. 189. So *confusion* often=destruction, ruin ; as in iv. 5. 61 below. See also *M. N. D.* p. 129.

15. *Too swift,* etc. "He that travels too fast is as long before he comes to the end of his journey as he that travels slow. Precipitation procures mishap" (Johnson). As the old proverb puts it, "The more haste, the worse speed."

17. *Will ne'er wear out,* etc. As W. remarks, the reading of the 1st quarto, "So light a foot ne'er hurts the trodden flower," is "a daintier and more graceful, and therefore, it would seem, a more appropriate figure."

18. *Gossamer.* Light filaments floating in the air, especially in autumn. Their origin was formerly not understood, but they are now known to be the webs of certain species of spiders. Cf. *Lear*, iv. 6. 49 : "Hadst thou been aught but gossamer, feathers, air." Steevens quotes Nabbes, *Hannibal and Scipio*, 1637 :

> " Fine as Arachne's web, or gossamer,
> Whose curls, when garnish'd by their dressing, shew
> Like that spun vapour when 't is pearl'd with dew ;"

and Malone adds from Bullokar's *English Expositor*, 1616 : "*Gossomor* : Things that flye like cobwebs in the ayre."

20. *Vanity.* "Here used for 'trivial pursuit,' 'vain delight.' The word was much used in this sense by divines in Shakespeare's time ; and with much propriety is so put into the good old Friar's mouth" (Clarke).

21. *Confessor.* For the accent, cf. *M. for M.* iv. 3. 133 : "One of our covent and his confessor ;" and *Hen. VIII.* i. 2. 149 : "His confessor, who fed him every minute," etc. Gr. 492.

25. *And that.* For the use of *that*, see Gr. 285.

26. *Blazon it.* Set it forth. Cf. *Oth.* ii. 1. 63 : "One that excels the quirks of blazoning pens," etc.

29. *Encounter.* Meeting. See *Much Ado*, p. 154.

30. *Conceit.* Conception, imagination. Cf. *Ham.* iii. 4. 114 : "Conceit in weakest bodies strongest works," etc. So *conceited*=imaginative in *R. of L.* 1371 : "the conceited painter," etc.

32. *They are but beggars*, etc. Steevens quotes *A. and C.* i. 1. 15 : "There 's beggary in the love that can be reckon'd."

34. *Sum up half*, etc. The early eds. have "sum up sum of half my," or "sum up some of halfe my." The reading in the text is Capell's, and is generally adopted.

36. *Leaves.* For the plural, see *Macb.* p. 209, note on *Loves*, or *Rich. II.* p. 206, note on *Sights*.

ACT III.

SCENE I.—2. *The day is hot.* "It is observed that in Italy almost all assassinations are committed during the heat of summer" (Johnson).

3. *Scape.* Not "'scape," as often printed. See *Macb.* p. 214.

6. *Me.* See on ii. 4. 21 above. We have the same construction in *him*, two lines below, where many eds. adopt the "it" of 1st quarto.

7. *Operation.* Effect. Cf. *2 Hen. IV.* iv. 3. 104 : "A good sherris-sack hath a twofold operation in it," etc.

10. *Am I*, etc. "The quietness of this retort, with the slight but significant emphasis which we imagine thrown upon the *I*, admirably gives point to the humorous effect of Mercutio's lecturing Benvolio—the sedate and peace-making Benvolio, and lectured by Mercutio, of all people !—for the sin of quarrelsomeness" (Clarke).

11. *Jack.* See on ii. 4. 127 above.

12. *Moody.* Angry. Cf. *2 Hen. IV.* iv. 4. 39 : "But, being moody, give him line and scope," etc. See Wb. s. v.

14. *What to ?* The early eds. have "what too ?" which St. makes= "what else ?"

28. *Tutor me from.* Teach me to avoid. For *from* the 5th quarto has "for," which W. adopts.

36. *Good den.* See on i. 2. 56 above.

39. *Apt enough to.* Ready enough for. Cf. iii. 3. 157 below.

43. *Consort'st with.* Keepest company with. Cf. *V. and A.* 1041, *M. N. D.* iii. 2. 387, *T. and C.* v. 3. 9, etc.

44. *Consort.* The word (with accent on first syllable) sometimes meant a company of musicians. Cf. *T. G. of V.* iii. 2. 84 :

> "Visit by night your lady's chamber-window
> With some sweet consort ; to their instruments
> Tune a deploring dump," etc.

See also 2 *Hen. VI.* iii. 2. 327. In these passages the modern eds. generally read "concert." Milton has *consort* in the same sense in the *Ode at a Solemn Musick*, 27 :

> "O, may we soon again renew that song,
> And keep in tune with Heaven, till God ere long
> To his celestial consort us unite,
> To live with him, and sing in endless morn of light !"

Cf. *Ode on Nativ.* 132 : "Make up full consort to the angelic symphony ;" *Il Pens.* 145 : "With such consort as they keep," etc.

47. *Zounds.* Like *'swounds* (see *Ham.* p. 214), an oath contracted from "God's wounds !" and generally omitted or changed in the folio in deference to the statute of James I. against the use of the name of God on the stage. Here the folio has "Come." There is no reason for printing the word "'zounds" as some editors do. See Worc. or Wb.

50. *Reason coldly.* Talk coolly or dispassionately. Cf. *M. of V.* ii. 8. 27 : "I reason'd with a Frenchman yesterday ;" and *Much Ado*, iii. 2. 132 : "bear it coldly but till midnight," etc.

"Benvolio presents a triple alternative : either to withdraw to a private place, or to discuss the matter quietly where they were, or else to part company ; and it is supremely in character that on such an occasion he should perceive and suggest all these methods of avoiding public scandal" (W.).

51. *Depart.* Part (St.). Cf. 3 *Hen. VI.* ii. 6. 43 : "A deadly groan, like life and death's departing," etc. So *depart with*=part with; as in *K. John*, ii. 1. 563 :

> "John, to stop Arthur's title in the whole,
> Hath willingly departed with a part," etc.

In the Marriage Ceremony "till death us do part" was originally "us depart." The word is used in the same sense in Wiclif's Bible, *Matt.* xix. 6. On the other hand, *part* often=depart ; as in *T. N.* v. 1. 394, *Cor.* v. 6. 73, *T. of A.* iv. 2. 21, etc.

53. *I.* The repetition of the pronoun at the end of the sentence is common in S.* Cf. *T. G. of V.* v. 4. 132 : "I care not for her, I ;" *Rich. III.*

---

* St. also notes this, but the illustration he gives is not in point. It is *Temp.* iii. 3. 53 '

> "You are three men of sin, whom destiny
> (That hath to instrument this lower world
> And what is in 't) the never-surfeited sea
> Hath caus'd to belch up *you ;*"

iii. 2. 78 : " I do not like these several councils, I ;" *T. A.* v. 3. 113 : " I am no vaunter, I ;" *Id.* v. 3. 185 : " I am no baby, I," etc. See also iii. 5. 12 below.

60. *Love.* Delius says that this " is of course ironical," but the reiteration in the next speech shows that it is not. Romeo's love for Juliet embraces, in a way, all her kindred. His heart, as Talfourd expresses it in *Ion* (we quote from memory),

> " Enlarg'd by its new sympathy with one,
> Grew bountiful to all."

61. *Appertaining rage*, etc. That is, the rage appertaining to (belonging to, or becoming) such a greeting. Cf. *Macb.* iii. 6. 48 :

> " our suffering country
> Under a hand accurst."

For other examples, see Gr. 419*a*.

69. *Tender.* Regard, cherish. Cf. *Ham.* i. 3. 107 : " Tender yourself more dearly ;" and see *Rich. II.* p. 151.

72. *A la stoccata.* Capell's emendation of the " Alla stucatho " or " Allastucatho " of the early eds. *Stoccata* is the Italian term for a thrust or stab with a rapier (Steevens). It is the same as the " stoccado " of *M. W.* ii. 1. 234, the " stock " of *Id.* ii. 3. 26, and the " stuck " of *T. N.* iii. 4. 303 and *Ham.* iv. 7. 162.

75. *King of cats.* See on ii. 4. 18 above.

Nine lives. Cf. Marston, *Dutch Courtezan :* " Why then thou hast nine lives like a cat," etc. A little black-letter book, *Beware the Cat*, 1584, says that it was permitted to a witch " to take on her a cattes body nine times." Trusler, in his *Hogarth Moralized*, remarks : " The conceit of a cat's having nine lives hath cost at least nine lives in ten of the whole race of them. Scarce a boy in the streets but has in this point outdone even Hercules himself, who was renowned for killing a monster that had but three lives."

77. *Dry-beat.* Beat soundly. Cf. *L. L. L.* v. 2. 263 : " all dry-beaten with pure scoff." See also iv. 5. 116 below. S. uses the word only three times ; but we have " dry basting " in *C. of E.* ii. 2. 64.

78. *Pilcher.* Scabbard ; but no other example of the word in this sense has been found. *Pilch* or *pilche* meant a leathern coat, and the word or a derivative of it may have been applied to the leathern sheath of a rapier. Warb. substituted " pilche," and St. conjectures " pilch, sir." Sr. reads " pitcher," and sees a jocose allusion to the proverb, " Pitchers have ears."

82. *Passado.* See on ii. 4. 24 above.

---

but *you* there is a pleonastic repetition of *whom*, to be explained by the intervention of the parenthesis. Cf. *W. T.* v. 1. 136 :

> " your brave father, *whom*,
> Though bearing misery, I desire my life
> Once more to look on *him*."

See also Gr. 249. We know of no instance in which S. repeats *you* as he does *I* in the text. The nearest approach to it is in such vocative clauses as " you puppet you " (*M. N. D.* iii. 2. 288) " you minion you " (*C. of E.* iv. 4. 63), etc.

86. *Forbid this.* The reading of 2d quarto; the folio has "forbidden."
For *bandying*=contending, cf. 1 *Hen. VI.* iv. 1. 190: "This factious bandying of their favourites."

88. *O' both.* The quartos and 1st folio have "a both;" the later folios "of both." See on ii. 5. 50 above.

Sped. Dispatched, "done for." Cf. *M. of V.* ii. 9. 72: "So begone;
you are sped;" *T. of S.* v. 2. 185: "We three are married, but you two
are sped," etc. See also Milton, *Lycidas*, 122: "What need they? They
are sped" (that is, provided for).

95. *Grave.* Farmer cites Lydgate's *Elegy on Chaucer:* "My master
Chaucer now is grave;" and Steevens remarks that we have the same
quibble in *The Revenger's Tragedy*, 1608, where Vindice dresses up a
lady's skull, and says: "she has a somewhat grave look with her."

Coleridge remarks here: "How fine an effect the wit and raillery ha-
bitual to Mercutio, even struggling with his pain, give to Romeo's following speed, and at the same time so completely justifying his passionate
revenge on Tybalt!"

On the death of Mercutio, which is not from the poem or the novel,
Hallam observes: "It seems to have been necessary to keep down the
other characters that they might not overpower the principal one; and
though we can by no means agree with Dryden that if S. had not killed
Mercutio, Mercutio would have killed him, there might have been some
danger of his killing Romeo. His brilliant vivacity shows the softness
of the other a little to a disadvantage."

98. *That fights by the book*, etc. See on ii. 4. 22 above.

99. *I was hurt*, etc. See p. 29 above.

105. *Your houses.* "The ineffectual attempt to repeat his former sentence, 'A plague o' both your houses!'—the shadowy fragment of the one
phrase being but an insubstantial representation of the other—serves
exquisitely to indicate the faint speech of the dying man, and poetically
to image his failing powers" (Clarke).

107. *My very friend.* Cf. *T. G. of V.* iii. 2. 41: "his very friend;" *M.
of V.* iii. 2. 226: "my very friends and countrymen," etc.

110. *Cousin.* Some editors adopt the "kinsman" of 1st quarto.

114. *Aspir'd.* Not elsewhere used transitively by S. Cf. Chapman,
Iliad, ix.: "and aspir'd the gods' eternal seats;" Marlowe, *Tamburlaine:*
"our souls aspire celestial thrones," etc.

115. *Untimely.* Often used adverbially; as in *Macb.* v. 8. 16, *Ham.* iv.
1. 40, etc. See also v. 3. 258 below.

116. *Depend.* Impend (Schmidt). Cf. *R. of L.* 1615: "In me moe
woes than words are now depending;" and *Cymb.* iv. 3. 23: "our jealousy Doth yet depend."

120. *Respective.* Considerate. Cf. *M. of V.* v. 1. 156: "You should
have been respective," etc.

121. *Conduct.* Conductor, guide. Cf. *Temp.* v. 1. 244:

> "And there is in this business more than nature
>   Was ever conduct of;"

Rich. III. i. 1. 45: "This conduct to convey me to the Tower," etc. See
also v. 3. 116 below.

123. *For Mercutio's soul*, etc. The passage calls to mind one similar yet very different in *Hen. V.* iv. 6. 15 fol. :

> "And cries aloud, 'Tarry, dear cousin Suffolk!
> My soul shall keep thine company to heaven ;
> Tarry, sweet soul, for mine, then fly abreast,
> As in this glorious and well-foughten field
> We kept together in our chivalry !'"

127. *Consort.* Accompany. Cf. *C. of E.* i. 2. 28 : "And afterward consort you till bedtime," *J. C.* v. 1. 83 : "Who to Philippi here consorted us," etc. For the intransitive use of the word, see on 43 above.

131. *Doom thee death.* Cf. *Rich. III.* ii. 1. 102 : "to doom my brother's death ;" *T. A.* iv. 2. 114 : "The emperor, in his rage, will doom her death."

133. *Fortune's fool.* Made a fool of by fortune, the sport of fortune. Cf. *Lear*, iv. 6. 195 : "The natural fool of fortune." See also *Ham.* i. 4. 54 : "we fools of nature ;" and cf. *M. for M.* iii. 1. 11, *Macb.* ii. 1. 44, etc. Douce cites *T. of A.* iii. 6. 106 : "You fools of fortune ;" but there, as the context shows, it is used in a different sense (=you foolish followers of fortune).

139. *Discover.* Uncover, reveal. See on ii. 2. 106 above.

140. *Manage.* "Bringing about" (Schmidt) ; or we may say that *all the manage* is simply=the whole course. The word means management, administration, in *Temp.* i. 2. 70 : "the manage of my state ;" *M. of V.* iii. 4. 25 : "The husbandry and manage of my house," etc. It is especially used of horses. See *M. of V.* p. 153 or *A. Y. L.* p. 136.

150. *Spoke him fair.* Spoke gently to him. Cf. *M. N. D.* ii. 1. 199 : "Do I entice you ? do I speak you fair ?" *M. of V.* iv. 1. 275 : "Say how I lov'd you, speak me fair in death" (that is, speak well of me after I am dead), etc.

151. *Nice.* Petty, trivial. Cf. *Rich. III.* iii. 7. 175 : "nice and trivial ;" *J. C.* iv. 3. 8 : "every nice offence," etc. See also v. 2. 18 below.

154. *Take truce.* Make peace. Cf. *V. and A.* 82 : "Till he take truce with her contending tears ;" *K. John*, iii. 1. 17 : "With my vex'd spirits I cannot take a truce," etc.

Spleen. Heat, impetuosity. Cf. *K. John*, iv. 3. 97 : "thy hasty spleen ;" *Rich. III.* v. 3. 350 : "Inspire us with the spleen of fiery dragons !" etc. Cf. *M. N. D.* p. 129.

156. Coleridge observes : "This small portion of untruth in Benvolio's narrative is finely conceived."

161. *Retorts.* Throws back ; as in *T. and C.* iii. 3. 101 :

> "Heat them, and they retort that heat again
> To the first giver," etc.

165. *Envious.* Malicious ; as often. See *Rich. II.* p. 172.

167. *By and by.* Presently. See on ii. 2. 151 above, and cf. iii. 3. 76 and v. 3. 284 below.

174. *Affection makes him false.* "The charge, though produced at hazard, is very just. The author, who seems to intend the character of Benvolio as good, meant, perhaps, to show how the best minds, in a state of faction and discord, are detorted to criminal partiality" (Johnson). K

observes : "Dr. Johnson's remark upon this circumstance is worthy of his character as a moralist."

182. *Concludes.* For the transitive use (=end), cf. 2 *Hen. VI.* iii, 1. 153 : "Will not conclude their plotted tragedy."

184. *Exile.* For the accent, see Gr. 490. So also with the noun in iii. 3. 20 and v. 3, 211 below.

187. *Amerce.* Used by S. only here.

190. *Purchase out.* Cf. *buy out* in *C. of E.* i. 2. 5, *K. John,* iii. 1. 164, *Ham.* iii. 3. 60, etc.

192. *Hour.* Metrically a dissyllable, as often. Gr. 480.

194. *Mercy but murthers,* etc. Malone quotes Hale, *Memorials:* "When I find myself swayed to mercy, let me remember likewise that there is a mercy due to the country."

SCENE II.—1. *Gallop apace,* etc. Malone remarks that S. probably remembered Marlowe's *Edward II.* which was performed before 1593 :

> "Gallop apace, bright Phœbus, through the skie,
> And dusky night, in rusty iron car;
> Between you both, shorten the time, I pray,
> That I may see that most desired day;"

and Barnaby Rich's *Farewell,* 1583 : "The day to his seeming passed away so slowely that he had thought the stately steedes had bin tired that drawe the chariot of the Sunne, and wished that Phaeton had beene there with a whippe."

2. *Lodging.* Some editors substitute "mansion" from the 1st quarto.

3. *Phaethon.* For other allusions to the ambitious youth, see *T. G. of V.* iii. 1. 153, *Rich. II.* iii. 3. 178, and 3 *Hen. VI.* i. 4. 33, ii. 6. 12.

6. *That runaways' eyes may wink.* This is the great *crux* of the play, and more has been written about it than would fill a volume like this. The condensed summary of the comments upon it fills twenty-eight octavo pages of fine print in F., to which we must refer the curious reader. The early eds. have "runnawayes," "run-awayes," "run-awaies," or "run-aways." Those who retain this as a possessive singular refer it variously to Phœbus, Phaethon, Cupid, Night, the moon, Romeo, and Juliet ; those who make it a possessive plural generally understand it to mean persons running about the streets at night. No one of the former list of interpretations is at all satisfactory. The most ingenious and elaborate plea that has been made for any of them is perhaps the Rev. Mr. Halpin's in behalf of Cupid ; but, to our thinking, this has been completely refuted by W. The others merit no special attention here. Personally, we are quite well satisfied to read *runaways',* and to accept the explanation given by Hunter and adopted by Delius, Schmidt, Daniel, and others. It is the simplest possible solution, and is favoured by the *untalk'a of* that follows. W. objects to it that "*runaway* appears to have been used only to mean one who ran away, and that *runagate,* which had the same meaning then that it has now, would have suited the verse quite as well as *runaway;*" but, as Furnivall and others have noted, Cotgrave apparently uses *runaway* and *runagate* as nearly equivalent terms.*

* In a letter in the *Academy* for Nov. 30, 1878, Furnivall, after referring to his former

It is of course possible that there is some corruption in the text of the early eds., but the attempts at emendation have been far from successful. Among these are " Renomy's " (Fr. *Renommée*=Rumour), " Rumour's " (adopted by H.), " rumorous," " rumourers'," " Cynthia's," " enemies'." (Coll. MS.), " rude day's " (D.), " soon day's," " roving," " sunny day's," " curious," " envious," " sun away," " yonder," " runabouts'," " runaway spies," " runagate," etc.

10. *Civil.* Grave, sober. See *Much Ado,* p. 133, note on *Civil count.*

12. *Learn.* Teach. See *Much Ado,* p. 153, or *A. Y. L.* p. 141.

16. *Hood my unmann'd blood,* etc. The terms are taken from falconry. The hawk was *hooded* till ready to let fly at the game. Cf. *Hen. V.* iii. 7. 121 : " 't is a hooded valour ; and when it appears it will bate." An *unmanned* hawk was one not sufficiently trained to know the voice of her keeper (see on ii. 2. 159 above). To *bate* was to flutter or flap the wings, as the hawk did when unhooded and eager to fly. Cf. *T. of S.* iv. 1. 199 :

> " as we watch these kites
> That bate and beat and will not be obedient."

D. quotes Holmes, *Acad. of Armory :* " *Bate,* Bateing or Bateth, is when the Hawk fluttereth with her Wings either from Pearch or Fist, as it were striveing to get away ; also it is taken from her striving with her Prey, and not forsaking it till it be overcome ;" and Nares cites Bacon : " I would to God I were hooded, that I saw less ; or that I could perform more ; for now I am like a hawk that bates, when I see occasion of service ; but I cannot fly because I am ty'd to another's fist."

15. *Strange.* " Reserved, retiring " (Clarke). *Grown* is Rowe's emendation for the " grow " of the early eds.

17. *Come, night,* etc. Mrs. Jameson remarks : " The fond adjuration, 'Come, night, come, Romeo, *come thou day in night!*' expresses that fulness of enthusiastic admiration for her lover which possesses her whole soul ; but expresses it as only Juliet could or would have expressed it—in a bold and beautiful metaphor. Let it be remembered that, in this speech, Juliet is not supposed to be addressing an audience, nor even a confidante ; and I confess I have been shocked at the utter want of taste and refinement in those who, with coarse derision, or in a spirit of pru-

---

citations in favour of *runaways* =" runagates, runabouts." and to the fact that Ingleby and Schmidt have since given the same interpretation, adds, " But I still desire to cite an instance in which Shakspere himself renders Holinshed's ' runagates ' by his own ' runaways.' In the second edition of Holinshed's *Chronicle,* 1587, which Singer (*Shaksp.* vi. p. 53, note) shows that Shakspere used for his *Richard III.,* he found the passage (p. 756, col. 2) : ' You see further, how a company of traitors, thieves, outlaws, and *runagates,* be aiders and partakers of this feate and enterprise,' etc. And he turned it thus into verse (1st folio, p. 203) :

> ' Remember whom you are to cope withall,
> A sort of Vagabonds, Rascals, and *Run-awayes,*
> A scum of Brittaines, and base Lackey Pezants,
> Whom their o're-cloyed Country vomits forth
> To desperate Aduentures, and assur'd Destruction.
> You sleeping safe, they bring you to vnrest ;
> You hauing Lands, and blest with beauteous wiues,
> They would restraine the one, distaine the other.' "

dery, yet more gross and perverse, have dared to comment on this beautiful 'Hymn to the Night,' breathed out by Juliet in the silence and solitude of her chamber. She is thinking aloud; it is the young heart 'triumphing to itself in words.' In the midst of all the vehemence with which she calls upon the night to bring Romeo to her arms, there is something so almost infantine in her perfect simplicity, so playful and fantastic in the imagery and language, that the charm of sentiment and innocence is thrown over the whole; and her impatience, to use her own expression, is truly that of 'a child before a festival, that hath new robes and may not wear them.' It is at the very moment too that her whole heart and fancy are abandoned to blissful anticipation that the nurse enters with the news of Romeo's banishment; and the immediate transition from rapture to despair has a most powerful effect."

18. *For thou*, etc. "Indeed, the whole of this speech is imagination strained to the highest; and observe the blessed effect on the purity of the mind. What would Dryden have made of it?" (Coleridge).

20. *Black-brow'd night.* Cf. *King John*, v. 6. 17: "Why, here walk I in the black brow of night."

25. *The garish sun.* Johnson remarks: "Milton had this speech in his thoughts when he wrote in *Il Pens.* 'Till civil-suited morn appear,' and 'Hide me from day's garish eye.'" S. uses *garish* only here and in *Rich. III.* iv. 4. 89: "a garish flag."

30. *That hath new robes*, etc. Cf. *Much Ado*, iii. 2. 5: "Nay, that would be as great a soil in the new gloss of your marriage as to show a child his new coat and forbid him to wear it."

40. *Envious.* Malignant; as in i. 1. 143 and iii. 1. 165 above.

45. *But ay.* In the time of S. *ay* was commonly written and printed *I*, which explains the play upon the word here. Most editors print "but 'I'" here, but it does not seem necessary to the understanding of the quibble.

47. *Death-darting eye*, etc. The eye of the fabled cockatrice or basilisk was said to kill with a glance. Cf. *T. N.* iii. 4. 215: "they will kill one another by the look, like two cockatrices;" *Rich. III.* iv. 1. 55:

> "A cockatrice hast thou hatch'd to the world,
> Whose unavoided eye is murtherous," etc.

See also *Hen. V.* p. 183, note on *The fatal balls.*

51. *Determine of.* Decide. Cf. 2 *Hen IV.* iv. 1. 164:

> "To hear and absolutely to determine
> Of what conditions we shall stand upon."

See also *T. G. of V.* ii. 4. 181, *Rich. III.* iii. 4. 2, etc.

53. *God save the mark!* An exclamation of uncertain origin, commonly = saving your reverence, but sometimes, as here = God have mercy (Schmidt). Cf. 1 *Hen. IV.* i. 3. 56. So *God bless the mark!* in *M. of V.* ii. 2. 25, *Oth.* i. 1. 33, etc.

56. *Gore-blood.* Clotted blood. Forby remarks that the combination is an East-Anglian provincialism. Halliwell cites Vicars, trans. of *Virgil*, 1632: "Whose hollow wound vented much black gore-bloud."

Swounded. The reading of the 1st quarto; the other early eds. have "sounded," except the 5th quarto ("swouned") and the 4th folio ("swooned"). Similar variations of spelling are found in other passages; as in *M. N. D.* ii. 2. 154, where the 1st quarto has "swoun," the 1st folio "sound," the 2d quarto and later folios "swound." In *R. of L.* 1486 we have "swounds" rhyming with "wounds."

57. *Bankrupt.* The early eds. have "banckrout" or "bankrout," as often in other passages. K. and Delius retain the latter form. See Wb. s. v.

64. *Contrary.* For the accent of the word in S. see *Ham.* p. 227.

66. *Dear-lov'd.* From 1st quarto; the other early eds. and some modern ones have "dearest."

73. *O serpent heart*, etc. Cf. *Macb.* i. 5. 66:

> "look like the innocent flower,
> But be the serpent under it."

Malone cites *K. John*, ii. 1. 68, and *Hen. VIII.* iii. 1. 145.

Mrs. Jameson remarks on this passage: "This highly figurative and antithetical exuberance of language is defended by Schlegel on strong and just grounds; and to me also it appears natural, however critics may argue against its taste or propriety.* The warmth and vivacity of Juliet's fancy, which plays like a light over every part of her character—which animates every line she utters—which kindles every thought into a picture, and clothes her emotions in visible images, would naturally, under strong and unusual excitement, and in the conflict of opposing sentiments, run into some extravagance of diction."

76. *Dove-feather'd raven.* The reading of Theo. The 2d quarto has "Rauenous douefeatherd rauē" ("Rauen" in 3d quarto); the 1st folio, "Rauenous Doue-feather'd Rauen;" the other early eds., substantially, "Rauenous Doue, feather'd rauen."

79. *A damned saint.* The reading of 4th and 5th quartos and later folios; the 2d and 3d quartos have "A dimme saint," and the 1st folio "A dimne saint."

83. *Was ever book*, etc. Cf. i. 3. 66 above.

84. *O that deceit*, etc. Cf. *Temp.* i. 2. 468: "If the ill spirit have so fair a house," etc.

85–87. These lines form two in the early eds., the first ending with *men.* The text is Capell's. Fleay plausibly suggests:

> "There 's no trust,
> No faith, no honesty in men; all naught,
> All perjur'd, all dissemblers, all forsworn."

87. *Naught.* Worthless, bad. See *A. Y. L.* p. 142.

90. *Blister'd*, etc. "Note the Nurse's mistake of the mind's audible struggle with itself for its decisions *in toto*" (Coleridge).

92. *Upon his brow*, etc. Steevens quotes Paynter: "Is it possible that under such beautie and rare comelinesse, disloyaltie and treason may have

---

* "The censure," observes Schlegel, "originates in a fanciless way of thinking, to which everything appears unnatural that does not suit its tame insipidity. Hence an idea has been formed of simple and natural pathos which consists in exclamations destitute of imagery, and nowise elevated above every-day life; but energetic passions electrify the whole mental powers, and will, consequently, in highly favoured natures, express themselves in an ingenious and figurative manner."

their siedge and lodging?" The image of shame *sitting* on the brow is not in Brooke's poem. See p. 15 above.

98. *Poor my lord*. See Gr. 13.

Smooth. The figurative meaning of the word is sufficiently explained by the following *mangle*. Cf. i. 5. 94 above. Malone cites Brooke's poem:

> "Ah cruell murthering tong, murthrer of others fame:
> How durst thou once attempt to tooch the honor of his name?
>
>   *   *   *   *   *   *
>
> Whether shall he (alas) poore banishd man, now flye?
> What place of succor shall he seeke beneth the starry skye?
> Synce she pursueth him, and him defames by wrong:
> That in distres should be his fort, and onely rampier strong."

108. *Worser*. Cf. ii. 3. 29 above. Gr. 11.

116. *Sour woe delights*, etc. That is, "misfortunes never come single." Cf. *Ham.* iv. 5. 78:

> "When sorrows come, they come not single spies,
>   But in battalions."

117. *Needly will*. Needs must. Clarke remarks: "S. has here coined an excellent word, . . . which it would be well to adopt into our language as good English."

120. *Modern*. Trite, commonplace; the usual, if not the only meaning of the word in S. See *A. Y. L.* p. 167 or *Macb.* p. 243.

121. *Rearward*. Cf. *Sonn.* 90. 6:

> "Ah! do not, when my heart hath scap'd this sorrow,
> Come in the rearward of a conquer'd woe"

(that is, to attack me anew); and *Much Ado*, iv. 1. 128:

> "Myself would, on the rearward of reproaches
> Strike at thy life."

The metaphor is a military one, referring to a rear-guard or reserve which follows up the attack of the vanguard or of the main army. Coll. conjectures "rear-word" here, but no change is called for.

130. *Wash they*, etc. That is, let them wash, etc. We follow St., D., the Camb. ed., K., and F. in adopting the pointing of the 3d and 4th quartos and the folios. Most of the other eds. put an interrogation mark after *tears*, as the 2d quarto does.

137. *Wot*. Know. See *M. N. D.* p. 171.

SCENE III.—1. *Fearful*. Full of fear, afraid. See *J. C.* p. 175, note on *With fearful bravery*.

2. *Parts*. Gifts, endowments. Cf. iii. 5. 181 below: "honourable parts."

7. *Sour company*. Cf. "sour woe" in iii. 2. 116 above, "sour misfort- une" in v. 3. 82 below, etc.

10. *Vanish'd*. A singular expression, which Massinger has imitated in *The Renegado*, v. 5: "Upon those lips from which those sweet words vanish'd." In *R. of L.* 1041 the word is used of the breath. Heath would read "issued" here.

20. *Exile*. For the variable accent (cf. 13 above), see Gr. 490.

21. *Banishment.* From 1st quarto ; the other early eds. have "banished."

26. *Rush'd aside the law.* "Openly and with partial eagerness eluded the law" (Schmidt). Capell conjectured "push'd," and the Coll. MS. gives "brush'd."

28. *Dear mercy.* True mercy. Cf. *Much Ado,* i. 1. 129 : "A dear happiness to women," etc. The 1st quarto has "meer" (mere), which would mean quite the same. See *Temp.* p. 111 or *J. C.* p. 129.

29. *Heaven is here,* etc. "All deep passions are a sort of atheists, that believe no future" (Coleridge).

33. *Validity.* Value, worth. Cf. *A. W.* v. 3. 192 :

> "O, behold this ring,
> Whose high respect and rich validity
> Did lack a parallel."

See also *T. N.* i. 1. 12 and *Lear,* i. 1. 83.

34. *Courtship.* Courtesy, courtliness (as in *L. L. L.* v. 2. 363 : "Trim gallants, full of courtship and of state," etc.) ; with the added idea of privilege of courting or wooing. For a similar blending of the two meanings, cf. *A. Y. L.* iii. 2. 364.

38. *Who.* Needlessly changed to "Which" by Pope. Cf. i. 1. 104 and i. 4. 97 above. Gr. 264.

40–43. *But Romeo . . . death?* We follow W., F., and Daniel in the arrangement of these lines. The 2d quarto (followed by the other quartos) reads :

> "This may flyes do, when I from this must flie,
> And sayest thou yet, that exile is not death?
> But *Romeo* may not, he is banished.
> Flies may do this, but I from this must flie :
> They are freemen, but I am banished."

The 1st folio (followed by the other folios, Rowe, Theo., Warb., and Johnson) gives :

> "This may Flies doe, when I from this must flie
> And saist thou yet, that exile is not death?
> But *Romeo* may not, hee is banished."

For the various reconstructions of the lines in modern eds. we must refer the curious reader to F.

In 42 Daniel "strongly suspects" that *They are free men* should be "They free remain." He does not see the bitter sarcasm in *free men.*

45. *Mean.* Often used by S. in the singular, though oftener in the plural. Cf. *W. T.* iv. 4. 89 :

> "Yet nature is made better by no mean,
> But nature makes that mean." etc.

See also v. 3. 240 below.

48. *Howling attends.* The 1st folio has "Howlings attends ;" the later folios and many modern eds. "Howlings attend."

49. *Confessor.* For the accent, see on ii. 6. 21 above.

52. *Thou fond,* etc. The reading of 1st quarto. Some eds. follow the 4th quarto in reading "Thou fond mad man, hear me a little speak." *Fond*=foolish ; as often in S. See *M. N. D.* p. 163 or *M. of V.* p. 152.

55. *Adversity's sweet milk.*   Cf. *Macb.* iv. 3. 98 : "the sweet milk of concord," etc.

59. *Displant.*   Transplant.   S. uses the word only here and in *Oth.* ii. 1. 283 : "the displanting of Cassio."

60. *Prevails.*   Avails.   Cf. *unprevailing* in *Ham.* i. 2. 107, and see note in our ed. p. 180.

62. *When that.*   See Gr. 287.

63. *Dispute.*   That is, reason.   The verb is used transitively in a similar sense in *W. T.* iv. 4. 411 and *Macb.* iv. 3. 220.

70. *Taking the measure*, etc.   Cf. *A. Y. L.* ii. 6. 2 : "Here lie I down, and measure out my grave."

77. *Simpleness.*   Folly.   Elsewhere it is=simplicity, innocence ; as in *Much Ado*, iii. 1. 70, *M. N. D.* v. 1. 83, etc.   The 1st quarto and many modern eds. have "wilfulness."

85. *O woful sympathy*, etc.   The early eds. give this speech to the Nurse.   Farmer transferred it to the Friar, and is followed by most of the modern eds.   Ulrici, Delius, and Daniel defend the old arrangement.

90. *O.*   Grief, affliction.   For its use=circle, etc., see *Hen. V.* p. 144 and *M. N. D.* p. 165.   In *Lear*, i. 4. 212, it means a cipher.

94. *Old.*   Practised, experienced.   Cf. *L. L. L.* ii. 1. 254, v. 2. 552, *T. and C.* i. 2. 128, ii. 2. 75, etc.

98. *Conceal'd.*   "Secretly married" (Schmidt).

103. *Level.*   Aim ; as in *Sonn.* 117. 11 : "the level of your frown ;" *Hen. VIII.* i. 2. 2 : "the level Of a full-charg'd confederacy," etc.   Cf. the use of the verb in *Much Ado*, ii. 1. 239, *Rich. III.* iv. 4. 202, etc.

109. *Art thou*, etc.   Cf. Brooke's poem :

> "Art thou quoth he a man? thy shape saith, so thou art:
> Thy crying and thy weping eyes, denote a womans hart.
> For manly reason is quite from of thy mynd outchased,
> And in her stead affections lewd, and fancies highly placed.
> So that I stoode in doute this howre (at the least)
> If thou a man, or woman wert, or els a brutish beast."

113. *Ill-beseeming.*   Cf. i. 5. 72 above.

115. *Better temper'd.*   Of better temper or quality.   Cf. *2 Hen. IV.* i. 1. 115 : "the best temper'd courage in his troops."

118. *Doing damned hate.*   Cf. v. 2. 20 below : "do much danger," etc. Gr. 303.

119. *Why rail'st thou*, etc.   Malone remarks that Romeo has not here railed on his birth, etc., though in Brooke's poem he does :

> "And then, our Romeus, with tender handes ywrong:
> With voyce, with plaint made horce, w^t sobs, and with a foltring tong.
> Renewd with nouel mone the dolours of his hart,
> His outward dreery cheere bewrayde, his store of inward smart,
> Fyrst nature did he blame, the author of his lyfe,
> In which his ioyes had been so scant, and sorrowes aye so ryfe:
> The time and place of byrth, he fiersly did reproue,
> He cryed out (with open mouth) against the starres aboue," etc.

In his reply the Friar asks :

> "Why cryest thou out on loue? why doest thou blame thy fate?
> Why dost thou so crye after death? thy life why dost thou hate?"

122. *Wit.* See on i. 4. 47 above.

127. *Digressing.* Deviating, departing. It is=transgressing in *Rich. II.* v. 3. 66 : "thy digressing son."

132. *Like powder,* etc. See on ii. 6. 10 above. Steevens remarks : "The ancient English soldiers, using match-locks instead of flints, were obliged to carry a lighted *match* hanging at their belts, very near to the wooden *flask* in which they kept their powder."

134. *And thou,* etc. "And thou torn to pieces with thine own weapons" (Johnson).

144. *Pout'st upon.* The 4th quarto has "powts upon," the 5th "poutst upon ;" the other early eds. have "puts up" or "puttest up," except the 1st quarto, which has "frownst upon."

151. *Blaze.* Make public. Cf. *blazon* in ii. 6. 26 above, and *emblaze* in *2 Hen. VI.* iv. 10. 76.

154. *Went'st forth.* For the ellipsis cf. Gr. 390.

157. *Apt unto.* Inclined to, ready for. Cf. iii, 1. 29 above.

163. *Here, sir.* Daniel suggests "Here, sir's." The 1st quarto has "Here is a Ring sir, that she bad me giue you."

166. *Here stands,* etc. "The whole of your fortune depends on this" (Johnson).

171. *Good hap.* Piece of good luck. Cf. ii. 2. 190 above.

174. *So brief to part.* To part so soon. Gr. 1 and 420.

SCENE IV.—11. *Mew'd up.* Shut up. See *M. N. D.* p. 126.

12. *Desperate.* "Overbold" (Schmidt). "I will make a *confident offer* or promise of my daughter's love" (St.).

20. *O' Thursday.* The early eds. have "A Thursday." See Gr. 140 and cf. 176.

23. *Keep no great ado.* Elsewhere in S. the phrase is, as now, *make ado.* Cf. *T. G. of V.* iv. 4. 31, 1 *Hen. IV.* ii. 4. 223, *Hen. VIII.* v. 3. 159, etc.

25. *Held him carelessly.* Cf. *3 Hen. VI.* ii. 2. 109 : "I hold thee reverently ;" *Id.* ii. i. 102 : "held thee dearly," etc.

28. *And there an end.* Cf. *T. G. of V.* i. 3. 65, ii. 1. 168, *Rich. II.* v. 1. 69, etc. See also *Much Ado*, p. 130, note on *There 's an end.*

32. *Against.* Cf. iv. 1. 113 below : "against thou shalt awake." Gr. 142.

34. *Afore me.* "By my life, by my soul" (Schmidt). Cf. *Per.* ii. 1. 84 : "Now, afore me, a handsome fellow !" So *before me,* as in *T. N.* ii. 3. 194, *Oth.* iv. 1. 149, etc.

35. *By and by.* Presently. See on ii. 2. 151 above.

SCENE V.—*Juliet's Chamber.* The scene is variously given by the editors as "The Garden" (Rowe), "Anti-room of Juliet's Chamber" (Capell), "Loggia to Juliet's Chamber" (K. and V.), "An open Gallery to Juliet's Chamber overlooking the Orchard" (D.), "Juliet's Bedchamber ; a Window open upon the Balcony" (W.), "Capulet's Orchard" (Camb. ed.), etc. As Malone remarks, Romeo and Juliet probably appeared in the balcony at the rear of the old English stage. "The scene in the

Poet's eye was doubtless the large and massy projecting balcony before one or more windows, common in Italian palaces and not unfrequent in Gothic civil architecture. The *loggia,* an open gallery, or high terrace [see cut on p. 82], communicating with the upper apartments of a palace, is a common feature in Palladian architecture, and would also be well adapted to such a scene " (V.).

4. *Nightly.* It is said that the nightingale, if undisturbed, sits and sings upon the same tree for many weeks together (Steevens). Sr. adds that this may be accounted for by the fact that the male bird sings near where the female is sitting.

Pomegranate tree. "The preference of the nightingale for the pomegranate is unquestionable. 'The nightingale sings from the pomegranate groves in the daytime,' says Russel in his account of Aleppo. A friend . . . informs us that throughout his journeys in the East he never heard such a choir of nightingales as in a row of pomegranate-trees that skirt the road from Smyrna to Boudjia. In the truth of details such as these the genius of S. is as much exhibited as in his wonderful powers of generalization " (K.).

8. *Lace.* Cf. *Macb.* ii. 3. 118 : " His silver skin lac'd with his golden blood ;" *Cymb.* ii. 2. 22 :

> "white and azure lac'd
> With blue of heaven's own tinct," etc.

See on ii. 4. 39 above. We have the word used literally in *Much Ado,* iii. 4. 20 : " laced with silver."

The severing clouds. Cf. *J. C.* ii. 1. 103 :

> "yon grey lines
> That fret the clouds are messengers of day;"*

and *Much Ado,* v. 3. 25 : " Dapples the drowsy east with spots of grey."

9. *Night's candles,* etc. Blakeway compares Sophocles, *Ajax,* 285 :

> —ἄκρας νυκτός, ἡνίχ' ἕσπεροι
> Λαμπτῆρες οὐκέτ' ᾖθον.

13. *Some meteor,* etc. Cf. 1 *Hen. IV.* ii. 4. 351 : " My lord, do you see

---

* At the meeting of the New Shakspere Society, October 11, 1878, the chairman read a paper by Mr. Ruskin on the word *fret* in this passage. The following brief outline of the paper and the comments made upon it is from the report in the London *Academy :*

"*Fret* means primarily the rippling of the cloud—as sea by wind ; secondarily, the breaking it asunder for light to come through. It implies a certain degree of vexation, some dissolution, much order, and extreme beauty. The reader should have seen 'Daybreak,' and think what is broken, and by what. The cloud of night is broken up, by Day, which breaks out, breaks in, as from heaven to earth, with a breach in the cloud wall of it. The thing that the day breaks up is partly a garment *rent,* the blanket of the dark torn to be peeped through. . . . Mr. Sanjo of Japan, Mr. E. Rose, and Mr. Hetherington described the early dawns they had seen, which bore out Shakspere's and Mr. Ruskin's descriptions of the grey light bursting through ragged gashes in the clouds ; and Mr. Harrison instanced the parallel lines in *R. and J.* iii. 5. 7, 8 :

> 'look, love, what envious streaks
> Do lace the severing clouds in yonder east,'

where the streaks of light—grey light, too ('yon grey')—are not like lace *on* the clouds, but behind and bursting through the crevices that the severing clouds leave between them, ragged-edged, fretted like lace. In colour, form, fact, the two passages correspond with nature." See on ii. 3. 1 above.

these meteors? do you behold these exhalations?" and *Id.* v. 1. 19: "an exhal'd meteor."

14. *Torch-bearer.* See on i. 4. 11 above.

19. *Yon grey.* See on 8 (and foot-note) above.

20. *The pale reflex of Cynthia's brow.* That is, the pale light of the moon shining through or reflected from the breaking clouds. *Brow* is put for face (Schmidt); as in *M. N. D.* v. 1. 11: "Helen's beauty in a brow of Egypt," etc. The passage would seem to be clear enough without explanation, but some of the editors have done their best to obscure it. Coll. says that "Cynthia's *brow* would not occasion a *pale reflex*," and therefore adopts the "bow" of his MS. corrector. Ulrici favours "bow" because "the reflex of Cynthia's *bow* properly refers only to the setting moon, whereas the reflex of Cynthia's *brow* or *eye* would indicate that the moon was just rising." He apparently forgets that it is only when the moon is near the full that she can be setting just before sunrise. If her *bow* or thin crescent could be in the west at the early dawn, the reflection of its light on the eastern clouds would hardly be perceptible. Only a rising moon could light up "the severing clouds" in the way described. The *reflection* (if we take *reflex* in that literal sense) is from their *edges*, as the light from behind falls upon them. Have these critics ever seen

> "a sable cloud
> Turn forth her silver lining on the night,"

when the moon was behind it?

21. *Nor that is not.* Gr. 406.

22. *The vaulty heaven.* Cf. *K. John,* v. 2. 52: "the vaulty top of heaven;" and *R. of L.* 119: "her vaulty prison" (that is, Night's).

29. *Division.* "Variation, modulation" (Schmidt). Cf. 1 *Hen. IV.* iii. 1. 210:

> "Sung by a fair queen in a summer's bower,
> With ravishing division, to her lute."

31. *The lark,* etc. The toad having beautiful eyes, and the lark very ugly ones, it was a popular tradition that they had changed eyes (Warb.).

34. *Hunts-up.* The tune played to wake and collect the hunters (Steevens). Cf. Drayton, *Polyolbion:* "But hunts-up to the morn the feather'd sylvans sing;" and again in *Third Eclogue:* "Time plays the hunts-up to thy sleepy head." We have the full form in *T. A.* ii. 2. 1: "The hunt is up, the morn is bright and grey." The term was also applied to any morning song, and especially one to a new-married woman. Cotgrave (ed. 1632) defines *resveil* as "a Hunts-up, or morning song, for a new-maried wife, the day after the mariage."

43. *My lord,* etc. From 1st quarto; the other quartos and 1st folio have "love, Lord, ay husband, friend" ("ah Husband" in later folios). *Friend* was sometimes=lover; as in *Much Ado,* v. 2. 72, *Oth.* iv. 1. 3, *A. and C.* iii. 12. 22, *Cymb.* i. 4. 74, etc. Cf. Brooke's poem, where Juliet, referring to Romeo, says:

> "For whom I am becomme vnto my selfe a foe,
> Disdayneth me, his steadfast frend, and scornes my frendship so:"

and of their parting the poet says:

plain her conduct." They appear to crowd the measure, but possibly "I will not marry yet" ("I 'll not marry yet") may count only as two feet. Cf. Gr. 497.

122. *These*, etc.   See on 105 above.

125. *The air.*   The reading of 4th and 5th quartos ; the other early eds. have "the earth," which is adopted by K., Coll., St., H., and others. H. remarks : "This is scientifically true ; poetically, it would seem better to read *air* instead of *earth*." It happens, however, that science and poetry agree here ; for it is the watery vapour in the *air* that is condensed into dew. Malone, who also says that the reading *earth* is "philosophically true," cites *R. of L.* 1226 : "But as the earth doth weep, the sun being set ;" but this only means that the earth is wet with dew. To speak of the earth as *drizzling* dew is nonsense ; we might as well say that it "drizzles rain" (*Much Ado*, iii. 3. 111). Elsewhere S. refers to the "falling" dew ; as in *K. John*, ii. 1. 285, *Henry VIII.* i. 3. 57, *Cymb.* v. 5. 351, etc.

128. *Conduit.*   Probably alluding to the human figures that spouted water in fountains.   Cf. *R. of L.* 1234 :

> "A pretty while these pretty creatures stand,
> Like ivory conduits coral cisterns filling."

See also *W. T.* v. 2. 60.

134. *Who.*   See on i. 1. 104 above.

138. *She will none.*   Cf. *M. N. D.* iii. 2. 169 : "Lysander, keep thy Hermia ; I will none," etc.

140. *Take me with you.*   Let me understand you.   Cf. 1 *Hen. IV.* ii. 4. 506 : "I would your grace would take me with you : whom means your grace ?"

143. *Wrought.*   "Not = induced, prevailed upon, but brought about, effected" (Schmidt).   Cf. *Henry VIII.* iii. 2. 311 : "You wrought to be a delegate ;" *Cor.* ii. 3. 254 : "wrought To be set high in place," etc.

148. *Chop - logic.*   Sophist.   Steevens cites *The XXIIII Orders of Knaves* : "*Choplogyk* is he that whan his mayster rebuketh his seruaunt for his defawtes, he will gyue hym xx wordes for one, or elles he wyll bydde the deuylles pater noster in scylence."

150. *Minion.*   Originally = favourite, darling (see *Macb.* p. 153), then a spoiled favourite, and hence a pert or saucy person.

151. *Thank me no thankings*, etc.   Cf. *Rich. II.* ii. 3. 87 : "Grace me no grace, nor uncle me no uncle ;" and see note in our ed. p. 185.

152. *Fettle.*   Prepare, make ready.   It is the reading of the quartos and 1st folio ; the later folios have "settle," which may be what S. wrote. He does not use *fettle* elsewhere, and the long *s* (ſ) and *f* were easily confounded in printing.

155. *Out*, etc.   "Such was the indelicacy of the age of S. that authors were not contented only to employ these terms of abuse in their own original performances, but even felt no reluctance to introduce them in their versions of the most chaste and elegant of the Greek or Roman poets. Stanyhurst, the translator of Virgil, in 1582, makes Dido call Æneas *hedge-brat, cullion,* and *tar-breech* in the course of one speech. Nay, in the interlude of *The Repentance of Mary Magdalene,* 1567, Mary

Magdalene says to one of her attendants, '*Horeson*, I beshrowe your heart, are you here?'" (Steevens). Clarke observes: "Even in these coarsely abusive terms with which the irate old man loads his daughter, how well the dramatist contrives to paint and set before our imagination the pale face of Juliet, white with suppressed feeling, and almost livid under the momentary impulse to throw herself at her father's feet and confess all."

158. *Hang thee*, etc. "We see here the root of Juliet's prevarication; irrational violence if she attempt to offer remonstrance instead of blind obedience, or if she think for a moment of honest avowal. This is the way to convert original candour of disposition into timid misprision of truth, and artlessness into artfulness" (Clarke).

164. *Lent.* The 1st quarto has "sent," which may be what S. wrote. Clarke thinks it may be a misprint for "left," as Capulet (i. 2. 14) speaks as if he had had other children.

166. *Curse.* The 1st quarto has "crosse," which W. is disposed to favour.

167. *Hilding.* See on ii. 4. 38 above.

171. *God ye god den.* See on i. 2. 56 above. The early eds., except 4th and 5th quartos, give this to the Nurse.

172. *Peace.* Theo. repeated the word for the sake of the measure. Fleay suggests "speak t' ye?" *Peace* may be metrically a dissyllable, as in *A. Y. L.* ii. 4. 70. Cf. Gr. 484.

175–177. The text of the early eds. is evidently corrupt here. The 1st quarto has:

> "*Cap:* Gods blessed mother wife it mads me,
> Day, night, early, late, at home, abroad,
> Alone, in company, waking or sleeping,
> Still my care hath beene to see her matcht."

The 2d quarto, followed by the other early eds., gives:

> "*Fa.* Gods bread, it makes me mad,
> Day, night, houre, tide, time, worke, play,
> Alone in companie, still my care hath bene
> To haue her matcht," etc.

The reading in the text is Malone's, and, as W. remarks, perhaps it "very nearly approaches to what S. wrote on the revision of the play." Ulrici considers that the broken measure of the 2d quarto text "admirably suits old Capulet's blustering outburst of rage, and the imperfection thereby becomes an excellence;" but elsewhere the old fellow, though equally irate, raves in good verse enough.

180. *Train'd.* From 1st quarto; the 2d quarto has "liand," and the other early eds. "allied."

181. *Stuff'd*, etc. See *Much Ado*, p. 119. For *parts*, cf. iii. 3. 2 above.

184. *Mammet.* Puppet, doll. Cf. 1 *Hen. IV.* ii. 3. 95: "To play with mammets." The word is also written *mawmet*, and, according to Trench (see also Wb.), is a contraction of *Mahomet.* Minsheu makes it a diminutive of *mam*—"quasi dicat parvam matrem, seu matronulam."

In her fortune's tender. That is, when good fortune presents itself to her (Clarke). Cf. iii. 4. 12 above.

189. *Use.* See *A. Y. L.* p. 156.

190. *Lay hand on heart, advise.* Consider it seriously. Cf. Brooke's poem :

> "Aduise thee well, and say that thou art warned now.
> And thinke not that I speake in sporte, or mynd to breake my vowe."

198. *Sweet my mother.* Cf. iii. 2. 98 : "Ah, poor my lord," etc. Gr. 13.

212. *Faith, here 't is,* etc. S. here follows Brooke's poem :

> "She setteth foorth at large the fathers furious rage,
>   And eke she prayseth much to her the second mariage ;
>   And County Paris now she praiseth ten times more,
> By wrong, then she her selfe by right had Romeus praysde before," etc.

Mrs. Jameson remarks : "The old woman, true to her vocation, and fearful lest her share in these events should be discovered, counsels her to forget Romeo and marry Paris ; and the moment which unveils to Juliet the weakness and baseness of her confidante is the moment which reveals her to herself. She does not break into upbraidings ; it is no moment for anger ; it is incredulous amazement, succeeded by the extremity of scorn and abhorrence, which takes possession of her mind. She assumes at once and asserts all her own superiority, and rises to majesty in the strength of her despair."

220. *Green.* We have green eyes again in *M. N. D.* v. 1. 342 : "His eyes were green as leeks." Steevens cites *The Two Noble Kinsmen,* v. 1 : "With that rare green eye." Clarke remarks : "The brilliant touch of green visible in very light hazel eyes, and which gives wonderful clearness and animation to their look, has been admiringly denoted by various poets from time immemorial." Plautus, in his *Curculio,* speaks of a man "cum . . . oculis herbeis." In a sonnet by Drummond of Hawthornden, the gods are represented as debating of what colour a beauty's eyes shall be. Mars and Apollo vote for black ;

> "Chaste Phœbe spake for purest azure dyes,
>   But Jove and Venus green about the light,
>   To frame thought best, as bringing most delight,
> That to pin'd hearts hope might for aye arise."

Cf. Longfellow, *The Spanish Student:* "Ay, soft emerald eyes ;" and again :

> "in her tender eyes
> Just that soft shade of green we sometimes see
> In evening skies."

In a note on the former passage, the poet says : "The Spaniards, with good reason, consider this colour of the eyes as beautiful, and celebrate it in song ; as, for example, in the well-known *Villancico*

> 'Ay ojuelos verdes,
> ay los mis ojuelos,
> ay hagan los cielos
> que de mí te acuerdes !
>
> *   *   *   *
>
> Tengo confianza
> de mis verdes ojos.'

Dante speaks of Beatrice's eyes as emeralds (*Purgat.* xxxi. 116). Lami says in his *Annotazioni,* 'Erano i suoi occhi d' un turchino verdiccio, simile a quel del mare.'"

221. *Beshrew.* See on ii. 5. 51 above.

225. *Here.* Hanmer would read "hence ;" but, as Johnson observes, *here* may be=in this world.

233. *Ancient damnation.* Schmidt suggests that this may be "the abstract for the concrete=old sinner." Steevens cites *The Malcontent,* 1604 : "out, you ancient damnation !"

235. *Is it more sin,* etc. Mrs. Jameson remarks : "It appears to me an admirable touch of nature, considering the master-passion which, at this moment, rules in Juliet's soul, that she is as much shocked by the nurse's dispraise of her lover as by her wicked, time-serving advice. This scene is the crisis in the character ; and henceforth we see Juliet assume a new aspect. The fond, impatient, timid girl puts on the wife and the woman : she has learned heroism from suffering, and subtlety from oppression. It is idle to criticise her dissembling submission to her father and mother ; a higher duty has taken place of that which she owed to them ; a more sacred tie has severed all others. Her parents are pictured as they are, that no feeling for them may interfere in the slightest degree with our sympathy for the lovers. In the mind of Juliet there is no struggle between her filial and her conjugal duties, and there ought to be none."

ACT IV.

SCENE I.—3. *And I am nothing slow to slack his haste.* Paris here seems to say the opposite of what he evidently means, and various attempts have been made to explain away the inconsistency. Johnson thinks it may mean, "His haste shall not be abated by my slowness ;" but is inclined to read "back his haste." K. says it means "nothing slow (so as) to slack his haste." Coll. would change *nothing* to "something." We are satisfied that it is one of the peculiar cases of "double negative" discussed by Schmidt in his Appendix, p. 1420, though he does not give it there. "The idea of negation was so strong in the poet's mind that he expressed it in more than one place, unmindful of his canon that 'your four negatives make your two affirmatives.'" Cf. *Lear,* ii. 4. 142 :

> "You less know how to value her desert
> Than she to scant ["slack" in quartos] her duty ;"

that is, you are more inclined to depreciate her than she to scant her duty. See also *A. Y. L.* p. 156, note on *No more do yours.*

5. *Uneven.* Indirect. Cf. the use of *even* in *Ham.* ii. 2. 298 : "be even and direct with me," etc. Sometimes the word is=perplexing, embarrassing ; as in 1 *Hen. IV.* i. 1. 50 : "uneven and unwelcome news," etc.

11. *Marriage.* A trisyllable here ; as in *M. of V.* ii. 9. 13, etc. Gr. 479.

16. *Slow'd.* The only instance of the verb in S. Steevens cites Sir A. Gorges, *Lucan :* "thereby my march to slow."

20. *That may be must be.* That *may be* of yours must be. Some eds. print "may be, must be."

29. *Abus'd.* Marred, disfigured.

31. *Spite.* Cf. i. 5. 60 above.

38. *Evening mass.* Ritson, H., and W. say that Juliet means *vespers*, as there is no such thing as *evening mass.* St. expresses surprise that S. has fallen into this error, since he elsewhere shows a familiarity with the usages of the Roman Catholic Church. It is the critics who are in error, not S. It is possible, of course, that here he may use *mass* "in the general sense of *service*" (Clarke); but there *is* such a thing as *evening mass*, and S. may have been aware of it. Walafrid Strabo (*De Rebus Eccles.* xxiii.) says: "Tempus Missæ faciendæ interdum ante meridiem, interdum circa nonam, aliquando *ad vesperam.*" Amalarius, Bishop of Trèves (*De Eccles. Off.* iv. 40), says: "Addidimus propter nostram consuetudinem inolitam rationabiliter posse Missam celebrari *hora nona*, quia tunc Dominus emisit spiritum;" and he specifies Lent as the season for this hour. The *Generales Rubricæ* allow this at other times in the year: "In Adventu, Quadragesima, iv. Temporibus, etiam infra octavam Pentecostes, et Vigiliis quæ jejunantur, quamvis sint dies solemnes, Missa de tempore debet cantari post nonam." In Winkles's *French Cathedrals*, we are told that, on the occasion of the marriage of Henrietta of France, daughter of Henry IV., with the Duke of Chevreuse, as proxy for Charles I. of England, celebrated in Notre Dame at Paris, May 11th, 1625, "mass was celebrated in the evening." See *Notes and Queries* for Apr. 29 and June 3, 1876; also M'Clintock and Strong's *Biblical Cyclopædia*, under *Mass.*

41. *God shield.* God forbid. Cf. *A. W.* i. 3. 74: "God shield you mean it not." So "Heaven shield," in *M. for M.* iii. 1. 141, etc.

Devotion is here a quadrisyllable. Gr. 479.

45. *Cure.* The reading of 1st and 5th quartos; the other early eds. have "care," which K., Delius, and Ulrici prefer. Cf. *L. L. L.* v. 2. 28: "past cure is still past care."

48. *Prorogue.* See on ii. 2. 78 above.

54. *This knife.* It was the custom of the time for ladies to wear daggers at their girdles (W.).

57. *The label.* The seal appended by a slip to a deed, according to the custom of the day. In *Rich. II.* v. 2. 56, the Duke of York discovers, by the depending seal, a covenant which his son has made with the Duke of Aumerle (Malone). In *Cymb.* v. 5. 430 *label* is used for the deed itself.

60. *Of.* Walker (vol. ii. p. 172) cites this as an example of the metrical accentuation of the preposition. He does not seem to be aware that the trochee may take the place of the iambus in English heroic verse, and especially when, as here, followed by a spondee. *Therefore* is accented on the last syllable (see Gr. 490), but *of* should *not* be accented.*

---

* Many examples of the trochee followed by the spondee may be found in Pope and other poets, and they add to the music of the verse by breaking up its monotony. Cf. the *Essay on Criticism*, 366:

ant new Ballad of Two Lovers: "Hey hoe! my heart is full of woe (Steevens).

100. *Dump.* A melancholy strain in music. Calling it *merry* is a joke of Peter's. See *Much Ado,* p. 137, note on *Dumps.*

107. *Gleek.* Scoff. Cf. 1 *Hen. VI.* iii. 2. 123: "Now where's the Bastard's braves, and Charles his gleeks?" For the verb, see *M. N. D.* p. 159. *To give the gleek* was "to pass a jest upon, to make a person ridiculous" (Nares).

It is impossible to say what is the joke in *give you the minstrel,* unless it is a play upon *gleeman,* a minstrel. The reply of the musician may perhaps mean "that he will retort by calling Peter the servant to the minstrel" (W.).

111. *I will carry no crotchets.* I will bear none of your whims; with a play on *crotchets,* as in *Much Ado,* ii. 3. 58. Cf. *carry coals* in i. 1. 1 above. The play on *note* is obvious.

116. *Dry-beat.* See on iii. 1. 77 above, and cf. quotation in note on i. 1. 54.

119. *When griping grief,* etc. From a poem by Richard Edwards, in the *Paradise of Daintie Deuises.* See also Percy's *Reliques.*

123. *Catling.* A small string of *catgut.* Cf. *T. and C.* iii. 3. 306: "unless the fiddler Apollo get his sinews to make catlings on."

125. *Pretty.* From 1st quarto; corrupted in the other early eds. into "Prates," "Pratest," or "Pratee." The Coll. MS. gives "Thou pratest." Ulrici defends "Prates" as the plural of *prate*=gabble! Mommsen ridicules this, and suggests "Prat'ee," which is "formed like *look'ee, hark'ee, think'ee!*" These German critics are troubled by *pretty,* because Peter does not intend to praise; and irony, they say, would be out of place. It is simply a jocose patronizing expression=That's not bad in its way, but you haven't hit it.

Rebeck. A kind of three-stringed fiddle. Cf. Milton, *L' All.* 94: "And the jocund rebecks sound," etc.

136. *Jack.* See on iii. 1. 11 above; and for *stay*=wait for, on ii. 5. 36.

ACT V.

SCENE I.—1. *The flattering truth.* This is apparently=that which bears the flattering semblance of truth; but it has sorely perplexed the critics. The 1st quarto has "flattering eye," which St., D., H., and others adopt. The Coll. MS. has "flattering death," and W. "flattering sooth" (=augury, or prognostication). We fully agree with Clarke, who says: "We greatly prefer '*truth* of sleep;' poetically conveying, as it does, to our imagination the verisimilitude of visions presented during sleep. *Flattering* is here used in the sense of illusive; as in ii. 2. 141."

Some have wondered that S. here makes the presentiment a hopeful one; but as a writer in the *Cornhill Magazine* (October, 1866) remarks, the presentiment was true, but Romeo did not trust it. Had he done so, his fate would not have been so tragic.

curtains and the scene again becomes Juliet's chamber, where she is dis covered apparently dead. After the lamentations over her, the 1st quarto gives the direction, "*They all but the Nurse goe foorth, casting Rosemary on her and shutting the Curtens;*" and then follows the scene with Peter and the Musicians. The stage had no movable painted scenery. The name of the place of action in large letters was displayed on a board. "At times, when a change of scene was necessary, the audience was required to suppose that the performers, who had not quitted the stage, had passed to a different spot. A bed thrust forth showed that the stage was a bed-chamber; and a table with pen and ink indicated that it was a counting-house. Rude contrivances were employed to imitate towers, walls of towns, hell-mouths, tombs, trees, dragons, etc. Trap-doors had been early in use; but to make a celestial personage ascend to the roof of the stage was more than the mechanists of those days could always accomplish"* (D.).

SCENE IV.—2. *Pastry.* That is, the room where the paste was made (Malone). Cf. *pantry* (Fr. *paneterie*, from *pain*), the place where bread is kept, etc. St. quotes *A Floorish upon Fancie*, 1582:

> "Now having seene all this, then shall you see hard by
> The pastrie, mealehouse, and the roome whereas the coales do ly."

Nares cites Howell, *Letters*: "he was so amazd that he missd his way, and so struck into the pastry," etc. For the double meaning of the word, cf. *spicery* (Fr. *épicerie*), which was used both for the material (*Rich. III.* iv. 4. 424) and the place where it was kept. See Wb.

4. *Curfew-bell.* As the curfew was rung in the evening, the only way to explain this is to assume that it means "the bell ordinarily used for that purpose" (Schmidt). Nares says: "At the regular time it probably was called simply the *curfew;* at others, if it was known that the same bell was used, it might be said that the *curfew-bell* had rung."

5. *Baked meats.* "Pastry" (Schmidt). S. uses the term only here and in *Ham.* i. 2. 180. Nares says that it formerly meant "a meat pie, or perhaps any other pie." He cites Cotgrave, who defines *pastisserie* as "all kind of pies or bak'd meats;" and Sherwood (English supplement to Cotgrave), who renders "bak'd meats" by *pastisserie.* Cf. *The White Devil:*

> "You speak as if a man
> Should know what fowl is coffin'd in a bak'd meat
> Afore it is cut up;"

that is, what fowl is under the crust of the pie. Johnson does not recognize this meaning of *baked meats* in his *Dict.*, and none of the editors of S. refer to it.

Good Angelica. This probably means Lady Capulet, not the Nurse.

6. *Go, you cot-quean,* etc. Sr., V., H., and Keightley give this speech to Lady Capulet; on the ground that the Nurse is not present, having been sent for spices. It has also been suggested that a servant would not

---

* A stage direction at the end of Greene's *Alphonsus* is, "*Exit Venus; or, if you can conveniently, let a chair come down from the top of the stage and draw her up.*"

Receptacle. For the accent, cf. *T. A.* i. 1. 92 : "O sacred receptacle of my joys !" Gr. 492.

43. *Festering.* Corrupting ; as in *Hen. V.* iv. 3. 88 and *Sonn.* 94. 14.

47. *Mandrakes'.* The plant *Atropa mandragora* (cf. *Oth.* iii. 3. 130 and *A. and C.* i. 5. 4, where it is called "mandragora"), the root of which was thought to resemble the human figure, and when torn from the earth to utter shrieks which drove those mad who heard them. Cf. *2 Hen. VI.* iii. 2. 310: "Would curses kill, as doth the mandrake's groans," etc. Steevens quotes Webster, *Duchess of Malfi :*

> "I have this night digg'd up a mandrake
> And am grown mad with it;"

The Atheist's Tragedy, 1611:

> "The cries of mandrakes never touch'd the ear
> With more sad horror, than that voice does mine;"

A Christian Turned Turk, 1612:

> "I 'll rather give an ear to the black shrieks
> Of mandrakes," etc.

Coles, in his *Art of Simpling,* says that witches "take likewise the roots of mandrake, . . . and make thereof an ugly image, by which they represent the person on whom they intend to exercise their witchcraft." The plant was of repute also in medicine, as a soporific (see the passages noted above in which it is called *mandragora*) and for sundry other purposes. Sir Thomas More observes that "Mandragora is an herbe, as phisycions saye, that causeth folke to slepe, and therein to have many mad fantastical dreames." How the root could be got without danger is explained by Bullein, in his *Bulwark of Defence against Sicknesse,* 1575: "Therefore they did tye some dogge or other lyving beast unto the roote thereof wythe a corde, and digged the earth in compasse round about, and in the meane tyme stopped their own eares for feare of the terreble shriek and cry of this Mandrack. In whych cry it doth not only dye it selfe, but the feare thereof kylleth the dogge or beast which pulleth it out of the earth."

49. *Distraught.* Distracted. S. uses the word again in *Rich. III.* iii. 5. 4 : "distraught and mad with terror." Elsewhere he has *distracted* (as in *Temp.* v. i. 12, *Macb.* ii. 3. 110, etc.) or *distract* (as in *J. C.* iv. 3. 155, *Ham.* iv. 5. 2, etc.). Spenser has *distraught* often ; as in *F. Q.* iv. 3. 48 : "Thus whilest their minds were doubtfully distraught ;" *Id.* iv. 7. 31 : "His greedy throte, therewith in two distraught" (where it is=drawn apart, its original sense), etc.

58. *Romeo, I come,* etc. Coleridge remarks : "Shakespeare provides for the finest decencies. It would have been too bold a thing for a girl of fifteen ; but she swallows the draught in a fit of fright."

The 1st quarto has here the stage-direction, "*She fals vpon her bed within the Curtaines.*" The ancient stage was divided by curtains, called *traverses,* which were a substitute for sliding scenes. Juliet's bed was behind these curtains, and when they were closed in front of the bed the stage was supposed to represent the hall in Capulet's house for the next scene. When he summons the Nurse to call forth Juliet, she opens the

15. *Thrills.* For the ellipsis, see Gr. 244. This instance is somewhat peculiar from the fact that the relative is expressed in the next line. We should expect "thrilling" or "And almost."

23. *Lie thou there.* See on iv. 1. 54 above. Moreover, as Steevens notes, *knives*, or daggers, were part of the accoutrements of a bride. Cf. Dekker, *Match me in London:* "See at my girdle hang my wedding knives!" and *King Edward III.,* 1599: "Here by my side do hang my wedding knives," etc. D. remarks that the omission of the word *knife* "is peculiarly awkward, as Juliet has been addressing the vial just before;" but S. wrote for the stage, where the action would make the reference perfectly clear.

29. *Tried.* Proved; as in *J. C.* iv. 1. 28, *Ham.* i. 3. 62, etc.

34. *Healthsome.* Wholesome; used by S. only here.

36. *Like.* Likely; as often. See *Ham.* p. 186.

39. *As in a vault,* etc. *As* is here = to wit, namely. Cf. *Ham.* i. 4. 25, etc. Steevens remarks here: "This idea was probably suggested to S. by his native place. The charnel at Stratford-upon-Avon is a very large one, and perhaps contains a greater number of bones than are to be found in any other repository of the same kind in England." This charnel-house (removed since Steevens's day) is shown in the accompanying cut.

STRATFORD CHURCH, EAST END, WITH CHARNEL-HOUSE.

SCENE II.—2. *Twenty cunning cooks.* Ritson says : " Twenty cooks for half a dozen guests ! Either Capulet has altered his mind strangely, or S. forgot what he had just made him tell us " [iii. 4. 27]. But, as K. remarks, "Capulet is evidently a man of ostentation ; but his ostentation, as is most generally the case, is covered with a thin veil of indifference." Cf. i. 5. 120 : " We have a trifling foolish banquet towards ;" and iii. 4. 23 : " We 'll keep no great ado,—a friend or two."

According to an entry in the books of the Stationers' Company for 1560, the preacher was paid six shillings and twopence for his labour ; the minstrel, twelve shillings ; and the cook, fifteen shillings. But, as Ben Jonson tells us, a master cook is

> "a man of men
> For a professor ; he designs, he draws,
> He paints, he carves, he builds, he fortifies,
> Makes citadels of curious fowl and fish.
>   *   *   *   *   *
> He is an architect, an engineer,
> A soldier, a physician, a philosopher,
> A general mathematician."

6. '*T is an ill cook*, etc. Steevens quotes Puttenham, *Arte of English Poesie,* 1589 :

> "As the old cocke crowes so doeth the chick :
>   A bad cooke that cannot his owne fingers lick."

14. *Harlotry.* S. uses the noun only in this concrete sense : literally in *Oth.* iv. 2. 239 ; and in a loose contemptuous way, as here (=silly wench), in 1 *Hen. IV.* iii. 1. 198 : " a peevish, self-willed harlotry, one that no persuasion can do good upon." For *peevish*=foolish, childish, see *Hen. V.* p. 171.

17. *Learned me.* Taught myself, learned ; not elsewhere used reflexively by S. Cf. iii. 2. 12 above.

26. *Becomed.* Becoming. Cf. "lean-look'd "=lean-looking in *Rich. II.* ii. 4. 11 ; and see Gr. 294 and 374.

33. *Closet.* Chamber ; as in *Ham.* ii. 1. 77, iii. 2. 344, iii. 3. 27, etc. Cf. *Matt.* vi. 6.

34. *Sort.* Select. Cf. iii. 5. 108 above.

37. *We 'll to church.* See *Much Ado*, p. 134, note on *To go to church.*

38. *Short in our provision.* Cf. *Lear*, ii. 4. 208 :

> " I am now from home, and out of that provision
>   Which shall be needful for your entertainment."

41. *Deck up her.* The transposition is most common when the pronoun is emphatic ; and in 45 just below, the folio reading, " prepare him up," is on this account to be preferred to the " prepare up him " of the quartos. The rule is not so invariable that we are justified in making a change when, as here, all the early eds. agree in the reading.

SCENE III.—5. *Cross* (Schmidt). Perverse. Cf. *Hen. VIII.* iii. 2. 214

> "what cross devil
> Made me put this main secret in the packet
> I sent the king ?"

8. *Behoveful.* Befitting ; used by S. nowhere else.

be broad daylight on an Italian summer morning. Maginn's three o'clock is none too early for v. 3 ; and since we can hardly send Juliet to bed before nine in the evening, *thirty* hours is the most that can be allowed for the interval, unless we add another day and accept the fifty-two of Maginn. But this does not seem required by anything in act v.—not even by the "two days buried" of v. 3. 176, for Thursday would be the second day that she had lain in the tomb. The marriage was to be early on Wednesday morning, and the funeral took its place. Balthasar "presently took post" (v. 1. 21) to tell the news to Romeo at Mantua, less than twenty-five miles distant. He arrives before evening (cf. v. 1. 4 : "all this day," which indicates the time), and Romeo at once says, "I will hence *to-night.*" He has ample time to make his preparations and to reach Verona before two o'clock the next morning. He has been at the tomb only half an hour or so (v. 3. 130) before the Friar comes. It must have been near midnight (see v. 2. 24) when Friar John returned to Laurence's cell ; so that even if he had not been dispatched to Mantua until that morning, he would have had time to go and return, but for his unexpected detention. We see no difficulty, therefore, in assuming that the drama closes on Thursday morning ; the difficulty would be in prolonging the time to the next morning without making the action drag.

110. *In thy best robes,* etc. Malone remarks : "The Italian custom here alluded to, of carrying the dead body to the grave richly dressed and with the face *uncovered* (which is not mentioned by Painter) S. found particularly described in *Romeus and Juliet :*

> 'Now throughout Italy this common vse they haue,
>   That all the best of euery stocke are earthed in one graue ;
>   *   *   *   *   *   *
> An other vse there is, that whosoeuer dyes,
> Borne to their church with open face vpon the beere he lyes,
> In wonted weede attyrde, not wrapt in winding sheete.' "

Cf. *Ham.* iv. 5. 164 : "They bore him barefac'd on the bier."

K. remarks that thus the maids and matrons of Italy are still carried to the tomb ; and he quotes Rogers, *Italy :*

> "And lying on her funeral couch,
> Like one asleep, her eyelids closed, her hands
> Folded together on her modest breast
> As 't were her nightly posture, through the crowd
> She came at last—and richly, gaily clad,
> As for a birthday feast."

114. *Drift.* Scheme. Cf. ii. 3. 55 above.

119. *Inconstant toy.* Fickle freak or caprice. Cf. *Ham.* i. 3. 5 : "a fashion and a toy in blood ;" *Id.* 1. 4. 75 : "toys of desperation ;" *Oth.* iii. 4. 156 : "no jealous toy," etc. *Inconstant toy* and *womanish fear* are both from Brooke's poem :

> "Cast of from thee at once the weede of womannish dread,
>   With manly courage arme thy selfe from heele vnto the head ;
>   *   *   *   *   *   *
> God graunt he so confirme in thee thy present will,
> That no inconstant toy thee let thy promesse to fulfill."

121. *Give me, give me !* Cf. *Macb.* i. 3. 5 : " 'Give me,' quoth I."

122. *Get you gone.* See Gr. 296.

But thou shalt lye as she that dyeth in a traunce :
Thy kinsmen and thy trusty frendes shall wayle the sodain chaunce ;
The corps then will they bring to graue in this church yarde,
Where thy forefathers long agoe a costly tombe preparde,
Both for them selfe and eke for those that should come after,
Both deepe it is, and long and large, where thou shalt rest, my daughter,
Till I to Mantua sende for Romeus, thy knight ;
Out of the tombe both he and I will take thee forth that night."

97. *Surcease.* Cf. *R. of L.* 1766 : " If they surcease to be that should survive ;" and *Cor.* iii. 2. 121 : " Lest I surcease to honour mine own truth." For the noun, see *Macb.* i. 7. 74.

100. *Paly.* Cf. *Hen. V.* iv. chor. 8 ; "paly flames ;" and 2 *Hen. VI.* iii. 2. 141 : " his paly lips."

105. *Two and forty hours.* See p. 15, foot-note. It is difficult to make this period agree with the time of the events that follow. Maginn says : " Juliet retires to bed on Tuesday night at a somewhat early hour. Her mother says, after she departs, ' 'T is now near night.' Say it is eleven o'clock ; forty-two hours from that hour bring us to five o'clock in the evening of Thursday ; and yet we find the time of her awakening fixed in profound darkness, and not long before the dawn. We should allow at least ten hours more, and read 'two and fifty hours,' which would fix her awakening at three o'clock in the morning, a time which has been marked in a former scene (cf. iv. 4. 4 and 21) as the approach of day." But was it on " Tuesday night " that Juliet took the sleeping-potion ? In iv. 1. 90 the Friar says to her ;

> *"Wednesday* is to-morrow:
> To-morrow night look that thou lie alone," etc.

This agrees with the preceding dates. The conversation in iii. 4 is late on Monday evening (cf. lines 5 and 18), and Lady Capulet's talk with Juliet about marrying Paris (iii. 5. 67 fol.) is early the next (Tuesday) morning. The visit to the Friar is evidently on the same day ; and the next scene (iv. 2) is in the evening of that day. Juliet comes home and tells her father that she has been to the Friar's, and is ready to marry Paris. The old man at once decides to have the wedding "to-morrow morning " (that is, Wednesday) instead of Thursday. Lady Capulet objects, but finally yields to her husband's persistency ; and so Juliet goes to her chamber, and drinks the potion on *Tuesday* evening, or twenty-four hours earlier than the Friar had directed. We need not suppose that here, as in the *M. N. D.* (see our ed. p. 122) S. has been careless in his dates ; on the contrary, as more than one critic has noted, he seems to have indicated the time very carefully throughout the play. This hastening of the wedding-day was doubtless a part of his plan, and as the Friar is notified of it, being called in to perform the ceremony, he of course understands that Juliet has anticipated the time of taking the potion, and that she will wake on *Thursday* morning instead of Friday. If so, instead of extending the "two and forty hours," as Maginn does, we need rather to shorten the interval. A writer in *Notes and Queries* (Dec. 1, 1877) suggests "two and thirty hours," that is, from nine o'clock on *Wednesday* evening to five o'clock on *Friday* morning. The days, as we have seen, should be Tuesday and Thursday ; and five o'clock would

62. *Extremes.* Extremities, sufferings. Cf. *R. of L.* 969 :

> "Devise extremes beyond extremity,
> To make him curse this cursed crimeful night;"

T. of C. iv. 2. 108 :

> "Time, force, and death,
> Do to this body what extremes you can," etc.

The meaning of the passage is, "This knife shall decide the struggle between me and my distresses" (Johnson).

64. *Commission.* Warrant, authority. Cf. *A. W.* ii. 3. 279 : "you are more saucy with lords and honourable personages than the commission of your birth and virtue gives you heraldry."

66. *Be not so long to speak.* That is, so long silent, so slow to speak.

Clarke remarks here : "The constraint, with sparing speech, visible in Juliet when with her parents, as contrasted with her free outpouring flow of words when she is with her lover, her father confessor, or her nurse—when, in short, she is her natural self and at perfect ease—is true to characteristic delineation. The young girl, the very young girl, the girl brought up as Juliet has been reared, the youthful Southern maiden, lives and breathes in every line by which S. has set her before us."

69. *As desperate,* etc. "It is interesting to observe how different is the style here, in one of Shakespeare's earlier plays, from the style in his later ones. The repetition of the word *desperate,* the precision of statement in this comparison, is utterly contrary to the conciseness, the elliptical condensedness, which we find in the comparisons from Shakespeare's hand at a later date" (Clarke).

78. *Yonder.* From 1st quarto ; "any" in the other early eds. Ulrici considers "any (no matter how high) tower" more vigorous than "from that tower there," and he "cannot perceive why Juliet must designate a particular, actual tower, since all that follows is purely imaginary ;" but to us the reference to a tower in sight seems both forcible and natural, and the transition to imaginary ordeals is equally natural.

83. *Reeky.* Reeking with foul vapours, or simply = foul, as if soiled with smoke or *reek.* Cf. *reechy* (another form of the same word) in *Much Ado,* iii. 3. 143, *Ham.* iii. 4. 184, etc. See *Ham.* p. 240.

93. *Take thou this vial,* etc. Cf. Brooke's poem :

> "Receiue this vyoll small and keepe it as thine eye ;
> And on the mariage day, before the sunne doe cleare the skye,
> Fill it with water full vp to the very brim,
> Then drinke it of, and thou shalt feele throughout eche vayne and lim
> A pleasant slumber slide, and quite dispred at length
> On all thy partes, from euery part reue all thy kindly strength ;
> Withouten mouing thus thy ydle parts shall rest,
> No pulse shall goe, ne hart once beate within thy hollow brest,

---

> "Soft is the strain when Zephyr gently blows,
> And the smooth stream in smoother numbers flows."

In the first line we have the trochee followed by the iambus ("Sòft is the stràin," not "Soft ìs "), and in the second followed by the spondee ("And the smoòth streàm," not "And thè smooth streàm"). So again in 378 just below : "Now his fierce eyes with sparkling fury glow."

3. *My bosom's lord.* That is, my heart; not Love, or Cupid, as Malone and Delius would make it. Schmidt defines it "the genius that rules my affections." Lines 3–5 seem to us only a highly poetical description of the strange new cheerfulness and hopefulness he feels—a reaction from his former depression which is like his dream of rising from the dead an emperor. The 2d quarto prints here: "My bosomes L. sits," etc.

10. *Ah me!* Elsewhere S. has "Ay me!" See *M. N. D.* p. 128.

17. *She is well.* See on iv. 5. 72 above.

18. *Capel's.* The early eds. have "*Capels;*" the modern ones generally "Capels'." The singular seems better here, on account of the omission of the article; but the plural in v. 3. 127 : "the Capels' monument." S. uses this abbreviation only twice. Cf. the quotation in note on i. 1. 24 above.

21. *Presently.* Immediately; the usual meaning in S. Cf. iv. 1. 54 and 95 above.

24. *Defy.* From 1st quarto, which has "defie my Starres;" the other early eds. have "denie you." Cf. v. 3. 111 below, and see p. 33 above.

27. *Patience.* A trisyllable, as in v. 3. 221 and 261 below. Gr. 479.

29. *Misadventure.* Mischance, misfortune; used by S. only here and in v. 3. 188 below. *Misadventured* occurs only in prol. 7 above.

36. *In.* Into. See Gr. 159.

37. *I do remember,* etc. Joseph Warton objects to the detailed description here as very improperly put into the mouth of a person agitated with such passion." "But," as K. remarks, "the mind once made up, it took a perverse pleasure in going over every circumstance that had suggested the means of mischief. All other thoughts had passed out of Romeo's mind. He had nothing left but to die; and everything connected with the means of death was seized upon by his imagination with an energy that could only find relief in words. S. has exhibited the same knowledge of nature in his sad and solemn poem of *R. of L.* where the injured wife, having resolved to wipe out her stain by death,

'calls to mind where hangs a piece
Of skilfull painting, made for Priam's Troy.'

She sees in that painting some fancied resemblance to her own position, and spends the heavy hours till her husband arrives in its contemplation." See *R. of L.* 1366 fol. and 1496 fol.

39. *Overwhelming.* Overhanging. Cf. *V. and A.* 183 : "His lowering brows o'erwhelming his fair sight." See also *Hen. V.* iii. 1. 11. For *weeds* = garments, see *M. N. D.* p. 149, and cf. quotation in note on iv. 5. 80 above.

40. *Culling of.* See Gr. 178. For *simples* = medicinal herbs, see *A. Y. L.* p. 185.

43. *An alligator stuff'd.* The 1st quarto reads : "And in the same an *Aligarta* hangs ;" the 2d, " An allegater stuft," etc. This was a regular part of the furniture of an apothecary's shop in the time of S. Nash, in his *Have With You,* etc., 1596, refers to "an apothecary's crocodile or dried alligator." Steevens says that he has met with the alligator, tortoise, etc., hanging up in the shop of an ancient apothecary at Limehouse, as well as in places more remote from the metropolis. See Hogarth,

Marriage à la Mode, plate iii. In Dutch art, as Fairholt remarks, these marine monsters often appear in representations of apothecaries' shops.

45. *A beggarly account*, etc. Cf. Brooke's poem :

"And seeking long (alac too soone) the thing he sought, he founde.
An Apothecary sate vnbusied at his doore,
Whom by his heauy countenaunce he gessed to be poore.
And in his shop he saw his boxes were but fewe,
And in his window (of his wares) there was so small a shew;
Wherfore our Romeus assuredly hath thought,
What by no frendship could be got, with money should be bought;
For nedy lacke is lyke the poore man to compell
To sell that which the cities lawe forbiddeth him to sell.
Then by the hand he drew the nedy man apart,
And with the sight of glittring gold inflamed hath his hart :
Take fiftie crownes of gold (quoth he) I geue them thee.

*   *   *   *   *   *   *

Fayre syr (quoth he) be sure this is the speeding gere,
And more there is then you shall nede for halfe of that is there
Will serue, I vnder take, in lesse than halfe an howre
To kill the strongest man aliue ; such is the poysons power."

51. *Present.* Immediate ; as in iv. 1. 61 above. Cf. *presently* in 21 above.

Secret poisoning became so common in Europe in the 16th century that laws against the sale of poisons were made in Spain, Portugal, Italy, and other countries. K. says : "There is no such law in our own statute-book ; and the circumstance is a remarkable exemplification of the difference betweer English and Continental manners." But that this practice of poisoning prevailed to a considerable extent in England in the olden time is evident from the fact that in the 21st year of the reign of Henry VIII. an act was passed declaring the employment of secret poisons to be high-treason, and sentencing those who were found guilty of it to be boiled to death.

60. *Soon-speeding gear.* Quick-dispatching stuff. Cf. the extract from Brooke just above. For *gear*, see ii. 4. 85 above.

63. *As violently*, etc. See on ii. 6. 10 above.

67. *Any he.* Cf. *A. Y. L.* iii. 2. 414 : "that unfortunate he ;" 3 *Hen. VI.* i. 1. 46 : "The proudest he ;" *Id.* ii. 2. 97 : "Or any he the proudest of thy sort," etc. Gr. 224.

Utters them. Literally, sends them *out*, or lets them go from his possession ; hence, sells them. Cf. *L. L. L.* ii. 1. 16 and *W. T.* iv. 4. 330.

70. *Starveth.* That is, look out hungrily ; a bold but not un-Shake-spearian expression, for which Otway's "stareth" (adopted by Sr. and D.) is a poor substitution. See on i. 1. 211 above ; and for the inflection, on prol. 8.

71. The 1st quarto has "Vpon thy backe hangs ragged Miserie," which Steevens adopts. For *hangs*, see Gr. 336.

76. *Pay.* The 2d and 3d quartos and the folios have "pray," which K. prefers.

SCENE II.—5. *A barefoot brother.* Friars Laurence and John are evidently Franciscans. "In his kindliness, his learning, and his inclination to mix with and, perhaps, control the affairs of the world, he is no unapt

representative of this distinguished order in their best days" (K.). Warton says that the Franciscans "managed the machines of every important
operation and event, both in the religious and political world."

Cf. Brooke's poem :

> " Apace our frier Iohn to Mantua him hyes;
> And, for because in Italy it is a wonted gyse
> That friers in the towne should seeldome walke alone,
> But of theyr couent ay should be accompanide with one
> Of his profession, straight a house he fyndeth out,
> In mynde to take some frier with him, to walke the towne about."

Each friar has a companion assigned him by the superior when he asks
leave to go out ; and thus they are a check upon each other (Steevens).

9. *A house.* According to both the poem and the novel, this was the
convent to which the "barefoot brother" belonged. See p. 12, foot-note.

16. *Infection.* A quadrisyllable. Gr. 479. Cf. iv. 1. 41 above.

18. *Nice.* Trifling, unimportant. See on iii. 1. 151 above. For *charge,*
cf. *W. T.* iv. 4. 261 : " I have about me many parcels of charge."

19. *Dear.* Cf. v. 3. 32 below : "dear employment." See *Temp.* p. 124
(note on *The dear'st o' th' loss*), or *Rich. II.* p. 151.

20. *Do much danger.* See on iii. 3. 118 above.

25. *This three hours.* Cf. iv. 3. 40 above : "these many hundred years ;"
and v. 3. 176 below : "these two days." In both passages the 2d quarto
has "this." See Gr. 87.

26. *Beshrew.* See on ii. 5. 51 above.

SCENE III.—*A Churchyard*, etc. Hunter says : "It is clear that S.,
or some writer whom he followed, had in mind the churchyard of Saint
Mary the Old in Verona, and the monument of the Scaligers which stood
in it." He may, however, have been indebted only to Brooke, who refers
to the Italian custom of building large family tombs :

> " For euery houshold, if it be of any fame ;
> Doth bylde a tombe, or digge a vault, that beares the housholdes name :
> Wherein (if any of that kindred hap to dye)
> They are bestowde ; els in the same no other corps may lye.
> The Capilets her corps in such a one dyd lay
> Where Tybalt slaine of Romeus was layde the other day."

At the close of the poem we are told that

> " The bodies dead, remoued from vaulte where they did dye,
> In stately tombe, on pillers great of marble, rayse they hye.
> On euery syde aboue were set, and eke beneath,
> Great store of cunning Epitaphes, in honor of theyr death.
> And euen at this day the tombe is to be seene :
> So that among the monumentes that in Verona been,
> There is no monument more worthy of the sight,
> Then is the tombe of Iuliet and Romeus her knight."

See also the quotation in note on iv. 1. 93 above.

3. *Lay thee all along.* That is, at full length. Cf. *A. Y. L.* ii. 1. 30 :
"As he lay along Under an oak ;" *J. C.* iii. 1. 115 : "That now on Pom-
pey's basis lies along," etc.

6. *Unfirm.* Cf. *J. C.* i. 3. 4, *T. N.* ii. 4. 34, etc. S. also uses *infirm,* as
in *Macb.* ii. 2. 52, etc. See Gr. 442.

11. *Adventure.* Cf. ii. 2. 84 above.

14. *Sweet water.* Perfumed water. Cf. *T. A.* ii. 4. 6 : "call for sweet water ;" and see quotation in note on iv. 5. 75 above.

20. *Cross.* Thwart, interfere with. Cf. iv. 5. 91 above.

21. *Muffle.* Cover, hide. Cf. i. 1. 163 above ; and see *J. C.* iii. 2. 191, etc.*

22. *Enter Romeo and Balthasar.* The 2d and 3d quartos and the folios have "*Enter* Romeo *and* Peter."

33. *Jealous.* Suspicious ; as in *Lear*, v. 1. 56, *J. C.* i. 2. 71, etc.

34. *In.* Into. See on v. 1. 36 above.

37. *Savage-wild.* See Gr. 2, and cf. ii. 2. 141 above.

39. *Empty.* Hungry. Cf. *V. and A.* 55 : "Even as an empty eagle, sharp by fast" (see also *2 Hen. VI.* iii. 1. 248 and *3 Hen. VI.* i. 1. 268) ; and *T. of S.* iv. 1. 193 : "My falcon now is sharp and passing empty."

44. *Doubt.* Distrust ; as in *J. C.* ii. 1. 132, iv. 2. 13, etc.

45. *Detestable.* See on iv. 5. 52 above.

47. *Enforce.* Force. See *Much Ado*, p. 170.

50. *With.* For *with* expressing the relation of cause, see Gr. 193.

59. *Good gentle youth*, etc. "The gentleness of Romeo was shown before [iii. 1. 60 fol.] as softened by love, and now it is doubled by love and sorrow, and awe of the place where he is" (Coleridge).

68. *Conjurations.* Obsecrations (Schmidt) ; as in *Rich. II.* iii. 2. 23, *Ham.* v. 2. 38, etc. Some have taken it to mean incantations.

74. *Peruse.* Scan, examine. See *Ham.* p. 257.

76. *Betossed.* Agitated ; used by S. nowhere else.

82. *Sour.* See on iii. 3. 7 above.

84. *Lantern.* Used in the architectural sense of "a turret full of windows" (Steevens). Cf. Parker, *Glossary of Architecture :* "In Gothic architecture the term is sometimes applied to *louvres* on the roofs of halls, etc., but it usually signifies a tower which has the whole height, or a considerable portion of the interior, open to the ground, and is lighted by an upper tier of windows ; lantern-towers of this kind are common over the centre of cross churches, as at York Minster, Ely Cathedral, etc. The same name is also given to the light open erections often placed on the top of towers, as at Boston, Lincolnshire," etc.

86. *Presence.* Presence-chamber, state apartment ; as in *Rich. II.* i. 3. 289 and *Hen. VIII.* iii. 1. 17.

87. *Death.* The abstract for the concrete. D. adopts Lettsom's conjecture of "Dead."

A dead man. That is, Romeo, who is so possessed with his suicidal purpose that he speaks of himself as dead. Steevens perversely calls it one of "those miserable conceits with which our author too frequently counteracts his own pathos."

88–120. "Here, here, is the master example how beauty can at once increase and modify passion" (Coleridge).

---

* Steevens intimates that it was "a low word" in his day ; but, if so, it has since regained its poetical character. Tennyson uses it repeatedly ; as in *The Talking Oak :* "O muffle round thy knees with fern ;" *The Princess :* "A full sea glazed with muffled moonlight ;" *Id. :* "the muffled cage of life ;" *In Memoriam :* "muffled round with woe," etc.

90. *A lightning before death.* "A last blazing-up of the flame of life" (Schmidt). Steevens quotes *The Downfall of Robert Earl of Huntington*, 1601 :

> "I thought it was a lightning before death,
> Too sudden to be certain."

"The mingling here of words and images full of light and colour with the murky grey of the sepulchral vault and the darkness of the midnight churchyard, the blending of these images of beauty and tenderness with the deep gloom of the speaker's inmost heart, form a poetical and metaphysical picture unequalled in its kind" (Clarke).

92. *Suck'd the honey,* etc. Cf. *Ham.* iii. 1. 164 : "That suck'd the honey of his music vows." Steevens quotes Sidney, *Arcadia :* "Death being able to divide the soule, but not the beauty from her body."

96. *Death's pale flag.* Steevens compares Daniel, *Complaint of Rosamond :*

> "And nought-respecting death (the last of paines)
> Plac'd his pale colours (th' ensign of his might)
> Upon his new-got spoil."

97. *Tybalt,* etc. Cf. Brooke's poem :

> "Ah cosin dere, Tybalt, where so thy restles sprite now be,
> With stretched handes to thee for mercy now I crye,
> For that before thy kindly howre I forced thee to dye.
> But if with quenched lyfe not quenched be thine yre,
> But with revenging lust as yet thy hart be set on fyre,
> What more amendes, or cruell wreke desyrest thou
> To see on me, then this which here is shewd forth to thee now?
> Who reft by force of armes from thee thy living breath,
> The same with his owne hand (thou seest) doth poyson himselfe to death."

101. *Forgive me,* etc. "Inexpressibly beautiful and moving is this gentleness of Romeo's in his death hour. His yearning to be at peace with his foe, his beseeching pardon of him and calling him kinsman in token of final atonement, his forbearance and even magnanimity towards Paris, his words of closing consideration and kindly farewell to his faithful Balthasar, all combine to crown Romeo as the prince of youthful gentlemen and lovers" (Clarke).

106. *Still.* Constantly, always ; as very often. Gr. 69.

107. *This palace,* etc. "By these few words—a concentrated amalgamation of richest splendours with dunnest obscurity—the poet brings his grandly-blended imagery in this speech to a fitting climax" (Clarke).

110. *Set up my everlasting rest.* That is, remain forever. To *set up one's rest* was a phrase taken from gaming, the *rest* being the highest stake the parties were disposed to venture ; hence it came to mean to have fully made up one's mind, to be resolved (D. and Schmidt). See *M. of V.* p. 139. Here the form of expression seems to be suggested by the gaming phrase rather than to be a figurative example of it.

112–118. *Eyes . . . bark.* Whiter points out a coincidence between this last speech of Romeo's and a former one (i. 4. 103 fol.) in which he anticipates his misfortunes. "The ideas drawn from the *stars,* the *law,* and the *sea* succeed each other in both speeches, in the same order, though with a different application."

115. *Dateless.* Limitless, eternal. Cf. *Sonn.* 30. 6 : "death's date-

less night;" *Rich. II.* i. 3. 151 : "The dateless limit of thy dear exile," etc.

Engrossing. Malone says that the word "seems here to be used in its clerical sense." There seems to be at least a hint of that sense, suggested by *seal* and *bargain*; but the leading meaning is that of all-seizing, or "taking the whole," as Schmidt explains it.

116. *Conduct.* See on iii. 1. 121 above.

Unsavoury. Cf. *V. and A.* 1138 : "sweet beginning, but unsavoury end." Schmidt, who very rarely makes such a slip, treats both of these examples as literal rather than metaphorical. The only example of the former sense in S. is *Per.* ii. 3. 31 : "All viands that I eat do seem unsavoury."

118. *Thy.* Pope substituted "my," which D. also adopts. *Thy* might be defended on the nautical principle that the pilot is the master of the ship after he takes her in charge. That seems to be Romeo's thought here; he gives up the helm to the "desperate pilot," and says, "The ship is yours, run her upon the rocks if you will."

121. *Be my speed.* Cf. *Hen. V.* v. 2. 194 : "Saint Denis be my speed !" *A. Y. L.* i. 2. 222 : "Hercules be thy speed !" etc.

122. *Stumbled at graves.* The idea that to stumble is a bad omen is very ancient. Cicero mentions it in his *De Divinatione.* Melton, in his *Astrologaster*, 1620, says that "if a man stumbles in a morning as soon as he comes out of dores, it is a signe of ill lucke." Bishop Hall, in his *Characters*, says of the "Superstitious Man" that "if he stumbled at the threshold, he feares a mischief." Stumbling at graves is alluded to in *Whimzies, or a New Cast of Characters*, 1631 : "His earth-reverting body (according to his mind) is to be buried in some cell, roach, or vault, and in no open space, lest passengers (belike) might stumble on his grave." Steevens cites 3 *Hen. VI.* iv. 7. 11 and *Rich. III.* iii. 4. 86.

127. *Capels'.* See on v. 1. 18 above.

136. *Unlucky.* The 2d quarto has "vnthriftie," which is adopted by Coll., Halliwell, and H.

137. *Yew tree.* Pope's emendation for the "yong tree" or "young tree" of the early eds.

138. *I dreamt,* etc. As Steevens observes, this is a touch of nature : "What happens to a person under the manifest influence of fear will seem to him, when he is recovered from it, like a dream."

143. *To lie.* For the "indefinite use" of the infinitive, see Gr. 356.

145. *Unkind.* Usually accented on the first syllable before a noun, but otherwise on the second (Schmidt). For many similar cases of dissyllabic adjectives and participles, see Schmidt, Appendix, p. 1413 fol.

Unkind and its derivatives are often used by S. in a much stronger sense than at present. In some cases, the etymological sense of *unnatural* (cf. *kind* and *kindly*=natural) seems to cling to them. Cf. *J. C.* iii. 2. 187, *Lear*, i. 1. 263, iii. 4. 73, etc.

148. *Comfortable.* Used in an active sense=ready to comfort or help; as in *A. W.* i. 1. 86, *Lear*, i. 4. 328, etc. Cf. Gr. 3.

155. *Thy husband,* etc. On the ending of the story in Da Porta, see p. 25 above.

158. *The watch.* It has been asserted by some of the critics that there was no watch in the old Italian cities; but, however that may have been, S. follows Brooke's poem:

> "The watchmen of the towne the whilst are passed by,
> And through the gates the candel light within the tombe they spye."

162. *Timeless.* Untimely. Cf. *T. G. of V.* iii. 1. 21: "your timeless grave;" *Rich. II.* iv. 1. 5: "his timeless end," etc.

170. *There rest.* From 1st quarto; the other early eds. have "rust," which some editors prefer. Clarke remarks: "The expression *O happy dagger*, though meaning 'O happily-found dagger! opportune dagger!' yet conveys an included sense that is in keeping with the word *rest*, which also affords antithetical effect with 'let me die.' Poetically calling her bosom the *sheath* to Romeo's dagger, *rest* seems more in harmony than *rust* with the image presented."

The tragedy here ends in Booth's Acting Copy (F.).

173. *Attach.* Arrest; as in *C. of E.* iv. 1. 6, 73, iv. 4. 6, *Rich. II.* ii. 3. 156, *Hen. VIII.* i. 1. 217, i. 2. 210, etc.

176. *These two days.* See on iv. 1. 105 above.

181. *Without circumstance.* Without further particulars. Cf. ii. 5. 36 above.

194. *Our.* Johnson's emendation of the "your" of the early eds. K. and W. read "your."

203. *His house.* Its sheath. For *his*, see Gr. 228.

204. *On the back.* The dagger was commonly turned behind, and worn at the back (Coll.); as Steevens shows by sundry quotations.

205. *And is.* The 2d quarto has "And it."

207. *Old age.* A slip. See on i. 3. 51 above.

211. *Grief of my son's exile.* Cf. *Much Ado,* iv. 2. 65: "and upon the grief of this suddenly died." For the accent of *exile*, see Gr. 490, and cf. iii. 1. 184 and iii. 3. 20 above.

After this line the 1st quarto has the following: "And yong *Benuolio* is deceased too." D. is inclined to insert this in the text; but, as Ulrici remarks, "the pacific, considerate Benvolio, the constant counsellor of moderation, ought not to be involved in the fate which had overtaken the extremes of hate and passion."

214. *Manners.* S. makes the word either singular or plural, like *news, tidings* (see on iii. 5. 105 above), etc. Cf. *A. W.* ii. 2. 9, *W. T.* iv. 4. 244, etc., with *T. N.* iv. 1. 53, *Rich. III.* iii. 7. 191, etc. See also Gr. 333.

216. *Outrage.* The Coll. MS. gives "outcry," which H. adopts; but, as St. observes, no change is needed. Cf. *1 Hen. VI.* iv. 1. 126:

> "Are you not asham'd
> With this immodest clamorous outrage
> To trouble and disturb the king and us?"

There, as here, it means a mad outcry. D. quotes Settle, *Female Prel ate:* "Silence his outrage in a jayl, away with him!"

229. *I will be brief,* etc. Johnson and Malone criticise S. for following Brooke in the introduction of this long narrative. Ulrici defends it as preparing the way for the reconciliation of the Capulets and Montagues over the dead bodies of their children, the victims of their hate.

Date. See on i. 4 105 above.

237. *Siege.* Cf. the same image in i. 1. 204 (Delius).

238. *Perforce.* By force, against her will. See *A. Y. L.* p. 141.

241. *Marriage.* A trisyllable. See on iv. 1. 11 above.

247. *As this dire night.* For this redundant use of *as* in statements of time, see *Temp.* p. 113, note on *As at that time.* See also Gr. 114.

257. *Some minute.* We should now say "some minutes," which is Hanmer's reading. Cf. "some hour" in 268 below.

258. *Untimely.* For the adverbial use, see on iii. 1. 115 above.

260. *Come.* For the omission of *to,* see Gr. 349.

270. *Still.* Always. See on 106 above.

273. *In post.* In haste, or "post-haste." Cf. v. 1. 21 above. In *Rich. II.* ii. 1. 296, the 1st and 2d folios have "in post," the 3d and 4th "in haste." We find "in all post" in *Rich. III.* iii. 5. 73, and "all in post" in *R. of L.* 1.

276. *Going in.* See on v. 1. 36 above.

280. *What made your master?* What was your master doing? See *A. Y. L.* p. 136, note on *What make you here?*

284. *By and by.* Presently. See on ii. 2. 151 above.

289. *Pothecary.* Generally printed "'pothecary" in the modern eds., but not in the early ones. It was a common form of the word. See Schmidt or Wb. s. v. Cf. Chaucer, *Pardoneres Tale:*

> "And forth he goth, no lenger wold he tary,
> Into the toun unto a potecary."

Therewithal. Therewith, with it. Cf. *T. G. of V.* iv. 4. 90:

> "Well, give her that ring and therewithal
> This letter," etc.

291. *Be.* Cf. *Ham.* iii. 2. 111, v. 1. 107, etc. Gr. 299.

295. *A brace of kinsmen.* Mercutio and Paris. For the former, see iii. 1. 106; and for the latter, iii. 5. 179 (where the 1st quarto has "Of Princely parentage") and v. 3. 75. Steevens remarks that *brace* as applied to men is generally contemptuous; as in *Temp.* v. 1. 126: "But you, my brace of lords," etc. As a parallel to the present passage, cf. *T. and C.* iv. 5. 175: "You brace of warlike brothers, welcome hither!"

302. *True.* The Coll. MS. substitutes "fair."

305. *Glooming.* The 1st quarto has "gloomie," and the 4th folio "gloomy," which D. adopts and W. favours. *Glooming* occurs nowhere else in S. Steevens cites *Tom Tyler and his Wife,* 1578: "If either he gaspeth or gloometh;" and *The Spanish Tragedy,* 1603: "shades of ever-glooming night." Cf. Spenser, *F. Q.* i. 14: "A little glooming light, much like a shade 'Young uses the verb in his *Night Thoughts,* ii.: "A night that glooms us in the noontide ray."

308. *Some shall be pardoned,* etc. In the novel, Juliet's attendant is banished for concealing the marriage; Romeo's servant set at liberty because he had acted under his master's orders; the apothecary tortured and hanged; and Friar Laurence permitted to retire to a hermitage, where he ends his life in penitence and peace (Steevens).

ADDENDA.

The "Time-Analysis" of the Play.—This is summed up by Mr. P. A. Daniel in his valuable paper "On the Times or Durations of the Actions of Shakspere's Plays" (*Trans. of New Shaks. Soc.* 1877–79, p. 194) as follows :

"Time of this Tragedy, six consecutive days, commencing on the morning of the first, and ending early in the morning of the sixth.

Day 1. (Sunday) Act I., and Act II. sc. i. and ii.
" 2. (Monday) Act II. sc. iii.–vi., Act III. sc. i.–iv.
" 3. (Tuesday) Act III. sc. v., Act IV. sc. i.–iv.
" 4. (Wednesday) Act IV. sc. v.
" 5. (Thursday) Act V.
" 6. (Friday) End of Act V. sc. iii."

After the above was printed, Mr. Furnivall called Mr. Daniel's attention to our note on p. 202 above, in which we show that the drama may close on Thursday morning instead of Friday. Mr. Daniel was at first disinclined to accept this view, but on second thought was compelled to admit that we were right.

The Text of the Play.—In preparing the text of this edition, we have made use of the collations in Furness's "New Variorum" and the "Cambridge" editions; and also of the reprints of the Quartos of 1597 and 1599, and Daniel's "revised edition" of the latter, all three published by the New Shakspere Society.

In the notes we have been specially indebted to Furness. There is little left for the gleaner in any field where he has been reaping; but he has generously allowed us to draw at pleasure from his rich garners to help "upfill this osier cage of ours." In some cases where he has merely recorded criticisms, we have ventured to discuss them; and we have also been able to pick up some things from the additions made to the literature of the play in the seven years since his edition appeared. The *teacher*, of course, cannot afford to do without his edition, which is a library distilled into a volume.

Da Porto's "La Giulietta" (p. 14).—A translation of this novel (with an historical and critical introduction by the present writer) has been published by the Joseph Knight Co. (Boston, 1893).

List of Characters in the Play, with the Scenes in which they Appear, etc.—The numbers in parentheses indicate the lines the characters have in each scene.

Escalus: i. 1(23); iii. 1(16); v. 3(36). Whole no. 75.
Paris: i. 2(4); iii. 4(4); iv. 1(23), 5(6); v. 3(32). Whole no. 69.
Montague: i. 1(28); iii. 1(3); v. 3(10). Whole no. 41.
Capulet: i. 1(3), 2(33), 5(56); iii. 4(31), 5(63); iv. 2(26), 4(19), 5(28); v. 3(10). Whole no. 269.
2d Capulet: i. 5(3). Whole no. 3.

Romeo: i. 1(65), 2(29), 4(34), 5(27) ; ii. 1(2), 2(86), 3(25), 4(54), 6(12 ; iii. 1(36), 3(71), 5(24); v. 1(71), 3(82). Whole no. 618.

Mercutio: i. 4(73); ii. 1(34), 4(95); iii. 1(71). Whole no. 273.

Benvolio: i. 1(51), 2(20), 4(13), 5(1); ii. 1(9), 4(14); iii. 1(53). Whole no. 161.

Tybalt: i. 1(5), 5(17); iii. 1(14). Whole no. 36.

Friar Laurence: ii. 3(72), 6(18); iii. 3(87); iv. 1(56), 5(25); v. 2(17), 3(75). Whole no. 350.

Friar John: v. 2(13). Whole no. 13.

Balthasar: v. 1(11), 3(21). Whole no. 32.

Sampson: i. 1(41). Whole no. 41.

Gregory: i. 1(24). Whole no. 24.

Peter: iii. 4(7); iv. 5(30). Whole no. 37.

Abram: i. 1(5). Whole no. 5.

Apothecary: v. 1(7). Whole no. 7.

1st Musician: iv. 5(16). Whole no. 16.

2d Musician: iv. 5(6). Whole no. 6.

3d Musician: iv. 5(1). Whole no. 1.

1st Servant: i. 2(21), 3(5), 5(11); iv. 4(1). Whole no. 38.

2d Servant: i. 5(7); iv. 2(5), 4(2). Whole no. 14.

1st Watchman: v. 3(19). Whole no. 19.

2d Watchman: v. 3(1). Whole no. 1.

3d Watchman: v. 3(3). Whole no. 3.

1st Citizen: i. 1(2); iii. 1(4). Whole no. 6.

Page: v. 3(9). Whole no. 9.

Lady Montague: i. 1(3). Whole no. 3.

Lady Capulet: i. 1(1), 3(36), 5(1); iii. 1(11), 4(2), 5(37); iv. 2(3), 3(3), 4(3), 5(13); v. 3(5). Whole no. 115.

Juliet: i. 3(8), 5(19); ii. 2(114), 5(43), 6(7); iii. 2(116), 5(105); iv. 1(48), 2(12), 3(56); v. 3(13). Whole no. 541.

Nurse: i. 3(61), 5(15); ii. 2(114), 6(43), 7(7); iii. 2(116), 5(105); iv. 1(48), 2(12), 3(56); v. 3(13). Whole no. 290.

"*Prologue*": (14). Whole no. 14.

"*Chorus*": end of act i. (14). Whole no. 14.

In the above enumeration, parts of lines are counted as whole lines, making the total in the play greater than it is. The actual number in each scene is as follows : Prologue (14); i. 1(244), 2(106), 3(106), 4(114), 5(147); Chorus (14); ii. 1(42), 2(190), 3(94), 4(233), 5(80), 6(37); iii. 1(202), 2(143), 3(175), 4(36), 5(241); iv. 1(126), 2(47), 3(58), 4(28), 5(150); v. 1(86), 2(30), 3(310). Whole number in the play, 3053. The line-numbering is that of the Globe ed.

INDEX OF WORDS AND PHRASES EXPLAINED.

marriage (trisyllable), 199, 218.
married (figurative), 152.
me (ethical dative), 171, 179.
mean (noun), 189.
measure (=dance), 153.
merchant (contemptuous), 175.
mewed up, 191.
mickle, 169.
minion, 196.
misadventure, 211.
mistempered, 142.
modern (=trite), 188.
moody (=angry), 179.
mouse-hunt, 208.
moved, 142.
much upon these years, 151.
muffle, 214.

natural (=fool), 174.
naught, 187.
needly, 188.
needy, 195.
new (adverbial), 143.
news (number), 178.
nice (=petty, trifling), 183, 213.
nothing (adverb), 142.
nuptial, 159.

O (=grief), 190.
o'er-perch, 165.
of (=on), 141.
of the very first house, 171.
old (=practised), 190.
on (=of), 178, 182.
once, 151.
one is no number, 147.
operation (=effect), 179.
orchard (=garden), 163.
osier cage, 169.
outrage (=outcry), 217.
overwhelming, 211.
owe (=possess), 165.

paly, 202.
pardonnez-mois, 172.
partisan, 141.
parts (=gifts), 188.
passado, 171, 181.
passing (adverbial), 145.
pastry, 207.
patience (trisyllable), 211.
patience perforce, 161.
perforce (=by force), 218.
peruse (=scan), 214.
Phaethon, 184.
pilcher, 181.
pin (in archery), 170.
plantain, 147.
pluck, 168.
portly, 160.

pothecary, 218.
pout'st upon, 191.
powerful grace, 169.
predominant, 170.
presence, 214.
present (=immediate), 212.
presently, 211.
preserving, 144.
prevails (=avails), 190.
prick of noon, 175.
prick-song, 171.
prince of cats, 171.
princox, 161.
procure, 194.
prodigious, 163.
proof (=experience), 144.
proof (of armour), 144.
properer, 176.
prorogued, 165, 200.
pump (=shoe), 173.
punto reverso, 171.
purchase out, 184.

question (=conversation), 145.
quit (=requite), 176.
quote (=note), 154.

R, the dog's letter, 177.
rearward, 188.
reason coldly, 180.
rebeck, 210.
receipt, 195.
receptacle (accent), 206.
reckoning, 146.
reeky, 201.
remember (reflexive), 150.
respective, 182.
rest you merry! 148.
retort (=throw back), 183.
riddling, 170.
roe (play upon), 172.
rood (=cross), 151.
ropery, 175.
rosemary, 208.
runaways' eyes, 184.
rushed aside the law, 189.
rushes, 154.

sadly (=seriously), 144.
sadness, 144.
savage-wild, 214.
scales (singular), 149.
scant, 149.
scape, 179.
scathe, 161.
scorn at, 160.
season, 170.
set abroach, 142.
set up my rest, 215.
sick and green, 164.
silver-sweet, 168.
simpleness, 190.

simples (=herbs), 211.
single-soled, 174.
sir-reverence, 155.
skains-mates, 176.
slip (=counterfeit), 173.
slops, 173.
slow (verb), 199.
so (omitted), 195.
so brief to part, 191.
so ho! 175.
solemnity, 160.
some minute, 218.
some other where, 144.
sometime, 157.
soon-speeding, 212.
sorrow drinks our blood, 95.
sort (=select), 204.
sorted out, 195.
soul (play upon), 154.
sour, 188, 214.
sped, 182.
speed, be my, 216.
spinners, 156.
spite, 141, 164, 200.
spleen, 183.
spoke him fair, 183.
stand on sudden haste, 170.
star-crossed, 140.
starved, 145.
starveth, 212.
stay (=wait for), 210.
stay the circumstance, 178
steads, 170.
still (=always), 215, 218.
strained, 169.
strange, 166, 185.
strucken, 145.
stumbling at graves, 216.
substantial (quadrisyllable) 167.
surcease, 202.
swashing blow, 141.
sweet water, 214.
sweet-heart (accent), 208.
sweeting, 174.
sweetmeats, 156.
swounded, 186.
sycamore, 143.

tables (turned up), 159.
tackled stair, 176.
take me with you, 196.
take truce, 183.
tassel-gentle, 167.
teen, 150.
temper (=mix), 195.
tender (noun), 197.
tender (=regard), 181.
tetchy, 151.
thank me no thankings, 196.
therefore (accent), 200.
therewithal, 218.
this three hours, 213.

SHAKESPEARE'S MONUMENT, WESTMINSTER ABBEY.